TRANSFORMING EAST ASIAN DOMESTIC AND INTERNATIONAL POLITICS

The International Political Economy of New Regionalisms Series

The International Political Economy of New Regionalisms Series presents innovative analyses of a range of novel regional relations and institutions. Going beyond established, formal, interstate economic organizations, this essential series provides informed interdisciplinary and international research and debate about myriad heterogeneous intermediate level interactions.

Reflective of its cosmopolitan and creative orientation, this series is developed by an international editorial team of established and emerging scholars in both the South and North. It reinforces ongoing networks of analysts in both academia and think-tanks as well as international agencies concerned with micro-, meso- and macro-level regionalisms.

Editorial Board

Timothy M. Shaw, University of London, London
Isidro Morales, Universidad de las Américas-Puebla, Mexico
Maria Nzomo, University of Nairobi, Kenya
Nicola Phillips, University of Warwick, UK
Johan Saravanamuttu, Munk Centre for International Studies, Canada
Fredrik Söderbaum, Göteborgs Universitet, Sweden

Other Titles in the Series

European Union and New Regionalism
Edited by Mario Telò
ISBN 0 7546 1748 3
South Africa's Multilateral Diplomacy and Global Change
Edited by Philip Nel, Ian Taylor and Janis van der Westhuizen
ISBN 0 7546 1653 3
Crises of Governance in Asia and Africa
Edited by Sandra J. MacLean, Fahimul Quadir and Timothy M. Shaw
ISBN 0 7546 1410 7

Transforming East Asian Domestic and International Politics
The Impact of Economy and Globalization

Edited by
ROBERT W. COMPTON, Jr.
State University of New York at Oneonta

LONDON AND NEW YORK

First published 2002 by Ashgate Publishing

Reissued 2018 by Routledge
2 Park Square, Milton Park, Abingdon, Oxon OX14 4RN
711 Third Avenue, New York, NY 10017, USA

Routledge is an imprint of the Taylor & Francis Group, an informa business

Copyright © Robert W. Compton 2002

All rights reserved. No part of this book may be reprinted or reproduced or utilised in any form or by any electronic, mechanical, or other means, now known or hereafter invented, including photocopying and recording, or in any information storage or retrieval system, without permission in writing from the publishers.

Notice:
Product or corporate names may be trademarks or registered trademarks, and are used only for identification and explanation without intent to infringe.

Publisher's Note
The publisher has gone to great lengths to ensure the quality of this reprint but points out that some imperfections in the original copies may be apparent.

Disclaimer
The publisher has made every effort to trace copyright holders and welcomes correspondence from those they have been unable to contact.

A Library of Congress record exists under LC control number: 2001099646

ISBN 13: 978-1-138-74150-8 (hbk)
ISBN 13: 978-1-138-74148-5 (pbk)
ISBN 13: 978-1-315-18282-7 (ebk)

Contents

List of Tables	vii
List of Abbreviations	viii
List of Contributors	x

1 Introduction: Globalization and the Changing Nature of East Asian Politics
   Robert W. Compton, Jr. — 1

2 Globalization and the Developmental State: Reflections on the Asian Financial Crisis
   Vincent Wei-Cheng Wang — 10

3 Chinese Elite Conflict over Globalization
   Lawrence C. Reardon — 36

4 Political Culture as a Source of Japanese Immobilism in the New World Order
   Robert W. Compton, Jr. — 68

5 Globalization, Asian Political Culture and State Control
   Kunihiko Imai — 83

6 South Korea as a Middle Power: The Growing Globalization of South Korean Foreign Policy in the 1990s
   Dlynn Armstrong-Williams — 100

7 East Timor Independence: The Changing Nature of International Pressure
   Thomas Ambrosio — 115

8 Japan's Regional Environmental Foreign Aid: Responding to Global and Regional Realities
   David M. Potter — 138

9 Prospects for a Regional Human Rights Mechanism in East Asia
   Hidetoshi Hashimoto — 161

10 Demilitarizing Okinawa: Globalization and Comparative
    Social Movements
    Vincent Kelly Pollard   180

Index   *201*

List of Tables

Table 2.1 Globalization– *déjà vu?* — 13

Table 2.2 Uneven Globalization – Internet Users by Region — 15

Table 2.3 Explaining the East Asian Miracle: Two Different Accounts — 18

Table 2.4 Rising Trade Dependence and External Debt — 21

Table 2.5 Uneven Globalization– Disparate Information Power — 23

Table 2.6 Asian Crisis: Shrinking Currency and Vanishing Wealth — 25

Table 2.7 Developmental State vs. Regulatory State — 28

Table 4.1 Interest Rates, Deficit Spending, and Economic Growth — 77

Table 5.1 Globalization and Civil Liberties: A Pooled Time-Series Analysis — 94

Table 6.1 South Korean ODA from 1987 to 2001 in US$ Millions — 110

Table 8.1 Japan's Environmental ODA, 1990-1999 — 146

Table 8.2 Japan's Bilateral ODA by Sector, Selected Years — 146

Table 8.3 MFA Support for NGOs by Category (%), Selected Years — 151

Table 8.4 MPT Support for NGOs by Sector (%), Selected Years — 151

Table 9.1 NGOs Surveyed — 165

Table 9.2 Characteristics of Leaders Interviewed — 166

Table 9.3 Salient Socioeconmic Factors and RIGO Formation — 171

Table 9.4 Signing and Ratifying International Human Rights Instruments — 176

List of Abbreviations

ADB- Asian Development Bank
AID- (US) Agency for International Development
AIDS- Acquired Immune Deficiency Syndrome
AMS- Agreement on Maintaining Security (Indonesia –Australia)
APEC- Asia Pacific Economic Cooperation
APODETI- Timorese Democratic People's Union
ASEAN- Association of South East Asian Nations
AU- Asian Union
CGIAR- Consultative Group on International Agricultural Research
CIS- Commonwealth of Independent States
COP3- Convention of Climate Change
DAC- Development Assistance Committee (OECD)
EAF- East Asian Forum
EDCF- Economic Development Cooperation Fund (Korea)
EIA- Environmental Impact Assessment
ELI- Export Led Industrialization
EPA- Economic Planning Agency (Japan)
EU- European Union
FAO- Food and Agriculture Organization
FDI- Foreign Direct Investment
FFYP- First Five-Year Plan
FRETILIN- Revolutionary Front for an Independent East Tuinr
GATT- General Agreement on Trade & Tariffs
GDI- Gross Domestic Investment
GDP- Gross Domestic Product
GEF- Global Environmental Fund
GLF- Great Leap Forward
GNP- Gross National Product
ICJ- International Court of Justice
IGO- Inter-governmental Organization
IMF- International Monetary Fund
INTERFET- International Force East Timor
ISD- Initiative for Sustainable Development
ISI- Import Substitution Industrialization
IT- Information Technology
ITTO- International Timber Trade Organization
JBIC- Japan Bank for International Cooperation
JICA- Japan International Cooperation Agency
JOCV- Japan Overseas Cooperation Volunteers
KOICA- Korea International Cooperation Agency
LDC- Less Developed Countries
LDP- Liberal Democratic Party
MFA- Minority of Foreign Affairs
MINURSO- *Mission des Nations Unies pour le Referendum au Sahara Occidental*
MITI- Ministry of Int. Trade & Industry
MPT- Ministry of Post & Tele Communications (Japan)

NGO- Non-Governmental Organization
NIC- Newly Industrialized Countries
NIDL- New Int. Division of Labor
OAS- Organization of American States
OAU- Organization of African Unity
OCS- Ordinary Feast Squares
ODA- Official Development Assistance
OECD- Organization for Economic Cooperation and Development
OECF- Overseas Economic Cooperation Fund (Japan)
OLS–Ordinary Least Squares
PRC- People's Republic of China
RDMHQ- Rapidly Deployable Mission Headquarters
RIGHRO- Regional Inter-governmental Human Rights Organization
RIGO- Regional Inter-government Organization
RMB- Renminbi (Chinese Yuan)
SAARC- South Asian Association for Regional Cooperation
SEZ- Special Economic Zone
SOE- State-owned enterprise
UDT- Timores Democratic Union
UNAMET- United Nations Mission in East Timor
UNAVEM III – United Nations Angola Verification Mission
UNDP- United Nations Development Program
UNEP- United Nations Environment Program
UNMOGIP- United Nations Military Observer Group in India & Pakistan
UNOMIG- United Nations Observer Mission in Georgia
UNOSOM- United Nations Operations in Somalia
UNTAET- United Nations Transitional Administration in East Timor
WTO- World Trade Organization

List of Contributors

Thomas Ambrosio, Ph.D., the University of Virginia, specializes in ethnic conflict theory, especially as applied to Eastern Europe. Having previously taught at Western Kentucky University (Bowling Green, KY), he is currently assistant professor at North Dakota State University. Recently, he published *Irredentism: Ethnic Conflict and International Politics* (Greenwood) and co-edited and contributed to *International Law and the Rise of Nations: The State System and the Challenge of Ethnic Groups* (Chatham House). He is also author of several articles and chapters on Russian security policy and Eastern European ethnic politics. Currently, he is working on an edited book on American Ethnic lobbies.

Robert W. Compton, Jr., Ph.D., graduated from the State University of New York at Binghamton in 1998. He specializes in East Asian and Sub-Saharan political development and political economy. He is currently assistant professor at the State University of New York at Oneonta. He previously published, *East Asian Democratization: Impact of Globalization, Culture, and Economy* (Greenwood), and several articles on political development and economic performance. Currently, he is working on a book chapter on AIDS and Asian regional security, an article linking political development and land reform in Zimbabwe and South Africa, and a larger project on comparative affirmative action policies in South Africa, Zimbabwe, and the United States.

Hidetoshi Hashimoto, Ph.D. (2000), graduated from the University of Maryland and focuses his research and teaching in the area of human rights and East Asian politics. A frequent guest speaker at the University of Maryland, he teaches courses at George Washington University and the University of Maryland. His primary area of current research involves the role of non-governmental organizations and their impact on a country's domestic and international human rights policies.

Kunihiko Imai, Ph.D. (1992) the State University of New York at Binghamton is currently Assistant Professor at Elmira College (Elmira, NY) where he teaches courses in comparative politics and international relations and serves as the college's liaison in Japan during the summer. Imai is the author of several articles and book chapters about foreign policy decision-making of major powers as well as globalization of national economies.

Vincent Kelly Pollard, Ph.D. (2000), University of Hawai'i, specializes in Filipino politics and East Asian foreign policy and teaches with the University of Hawai'i system and at the former Kansai Gaidai Hawaii College. A previous author of several articles based on interviews with top Filipino policy makers, he is currently completing a book on the impact of power sharing and society-society relations and its on foreign policy making in Asia.

David M. Potter, Ph.D. (1992), the University of California, Santa Barbara, currently teaches political science at Nanzan University in Japan. Previously, he taught at Northern Kentucky University (Covington, KY). An author of several articles on Japanese environmental policy and foreign power sharing and society-society relations and its effect on foreign in that country.

Lawrence C. Reardon, Ph.D., Columbia University, is an Associate Professor of Political Science at the University of New Hampshire and an Associate in Research at Harvard University's Fairbank Center. His publications include *The Reluctant Dragon: Crisis Cycles in Chinese Foreign Economic Policy* (University of Washington Press) and journal articles on China. He is currently preparing a book-length study of China's coastal development strategy of the 1980s.

Vincent Wei-Cheng Wang, Ph.D. (1995), University of Chicago, specializes in international relations and political economy, especially as it pertains to East Asia. Currently, he is an Associate Professor at the University of Richmond where he teaches courses on East Asia and international relations. A frequent guest on National Public Radio, Wang authored several articles on Chinese and East Asian political economy and international relations. His work in progress examines the political economy of globalization.

Dlynn Armstrong-Williams, Ph.D., graduated from Miami University (Ohio) and is assistant professor and coordinator of international programs at North Georgia College and State University. Armstrong-Williams' interests include political economy and East Asian politics, especially of South Korea, where she previously conducted extensive fieldwork. She has published several articles on South Korean politics.

Dedication

In memory of Robert W. Compton, Sr. (1932-2001)

Chapter 1

Introduction: Globalization and the Changing Nature of East Asian Politics

Robert W. Compton, Jr.

Introduction

In September 1998, a group of comparative and international relations scholars gathered for a panel at the American Political Science Association meeting to discuss the impact of globalization on East Asian domestic and international affairs, with the express purpose of bridging the gap between international relations and comparative politics. Based on the papers from that panel and through a process of competitive solicitation, nine papers became the basis for *Transforming East Asian International and Domestic Politics: The Impact of Globalization*. All scholars at the panel expressed a concern about the lack of integration between comparative politics and international relations in particular as they pertain to East Asia.

This chapter explores the theme of globalization and its impact on the conduct of international relations and the processes of domestic politics. It explores why domestic actors can no longer assume an insular political environment as they have in the past. In fact, throughout the world, domestic and international actors continuously receive stimuli to adjust their approaches in the conduct of domestic and international affairs. Furthermore, globalization leads to a proliferation of non-state actors as well as new issues. Old security issues, for example, take on new and altered realities, while new issues involving Acquired Immune Deficiency Syndrome (AIDS), environmental protection, and creating human rights norms become intertwined with issues of state security and the conduct of foreign affairs. Globalization's ubiquitous presence reflects a new reality for both state and non-state actors today. No policy maker can ignore or underemphasize its role in shaping or altering the course of public policy.

Globalization and the Nature of Power

A variety of definitions regarding globalization exist but most of them concentrate around notions of political economy, based especially on the increase of global trade and the role of transnational corporations. Thomas Friedman (2000, 7) defines globalization as:

> the inexorable integration of markets, nation-states and technologies to a degree never witnessed before– in a way that is enabling individuals, corporations and nation-states to reach around the world farther, faster, and deeper and cheaper than ever before, and in a way that is also producing a powerful backlash from those brutalized or left behind by this new system.

While many dispute the notion of a globalized economy, even skeptics seem to agree about the increased extent of internationalization. They refuse however, to assuage the notion of uncontrollable markets (Hirst and Thompson, 1996). Clearly, markets do not translate into the unequivocal death of the state, rather the emergence of a much more complicated system in which the state continues to play an important role.

As many of these chapters demonstrate, the state's power has both declined and increased simultaneously in the era of globalization. Clearly, the ability of the state to control international events and trade declined with the advent of increased transnational corporate activity and the rise of political entities with supranational powers including the World Trade Organization (WTO), the European Union (EU), and the International Court of Justice (ICJ). However, states developed the opportunity to influence and affect the outcome of numerous trade, health, and environmental issues in other countries, regions, and the entire globe through international cooperation, both bilateral and within the auspices of these international and supranational organizations.

At the same time, NGOs and interest groups, whether oriented toward domestic, regional, or global issues have both benefited and experienced difficulties as a result of globalization and the associated communication revolution. Not only have they become crucial in carrying out some of the objectives shared by states, they have also benefited from the moral and financial support of multilateral institutions. Thus, NGOs became a more active part of international relations during the era of rapid globalization and now form the core of addressing issues involving human rights, the environment, development issues, and women's rights.

Globalization and the Asian Political Economy

In the 1950 and early 1960s, many economists considered the East Asian economies as 'basket cases'. Import substitution policies and the lack of natural resources prevented them from exploiting comparative. Most East Asian countries lacked natural resources and a highly industrialized economy at that time. However, since then, many governments developed a strategy known as 'guided development' using the power of the state to economically develop. Many scholars discuss, in detail, the strategies of the developmental state (Woo-Cumings 1999; Johnson 1995 and 1982; Wade 1990; Amsden 1989; and Deyo 1987).

During the 1960s to the late 1990s, the developmental state provided the initial and often ongoing catalyst for economic development. While the impact of government on economic development varied from country to country– with the government playing the greatest role in South Korea and arguably the least in Hong Kong– many political scientists and sociologists recognize some major commonalities involved in the development of the entire regional economy. The successful ingredients for the rapid economic development of East Asia consist of:

- Targeted government subsidies to potentially successful industries;
- Protection and nurturing of infant industries;
- Emphases on the creation of a banking system with high levels of national savings;
- Use of traditional values to maintain political quiescence, curtail social welfare spending, and establish enterprise unions;
- The use of financial incentives and the manipulation of traditional symbols for maintaining the dominance of the ruling elite.

At the same time, many Asian states experienced a historically unprecedented psychological and economic sense of crisis resulting from the Cold War, or in the case of Japan, devastation from World War II. The siege mentality prevalent among the masses, hyped up by governmental speeches and policies spurred increased production from workers in South Korea, Japan, and Taiwan. Even in Indonesia, Malaysia, and Thailand, governments emphasized traditional values to maintain order in creating an environment wherein economic growth flourished.

Unlike much of the developing world, Asian economies performed well because they tapped into the global capitalist economy and benefited from an international division of labor that allowed labor-intensive production to shift away from the industrialized nations and toward those with low labor costs. Gradually, with increased value-added production, Japan rebuilt its economy after the war, and South Korea, Hong Kong, Taiwan and Singapore become industrialized nations.

All of this could not have occurred without the development of two integrated developments, one at the global scale and the other at the regional one. At the global level the Cold War coupled with the dramatic expansion of 'free trade' among the non-Communist systems promoted the economic development of Asian nations. With the United States locked in a Cold War battle with the Soviet Union, the US placed military security over economic security. As a result, it allowed the developmental state to thrive and ignored violations of 'free trade' principles provided these countries continued to resist communism and maintained solidarity with the Western camp. At the same time, the various rounds of GATT opened up the American markets more so than Asian ones. Clearly, however, the openness in trade manifested itself to a greater degree in the West than in an economically fragile Asia that lacked strong military security. In sum, the politically dammed up world, to adapt Thomas Friedman's terminology, coupled with an economically freed-up world allowed Asian states to maximize both economic and political security.

Secondly, the Asian economies, on a regional scale developed a high level of integration and division of labor as a subset of the international economy. In the 1980s, as the value of the Japanese yen increased in response to large trade surpluses, many firms sought to cut labor costs and transplant production to countries including South Korea, China, Taiwan, Indonesia, and Malaysia. As a result, a vast and comprehensive regional Japanese network of production and finance developed (Katzenstein and Shiraishi, 1997; Hatch and Yamamura, 1996). Under the rubric of Association of Southeast Asian Nations (ASEAN) and Asia Pacific Economic Cooperation (APEC), Japan and other East Asian countries worked to coordinate economic policies and foreign direct investment (FDI), especially from Japan (Pempel, 1997). In particular the Japanese, and to a lesser degree the South Korean, government began a concerted effort to provide foreign aid and fund capital projects throughout Asia. In addition, both governments began to encourage FDI into Southeast Asia as a vital part of its foreign policy initiatives. The end result was a more integrated Asian economy, with a commensurate division of labor with Japan and to a lesser extent Singapore and Hong Kong producing the highest value-added items and services, with South Korea and Taiwan a tier below, and the next group consisting of Malaysia, Thailand, Indonesia, and the Philippines producing much of the lowest value added products for export. Hong Kong and Japan became the primary financing source for expansion into the last tier. The end result was increased intra-Asian trade and Asian exports to the West with high levels of profitability for bankers and large multinational corporations.

The end of the Cold War altered the fundamental structures of the East Asian regional economy and produced profound alterations in states' domestic politics and foreign policies. As some of the chapters discuss, it created an environment leading to the demise of authoritarian systems that could no longer be maintained through the umbrella of anti-communist symbolism. Internationally, the end of the Cold War resulted in increased attention paid to 'low politics' of trade and democratization by the US and other regional foreign policy leaders, such as Japan and China, rather than issues of potential full-scale nuclear war. In other words, the United States and Western Europe, faced with its own economic problems of deindustrialization and perceived decline in national competitiveness, became less tolerant of the mercantilistic orientation of developmental states. The establishment of the Super 301 system, which targeted selected countries for retaliation for unfair trade practices, and the introduction of a European free-trade zone, meant more scrutiny on the practices of East Asian states and greater difficulty in penetrating new markets.

Impact of Globalization on Asian Domestic Politics

The stages of globalization impacted Asian domestic politics in two ways. First, it empowered specific domestic actors (such as the bureaucracy, the corporations, and social movements) and weakened others (including the military and some traditional political institutions). Asian states' interaction with external forces and interests created a much more complex political environment domestically. Second, globalization shaped the contours of democracy as East Asian countries experienced democratic transition and consolidation (Compton 2000a and Compton 2000b). Due to globalization, norms of acceptable behavior by the military and governmental entities and that of citizens experienced a systematic transformation.

Empowering and Weakening Actors

Throughout the Cold War period, an expansion of trade took place that impacted Asian politics in many ways. When the Cold War ended, corporations, a new middle class, and a plethora of special interest groups provided additional pressure and stress to the old existing political system. What actors became empowered in each of the two respective stages of globalization? Why did some actors do better than others? And what brought about the weakening and strengthening of actors in each stage?

At the beginning of the Cold War and in the early stages of political and economic development of East Asia (1950-75), authoritarian systems characterized the domestic environment throughout Asia. With the exception of Japan, where an ostensibly 'democratic' system existed, all political systems experienced some level of bureaucratic authoritarianism. To varying degrees, the military in collusion with the bureaucracy and a dominant party created by them dominated politics. As long as the elite could generate a modest and sustained level of economic growth through state activities, these actors strengthened their power. At the same time, independent unions, students, political leftists, and corporate leaders that sought to exercise influence from without the existing system or curtail and challenge the power of the existing elite were systematically weakened.

The insular developmental state took advantage of the increasing globalization of trade and simultaneously used the Cold War and the communist threat to its advantage in order to maintain domestic political tranquility. Those who opposed the regime would protest, demonstrate, and sometimes engage in violence, but that only sparked the harsh backlash of the authoritarian state. As long as the ruling elite, consisting of some variation of the military, bureaucracy, and the ruling party continued to derive benefit from the system and simultaneously maintain legitimacy in the eyes of the majority through economic growth and the use of traditional values, the system remained in equilibrium. By 1975, Taiwan, South Korea, Thailand, Indonesia, Singapore, and the Philippines could not be considered liberal democracies. In all cases, political development of parties atrophied. In Japan, the military did not assume any significant role in policy making, but the bureaucracy and the ruling Liberal Democratic Party (LDP) maintained a strong grip over politics.

After the demise of the Bretton Woods system, the United States' loss in Vietnam, and the Oil Crisis of the middle-to-late 1970s, Asian domestic political and economic systems received a severe externally produced shock. Asian economies experienced economic tribulations including inflation, temporarily reduced exports, and higher unemployment. However, these external events also created the foundation for the second stage of globalization by promoting the increased free-flow of currency by the use of floating exchange mechanisms, advances in free trade as evidenced by the Uruguay Round of GATT, and the need for corporations in the advanced industrialized nations to maximize their earnings by shifting production abroad. In particular, Japanese firms became active in seeking opportunities to lower labor costs by creating transplants in all countries, but especially in Southeast Asia and China. The sudden influx of FDI and the advantages that domestic corporations derived through increased openness upset the existing domestic political equilibrium.

During the 1980s and 1990s, the domestic political environment changed significantly as the previously authoritarian systems liberalized. One by one the bureaucratic, military, and dominant party elites received significant challenges. Challenges came from a new emerging middle class, more militant students, opposition politicians, and a new corporate elite that benefited from increased globalization and had become independent of the ruling elite. The previously powerful *ancien regimes* increasingly lost legitimacy as they could no longer maintain control over the increased quantity and strengths of new political actors. Further complicating the situation, any economic slowdown meant blame fell on the ruling elite. A more active press and increased political sophistication among the emerging middle class meant that the ruling elite could no longer operate in an insular manner. In other words, the entire region became more conducive for political liberalization and the inception of democracy in previously authoritarian systems. Even in Japan, the environment became ripe for dethroning the LDP from its pedestal.

Shaping Democratic Transitions and Consolidations

One of the major political developments within East Asian countries during the 1980s and 1990s consisted of increased political pluralism and democracy. The demise of the developmental state and the loosening of the previous elite configuration accounted for a shift in political development in the entire region. Globalization of the entire region created a new external and internal political and economic environment with greater levels of a diffusion of power.

Increased elite pluralism resulted in greater democratization with 'free and fair' elections in Taiwan, South Korea, the Philippines, and Thailand taking place in the 1980s and 1990s. In Japan, the ruling LDP even managed to lose power during the last decade. During the aftermath of the Asian Economic Crisis, South Korea and Taiwan underwent a peaceful transfer of power, with Kim Dae Jung and Chen Shui-bien. In Indonesia, General Suharto left the political scene and ushered in opposition leaders into power.

In other words, a new configuration of elites emerged as a result of globalization. The present contour of elite power includes elected officials and corporate elites in addition to many of the prior elites, including bureaucrats and former ruling party members. In fact, the developmental states' components still exert significant influence on domestic and foreign policies. Thus, while citizens' input will increase, the previously established patterns of interaction of elites and the basic decision-making structure will continue to operate, albeit through a more diffuse elite.

The public policies of these countries have become attuned to the diffuse power base. Issues of the environment, a more progressive foreign policy, and the development of welfare and domestic infrastructure are more likely to be emphasized. At the same time, increased political and policy immobilism becomes a major threat to governance. With a plethora of political actors juxtaposed against weak political institutions it becomes much more difficult to adopt new policies and to implement them. Clearly, domestic politics became much more complex as a result of globalization.

Impact of Globalization on Asian Foreign Policies

During the early part of the Cold War, the foreign policy of East Asian states consisted of anti-communism and an alliance with the United States. Caught up into the vortex of the conflict, most Asian states lacked an independent foreign policy. Most countries relied heavily on the United States for the transfer of military technology and military aid in order to protect national security. South Korea, Taiwan, and Thailand, in particular, expended large amounts of their national budgets for defense purposes. Most East Asian states hosted US military troops over an extended period of time.

Because of close relations with the United States, the 'free' East Asian nations did not interact cooperatively with North Korea, North Vietnam, or the People's Republic of China (PRC). At the same time, Japan failed to address issues related to its wartime activities and several Asian nations continued to harbor distrust and past grievances. The foreign policy world of most countries during the Cold War continued to remain centered on national security and the survival of each respective regime. The two components of national security consisted of economic development and military defense. As such most foreign policy initiatives fit around these two primary concerns.

With the approaching end of the Cold War, the economic success of the developmental states, and the Open Door Policy of PRC, East Asian states increasingly developed a more diversified foreign policy. US military presence in East Asia also declined with troops present in large numbers in South Korea and Japan only. Even in the cases of Japan and South Korea, the number of troops declined significantly from their peak.

Part of the foreign policy diversification included the increased importance of Association of Southeast Asian Nations (ASEAN) and regional cooperation issues. In particular, peacekeeping and environmental concerns became reflected in the foreign policies of Japan and South Korea, especially with a more active domestic constituency and the proliferation of Asian NGOs. Thus East Asian foreign policies have become more independent of the United States and more integrated with each other than during the Cold War.

Conclusion

Without a doubt, the Asian political realm reflects new levels of complexity resulting from globalization. Increased domestic and regional complexity, in terms of issues, actors, and linkages parallel developments in other regions of the world and in global affairs. This book brings together a variety of scholars committed to studying and understanding the transformation of the East Asian region in terms of domestic and foreign policies. The unique nature of this work consists of an attempt to place globalization as the unifying theme through which the foreign policies and domestic issues and politics intersect.

The various authors remain committed to the heterogeneity of approaches to exploring the phenomenon of regionalism in the context of globalization. Thus, some authors place greater emphasis on international systemic factors, such as the Cold War, while others emphasize the importance of changing domestic politics resulting from globalization. Many of the authors bring observations from extensive fieldwork to their analysis. All authors address the issue of globalization and the impact it has on these states as we move into the 21st century.

References

Amsden, A. (1989), *Asia's Next Giant: South Korea and Late Industrialization*, Oxford University Press, New York.
Compton, R. (2000a), *East Asian Democratization: Impact of Globalization, Culture, and Economy*, Praeger, Westport.
Compton, R. (2000b), "Reconstructing Political Legitimacy in Asia: Globalization and Political Development", *International Journal on World Peace*, vol. 17, 19-39.
Deyo, F. (1987), *The Political Economy of the New Asian Industrialism*, Cornell University Press, Ithaca.
Friedman, T. (2000), *The Lexus and Olive Tree*, New York, Farrar Straus and Giroux, New York.
Hatch, W. and Yamamura, K. (1996), *Asia in Japan's Embrace*, Cambridge University Press, Cambridge.
Hirst, P. and Thompson G. (1996), *Globalization in Question*, Polity Press, London.
Johnson, C. (1995), *Japan: Who Governs?*, W.W. Norton, New York.
Johnson, C. (1982), *MITI and the Japanese Miracle*, Berkeley,University of California Press, Berkeley.
Katzenstein, P.J. and Takashi S. (1997), *Network Power: Japan and Asia*, Cornell University Press, Ithaca.
Pempel, T. J. (1997), "Transpacific Torii: Japan and the Emerging Asian Regionalism", in P.J. Katzenstein and S. Takashi, (eds.), *Network Power: Japan and Asia*, Cornell University Press, Ithaca.
Wade, R. (1990), *Governing the Market: Economic Theory and the Role of Government in East Asian Industrialization*, Princeton University Press, Princeton.
Woo-Cumings, M. (1999), *The Developmental State (Cornell Studies in Political Economy)*, Cornell University Press, Ithaca.

Chapter 2

Globalization and the Developmental State: Reflections on the Asian Financial Crisis

Vincent Wei-Cheng Wang

Introduction

Mohamad Mahathir remarked, "All these countries have spent forty years to build up their economies and a moron like [George] Soros comes along" (Loh, 1997). Increasingly, political leaders in the developing nations witness the powerful market forces which render national fiscal, monetary, and regulatory policies weakened, if not totally ineffective. With increased economic globalization, national governments throughout the world see their power increasingly compromised and dependent on non-domestic factors, including global regimes of trade and finance. In essense, globalization became the paradigm (or cliché) of the post-Cold War era. Although its advent and presence seem irrefutable, its impact on domestic and international politics needs more studying.

A particularly important issue– the impact of globalization on governance in nation-states and the authority and legitimacy of the state– requires careful exploration. Will it cause the demise of the state, 'the withering away of the state', as Karl Marx put it? Or can globalization lead to the intensification of state powers?

Related to the issue of governance, globalization also affects economic performance. Globalization can propel countries to new economic heights or it can lead to dramatic domestic dislocations– a fact affirmed by the changing fortunes of East Asia. The rapid economic ascent in recent decades of such Asian countries as South Korea, Thailand, and Indonesia has often been attributed to their developmental state (Woo-Cumings, 1999; Johnson, 1982), whose astute stewardship of export-led industrialization coincided with the expansion of world trade. However, the Asian Financial Crisis of 1997-9 (Pempel, 1999) raised fundamental questions about the continued viability of developmental state and the perils of outward-looking development strategies in an increasingly globalized world economy.

This chapter discusses the challenges that globalization poses to the developmental state. It argues that the crisis induced by participation in the global economy has made it imperative to reform, but not jettison, the state. It will begin with an argument for placing the present globalization in a longer historical context. Then, it will contrast two different theories on the East Asian economic miracle that are relevant to the discussions on globalization. It will then show the degree of Asia's globalization in light of certain commonly used indicators so as to establish a partial account of the Asian financial crisis. It will conclude with a discussion of the future of the developmental state.

Globalization: New or Old?

The Cold War ended with the apparent dominance of liberal democracy over other forms of governance over Communist command economy based systems of Eastern Europe and Russia. As part of the resulting political analysis, Francis Fukuyama (1989) wrote of the dominance of liberal democratic systems into the future and prompted lively debate about the contours of the New World Order. Those who embrace and champion globalization emphasize the benign and potentially boundless promises that the current round of intensified globalization entails. In particular, advocates of globalization note that computerization and the digitization of communications lead to the 'the death of distance' (Cairncross, 1998). Increased international interactions created more porous borders and thereby transformed the state-centered Westphalian international system into a 'global village' (Falk, 1998).

Thomas L. Friedman, columnist for *The New York Times* and author of *The Lexus and the Olive Tree*, argues that globalization contributed to the emergence of a global marketplace and the rise of a 'homogeneous' global culture that reflects "the spread of Americanization on a global scale" (1999, 8). 'Globalphiles' like Friedman argue that free-market capitalism drives globalization, particularly since its apparent triumph over other ideological alternatives, as vindicated by the end of the Cold War (Fukuyama, 1989). Friedman asserts, "The globalization system has replaced the Cold War system... The world is 10 years old" (1999, xiii and 7). Others take a broader view on globalization, banking on its emancipating consequences. For example, the *1999 Human Development Report* (UNDP, 1999b) pins its hope that "global markets, global technology, global ideas, and global solidarity" can still "enrich the lives of people everywhere."

Many critics of globalization provide sober assessments about the social and economic costs of the entire process in order to help shape a more sustainable future path for globalization. Some fear that globalization may heighten communal and cultural conflicts (Barber, 1995). Others criticize that globalization exacerbates the gap between the 'haves' and the 'have-nots'– both between and within countries. Still others worry that the trade-off for interdependence is 'sovereignty at bay' with governments experiencing increasingly that external forces will undermine their ability to control their economies and to protect their citizens.

Still others question whether globalization represents a new phenomenon. In a thoughtful piece that places globalization in a broader historical context, Emma Rothschild (1999, 107) laments "globalization has been depicted, for much of the last 20 years, as a condition of the present and the future– a phenomenon without a past." Indeed, if one accepts a commonly used definition of globalization– "the intensification of economic, political, social, and cultural relations across borders" (Holm and Sørensen, 1995), then globalization not only occurred in history, but empirical evidence suggests its greater presence and integration before World War I.

Roger Burbach and William I. Robinson (1999) take a long-term historical perspective. They point out perceptively that the current era represents the fourth epoch in the world history of capitalism. Adapted from their analysis of capitalism, Table 2.1 summarizes the characteristics of each stage of globalization.

Table 2.1 shows that despite their similarities, each of these four epochs has its own driving forces, *zeitgeist*, and distinctive political events. The fourth and present epoch– since the 1970s– is characterized by the revolutionary impact of technology, particularly information technology (IT), which helps free market capitalism to expand globally with unprecedented speed and elan. The end of the Cold War and the apparent failure of other ideological alternatives are the most symbolic events.

As to the indicators for measuring globalization, Ankie Hoogvelt (1997, 69) points out that three key economic figures are conventionally marshaled to attest to the increasing internationalization of the world economy:

- world trade volume (in particular the allegedly rising ratio of world trade to output);
- the growth and spread of foreign direct investment through multinational corporations (also expressed in relation to world output and trade); and
- the expansion of *all* international capital flows (and their patterns of integration).

Table 2.1 Globalization– *déjà vu*?

Epochs	First	Second	Third	Fourth
Duration	1492-1789	1789-1900	1900-1970s	1970s-present
Age of	Discovery and conquest	Revolution, capital, and empire (Hobsbawn)	The 'Age of Extremes' (Hobsbawn)	The 'information age'
Discovery and Enlightenment				
Form of capitalism	Mercantilism and primitive accumulation	Industrial capitalism	'monopoly' capitalism	Globalization (world capitalism)
Symbolic events	Columbus' 'discovery' of the Americas	The French Revolution; England's 18th-century manufacturing revolution	World War I; Russia's Bolshevik revolution in Russia	The fall of the Berlin Wall; and the disintegration of the Soviet Union
Political manifestations	Capitalists emerging from 'feudal cocoon'	Rise of the bourgeoisie and the nation state	Rise of financial industrial corporations; imperialist wars; and a socialist alternative	End of the Bretton Woods system; collapse of socialism; failure of Third World national liberation movements

The use of the above three criteria leads to an identical conclusion with the United Nations Development Program (UNDP) *Human Development Report* (1999a, 30) which states: "globalization is not new: the world was more integrated a century ago; trade and investment as a proportion of GDP were comparable, and with borders open, many people were migrating abroad". So, what differentiates the current era of globalization from that of preceding periods?

As suggested earlier, revolutionary new technologies and the rapidity of change caused by these technologies characterize the current round of globalization. Friedman sums up the distinctive features as 'three democratizations'– of technology, of finance, and of information (1999, 39-58). Rothschild (1999, 107) thinks that "for both its admirers and its opponents, it [globalization] is associated with new and unprecedented technologies: the Internet, international capital markets, supersonic travel, cable news, and just-in-time deliveries across very large distances". Barber (1995, 4) argues that a new 'McWorld' will emerge that "demand(s) integration and uniformity and that mesmerize(s) people everywhere with fast music, fast computers, and fast food– MTV, Macintosh, and McDonald's– pressing nations into one homogeneous global theme park, one McWorld tied together by communications, information, entertainment, and commerce". As a UNDP publication states, what is really new about globalization is that it involves (1) new markets, (2) new actors, (3) new rules and norms, and (4) new (faster and cheaper) tools of communication (UNDP, 1999b).

Dramatic increase in speed and significant cost reductions in the communications arena lay the foundation for ensuing globalization. For instance, a three-minute call from New York to London in 1960 cost the equivalent of $46 in 1990 dollars, but in 1990 the cost for the same call dropped to $3. If the average cost of computers in 1990 is given an index of 100, the index for 1960 would be 12,500. The dramatic decline of cost and the simultaneous increase of speed inspires Friedman (1999, 9) to draw a contrast:

> While the defining measurement of the Cold War was weight– particularly the throw weight of missiles– the defining measurement of the globalization system is speed– speed of commerce, travel, communication and innovation. The Cold War was about Einstein's mass-energy equation, $e = mc^2$. Globalization is about Moore's law, which states that the computing power of silicon chips will double every eighteen to twenty-four months.

While these types of innovation benefit most developed nations, what impact could this have on the global South? Do they offer unprecedented opportunities or present insurmountable barriers to the less developed countries (LDCs) to tap into the current round of globalization? The answer to this question requires a reexamination of the world's economic structure (hierarchy and division of labor) in the context of the era's accelerated changes. If knowledge equates with power and its rapid dissemination promotes development, as the World Bank's *World Development Report* (1999) points out, then globalization– especially the computer and communication technology– reinforces and perhaps exacerbates the power differentials between the global North and South.

Measuring international power in the era of globalization requires an examination of Internet users rather than conventional military power, such as missiles. The Internet, which promotes international and domestic commerce and the dissemination of information epitomizes the current globalization. Table 2.2 presents a breakdown of Internet users by region.

Globalization and the Developmental State 15

Table 2.2 Uneven Globalization– Internet Users by Region

Region/Year	Millions online[a] 2000	Percentage of world's users 2000		1998	1997
North America (USA & Canada)	177.8	42.5		57.0	62.5
Europe	114.0	27.2		21.8	19.7
Asia-Pacific	104.9	25.1		17.0	14.7
South / Latin America	16.5	3.9		3.0	2.0
Africa	3.1	0.7		0.8	0.6
Middle East	2.4	0.6		0.5	0.5
World Total	418.6				

Note: [a] Estimated numbers as of December 2000, by Nua Internet Surveys.
Source: Compiled and calculated from NUA Internet Surveys (2001a; 1998; 1997).

Table 2.2 shows two important trends. First, it clearly affirms that America and globalization remain part and parcel, with Internet usage clustered strongly in that country. Among the estimated 418.6 million Internet users worldwide in 2000, 42.5 % of them lived in North America, mostly in the US and Canada. North America's dominance in the early years after the advent of the Worldwide Web was even higher– in 1997, five-eighths of all the world's Internet users lived in this region. English is the apparent *lingua franca* of the cyberspace, as more than 80% of all the websites are written in English. The ability of the U.S. to create the institutions and rules– defining protocols, allocating domains, standardizing languages– for the cyberworld characterizes what political scientist Stephen Krasner calls 'meta-power', which perpetuates and strengthens overall American power at lower cost.

Second, globalization progressed unevenly. Neither Africa nor the Middle East developed extensive Internet-based communications with the globalized world; their online populations remain negligible. One African official report described the huge gap in Internet connectivity between the global North and South by stating that "there are more phone lines in Manhattan than in all of sub-Sahara Africa" (Shapiro, 1999, 20).

However, European and Asian countries, including those traditionally considered 'developing,' steadily increased their Internet exposure during the past five years. In fact, some of the fast-growing countries in the Asia-Pacific region experienced explosive growth rates of their online populations. For example, in barely three years from 1997 to 2000, China's online population increased from 200,000 to 16.9 million (By contrast, the country's Internet 'penetration rate'– online population as a percentage of total population– rose from 0.001% to 1.34% during the same period). From June 1996 to July 2000, Taiwan's Internet penetration rate rose from

1.7% to 28.84% (NUA Internet Surveys, 2001b). The absorption of Internet technology in Asia illustrates an example of how countries utilize emerging technologies to partake in the globalization revolution. Asia continues to participate aggressively in the global economy and derive benefits from emerging technologies. Many analysts argued that globalization contributed to East Asia's dramatic post-World War II economic transformation, however, fewer scholars point out globalization's detrimental impact on East Asia. Studying the changing economic and political fortune of East Asia sheds light on the debate over the merits and perils of globalization for underdeveloped countries.

Asia's Ascendancy: Bringing the Global Factor back in

The rapid ascendancy of several Asian economies after World War II attracted much interest from scholars and policymakers alike. First Japan, then the 'Little Dragons' or Newly Industrialized Countries (NICs)– South Korea, Taiwan, Hong Kong, and Singapore– gained upward mobility in the international system by becoming important exporters of manufactured goods. Their ascent seemed to discredit the dependency theory in vogue during the 1970s (Cardoso and Faletto, 1979; Barrett and Chin, 1987; Evans, 1987), thereby enabling the liberals to tout the virtues for LDCs in maintaining outward-looking development strategies and access to global markets (World Bank, 1993). To varying degrees, Japanese and the NICs' strategies became replicated in several recently industrializing Southeast nations, such as Thailand, Malaysia, and Indonesia (MacIntyre 1994). The close economic relationships between the earlier industrializers and the later industrializers conjure up a 'flying geese' type of regional industrial development in East Asia (Bernard and Ravenhill, 1995).

Indeed, until the outbreak of the 1997 financial crisis, East Asia commanded attention and emulation. But many economists and commentators now scorn the same 'star tigers' after a sudden reversal of economic fortune for countries in the region. This raises a disturbing intellectual question: How can some of the same factors caused the successes of these nations– outward orientation, strong state, and market-coordinating intervention– also cause their economic demise? Do both earlier praise and present criticisms reflect premature judgements?

A quick settlement to this controversy remains unlikely. However, so far, some explanations offer more promise than others because of their comprehensive nature. Theoretical frameworks rooted in an analysis of global capitalism and its linkage to domestic economies provides useful sources of potential explanations. For example, according to the world system theory (Wallerstein, 1979), Asia joined the Western core-dominated capitalist system as part of the periphery. Consequently, Asia's rise and fall closely relate to globalization. Explanations for the Asian financial crisis that include both international and domestic-level factors are more intellectually satisfying than those that employ only domestic factors (e.g., 'crony capitalism').

The rapid ascent of dynamic Asian economies attracted much attention. Some analysts have admiringly described these Asian economies' success in the last three decades as 'miracle'. Others firmly believe that an East Asian model of development holds rich potential for other developing countries. Moreover, scholars have also long debated over how to explain Asia's economic success and whether this success story can be replicated elsewhere. A full treatment of this debate is beyond the scope of this chapter. However, discussions about certain aspects of globalization– specifically the merits of participating in the international economy and the proper role of the state in economic development– provide insight into Asia's economic development strategy.

Table 2.3 summarizes two competing perspectives explanations regarding the East Asian miracle.

While the dependency school depicts the forced participation in the world economy under an 'unjust' international division of labor as exploitation, both the neoclassical and the revisionist schools in Table 2.3 emphasize the benefits LDCs derive through their participation in the international economy. However, neoclassicalists and revisionists differ on the method by which LDCs should participate in the international economy. The neoclassical axiom states that LDCs should organize their participation based on the principle of comparative advantage arising from natural factor endowment. In contrast, the revisionists argue that the state must deliberately but judiciously employ incentives to promote industrial development that is anchored on an outward-oriented strategy. Specifically, they note that the most successful Asian countries adopted an export-led industrialization (ELI) strategy. By contrast, their Latin American counterparts that adopted an import-substituting industrialization (ISI) strategy that led to fewer successes (Haggard, 1990; Gereffi and Wyman, 1990).

Not only have the Asian economies been more integrated with the world economy than other regions, but their developments became more regionally integrated than Latin American counterparts. Some scholars (e.g., Cumings, 1987) suggest that a regional approach provides a more useful framework for understanding East Asia's patterns of development

Table 2.3 Explaining the East Asian Miracle: Two Different Accounts

	Neoclassical View	Revisionist View
Main reason for success	Getting the prices (basics) right	Getting the prices wrong
Market vs. state	State follows the market	State leads the market
More concerned about	Government failures	Market failures
View on external ties	Positive: They help achieve efficiency and gains	Positive: But they should be regulated by the state
Roles of government: nature of policies	Investing in human capital Promoting private enterprises Maintaining an open economy Maintaining macroeconomic stability ('fundamental' intervention policies)	Fundamental plus crafting and implementing selective intervention policies: Industrial and banking policies

and integration than single country analysis. Specifically, the development of regional political economy in East Asia has followed a 'flying geese' model (Bernard and Ravenhill, 1995; Romm, 1992). According to this model, countries gradually move up in technological development by following the patterns of those that preceded them in the development process (Radelet and Sachs, 1997). In this vision, Korea and Taiwan took over leadership in textiles and apparel from Japan as the latter moved into the higher technology sectors of electronics, transport, and other capital goods. A decade or so later, Korea and Taiwan would upgrade to electronics and auto components, while the textile and apparel industries moved to Indonesia, Thailand, Vietnam, and China.

Steven Radelet and Jeffrey Sachs argue that, to a certain extent, the flying geese pattern reflects the natural outcome of market forces, indicating that global economic forces also shape the patterns of regional industrialization. However, they also admit "even the simplest labor-intensive products (apparel, footwear, electronics assembly) are part of a sophisticated international division of labor, one increasingly determined by multinational enterprises and technological designs created in the advanced economies" (1997, 52).

From this discussion, one can understand why the neo-Marxist dependency writers contend that Asia owes its 'success' to a temporary comparative advantage entirely based on the exploitation of cheap labor in such designated export platforms as 'free export processing zones' with few linkages to the surrounding economy. This type of development, akin to what Peter Evans (1979) calls 'dependent development' in the Latin American context, resulted in deepening inequalities and marginalization. This neo-Marxist position becomes known as the new international division of labor (NIDL) thesis (Hoogvelt, 1997, 204).

Hoogvelt asks whether the developmental state phenomenon in East Asia reflects *historically* specific, rather than *culturally* specific (emphases original) factors:

> The historical specificity of the 'model' relates to the external environment of the geopolitics of the Cold War and its unique conjunction with a certain phase in the development of capitalism on a world scale (1997, 213).

Burbach and Robinson (1999) echo the NIDL view. They rebuke most of what they call 'detractors of globalization' that focus on global trade, and therefore the *market*. Instead, they argue, "The process of globalization is driven by the transnationalization of *production* and capital ownership, which in turns leads to the rise of a transnationalized bourgeoisie that sits at the apex of the global order" (1999, 7, 15). They conclude: "Global capitalism, therefore, is now represented in each nation-state by in-country representatives, who constitute transnationalized fractions of dominant groups" (1999, 34). These leftist scholars fill in a very important void in the mainstream rosy 'McWorld' interpretation of globalization. Clearly, it is important to consider the politics– class, democratic deficit, and civil society– of globalization, both at the domestic and international levels. Their influence led to calls for 'globalization with a human face' (UNDP, 1999b).

If politics is defined as a process of authoritatively allocating scarce resources, then political processes remain at the core of globalization, as it entails important distributional consequences that create a group of transnationalized bourgeoisie. In the neo-Marxist parlance, one can even argue that modern computer and communication technology constitutes a new means of production and creates new relations of production. It threatens to exacerbate existing class conflicts by increasing inequalities.

Stephen Gill (1999) offers an insightful neo-Marxist interpretation of the Asian crisis. He argues that the Asian crisis is partly attributable to geopolitics, namely, 'the third phase of a longer process involving the reassertion of U.S. strategic dominance', which is reflected in the ideology of neoliberalism and the mechanism of the International Monetary Fund's (IMF) strict conditionality. Did Western dominance contribute to East Asia's economic troubles?

With these caveats, we can proceed to discuss the relationship between globalization and the Asian financial crisis and speculate on the future of the developmental state model in an era of globalizing economies within the context of embedded neoliberalism.

The Globalization of Asia: Laying the Foundation for the Crisis?

Just how globalized has East Asia become? Has East Asia become a victim of its own success? Employing some of the most commonly used indicators in the study of globalization (i.e., growth of trade volume, trade share of GDP, growth of external debt, and external debt share of GNP), Table 2.4 depicts globalization trends in Asian countries over the past two decades. To the extent such increased exposure to the world market offers them more opportunities, it also makes them more vulnerable to the vicissitudes of the world economy.

Table 2.4 compares these indicators for two periods, 1980 and 1996, the year before the outbreak of the Asian financial crisis. The table reveals several important findings. First, all these countries had experienced a very large growth in merchandise trade (in current dollars) during the period under study. Trade indeed had served as one important– if not *the*– 'engine of growth'. Several Asian countries, particularly Japan and the NICs, have become important exporters of manufactured goods for the world markets.

Second, leading up to the onset of the Asian crisis in 1997, Thailand, the Philippines, and Malaysia had become more and more dependent upon trade (i.e., foreign markets)– measured by the percentage share of trade volume of gross domestic product (GDP). But other countries, such as Indonesia, South Korea, Taiwan, and Singapore experienced a decline in trade dependence, despite overall growth in absolute trade. This indicates the increased importance of their domestic markets. Hong Kong, historically an entrepôt, saw its trade share rise, mainly because of Mainland China's rapid economic development and expanding exports since 1980.

Third, apparently, a correlation between external debt and economic vulnerability exists. Not coincidentally, all of those countries most negatively affected by the Asian financial crisis previously assumed large external debt burdens in the leading to the crisis. In particular, Thailand and Indonesia accumulated such massive foreign debt that their debts matched or even exceeded their respective annual GNPs. The bad experience of these Asian debtors shared many important similarities with the Latin American debt crisis in the 1980s. During that crisis, a combination of factors– rising interest rates in the international financial markets, declining earnings from exports from these debtor nations, and pressure on these nations to devaluate their currencies– rapidly raised these nations' debt service ratios (export earnings/GNP) to unbearable levels, threatening a default. Only IMF's intervention averted the crisis (Frieden, 1991).

Table 2.4 Rising Asian Trade Dependence and External Debt

	Trade volume[a] ($ billions)		Trade share of GDP (%)		External debt ($ billions)		External debt as % of GNP
	1980	1996	1980	1996	1980	1996	1997
Thailand	15.8	129.1	54	83	8.3	90.8	61
Indonesia	32.7	92.6	54	51	20.9	129.0	62
Philippines	14.0	55.0	52	94	17.4	41.2	51
Malaysia	23.7	154.2	113	183	6.6	39.8	48
South Korea	39.7	269.1	74	69	–	–	33
Taiwan	39.5	218.3	95	80	–	–	–
Singapore	43.4	255.9	440	356	–	–	–
Hong Kong	41.7	379.3	181	285	–	–	–

Note: [a] Merchandise exports plus merchandise imports.
Sources: Compiled and calculated from World Bank (1999, 228-31; 2000, 268-71) and CEPD (1998, 204, 213).

Data show that Asian countries experienced increased globalization, in terms of trade and debt (both their blessing and curse), but the extent of each economy's globalization varies widely from country to country. Table 2.5 attempts to measure globalization by three indicators– Internet users (absolute numbers, shares of total population, and per 1,000 people), Internet hosts per 10,000 people, and personal computers per 1,000 people. The last three columns take into account population size by providing 'standardized' measures on the 'density' of personal computers and Internet users. The picture it presents– the disparate 'information power' in Asia– provides a new way to conceptualize power and plenty in the information age.

Table 2.5 emphasizes the central role that the modern information and communication technology plays in our current phase of globalization. Most of the proponents of globalization, considered 'technophiles' (Luke, 1989), view communication technology as a hallmark of globalization. In this paradigm, a country's 'information power', determines a country's overall strength, rather than traditional militaristic measurements.

In fact, some scholars speculate that as globalization progresses, the state, if it continues to exist, will become a 'virtual state' that thrives on ultra-mobile factors of production such as knowledge or human capital.

International relations, consisting of these virtual states, will be inherently peaceful (Rosecrance, 1996). If accurate, the prospects for prosperity or peace within regions and specific countries vary depending on the extent of information globalization.

As computer prices and Internet access fees continue to decline rapidly, increasingly more people will access a virtual world. The advent of the Worldwide Web in the mid-1990s was unquestionably a powerful boost to expanding the global Internet population. Table 2.5, which takes into account population size, compares the 'information density' of select countries.

Small nations with excellent communication infrastructure and extensive external economic ties fare exceptionally well under this new notion of national power. Singapore, Netherlands, and Finland rank as among the most globally integrated countries on *Foreign Policy's* (2001) index. Finland, with a population of just over 5 million and home of Nokia, is one of the 'most wired' nations. Meanwhile, the U.S. ranks as the country with the most Internet users in absolute numbers (estimated at 164.4 million, or close to 60% of the population– 4.25 times more than that of the next, Japan). In fact, fifteen countries account for 90% of all Internet users.

It should also be affirmed that those NICs that actively promoted the information technology (IT) industry, such as Taiwan and South Korea, fare quite well in terms of 'information power'. For example, Taiwan decided in the early 1980s to promote the IT industry as a strategic industry in anticipation of these broad trends in technology and trade (Wang, 1995/96; Lin, 1998). On a per capita basis, Taiwan's computer density is higher than Japan's and the NICs' Internet penetration rates (as a share of population) remain comparable to Japan's. However, in the long run, China seems to have limitless potential with estimates up to 37 million users by 2005 (NUA Internet Surveys, 2001b; 1999a; 1999b).

Tables 2.4 and 2.5 show that all the East Asian countries became much more globalized in recent years but simultaneously demonstrated variations in their dependence on trade, external debt, and foreign investment. Furthermore, variations exist in terms of their information power. In other words, each country accumulated a different mix of 'assets' and 'liabilities' associated with globalization, with each precise mix entailing important consequences. Table 2.5 also provides an unusual perspective for understanding the Asian financial crisis. Not coincidentally those countries that score low on 'information power'– for example, Indonesia and Thailand– received, *prima facie*, the most abrupt dislocations associated with the Asian financial crisis (see Table 2.6).

Table 2.5 Uneven Globalization– Disparate Information Power

	Internet users[a]	Internet users %[a]	Internet users[b]	Internet hosts[c]	Personal computers[c]
Thailand	1.0	1.65	16.2	.646	21.6
Indonesia	0.4	0.18	1.9	.1	8.2
Philippines	0.5	0.62	6.5	.158	15.1
Malaysia	1.5	6.88	66.1	2.543	58.6
South Korea	16.4	34.55	350.4	6.003	156.8
Taiwan	6.4	28.84	290.9	130.444	336.0
Singapore	1.9	44.58	578.1	4.522	458.4
Hong Kong	1.9	26.00	268.1	1.628	254.2
China	16.9	1.34	13.5	0.057	8.9
India	4.5	0.45	4.5	0.023	2.7
Japan	38.6	30.53	305.2	2.081	237.2
USA	164.4	59.86	602.4	193.997	458.6
Finland	2.8	43.93	436.5	121.842	349.2

Notes and Sources:
[a] Data for 2000; 'Internet users' in millions and percent as percent of total population. The months in which surveys were done varied. NUA Internet Surveys (2001b, 2001c, 2001d).
[b] Internet users / population as of 1999; expressed in 1,000s. NUA Internet Surveys (2001b, 2001c, 2001d) and World Bank (2000, 278-9).
[c] World Bank (2000, 310-1) employs data from International Telecommunication Union. All country data for 2000, except Taiwan. Taiwan's internet host data are internet subscribers per 10,000 people for 1999. Taiwan's computers per 1,000 people data are 1995 estimate, using the following formula: [(Units of desktop PCs produced in 1995) + (units of notebook PCs produced in 1995)] / (1995 total population). Compare figures in this column with caution. Admittedly many of these Taiwanese computers were exported. However, the World Bank/ITU data on other countries do not affirm they are for domestic use, not export. All data in 1,000s. See CEPD (2000, 20 and 142) and Figure 5.3 from World Technology Evaluation Center (1999).

This correlation seems to confirm the finding by Amartya Sen, the 1998 Nobel economics laureate, that accurate information flows are necessary to prevent man-made policy disasters (e.g., famine). If the financial crisis can be viewed as a 'man-made' crisis in the sense of policy failures, patron-client politics, and lack of accountability, then to what extent can the lack of transparency explain the downfall of such Asian countries as Indonesia and Thailand? And to what extent can weaknesses in 'information power' explain the negative impact of the Asian Crisis among countries? From this standpoint we can understand why developing the information technology (IT) industry is so important for Asian countries, because it not only produces new sources of growth, but also lays foundation for a more open and resilient society.

The Asian financial crisis dealt a devastating blow to several Asian high-fliers. Table 2.6 shows the effects by tracking several indicators from

1997, when the crisis started, in 1998, when the crisis reached maturity, and then again in 1999, when several countries began to slowly recover. All five of these affected countries experienced large currency devaluations, recession, and shrinking wealth. Furthermore, just as these Asian countries began to improve, the economic slowdown in the U.S. and the decline in technology related share prices on the US stock exchange 2000, severely dampened the momentum of East Asia's economic revival. Those countries that 'weathered' the 1997-9 crisis, such as Taiwan, now show surprisingly unusual economic difficulties in 2000 and 2001.

These aggregate statistics fail to accurately depict the human suffering, especially among the poor, resulting from the crisis. As a condition for accepting the IMF's conditionality, these countries slashed social spending (on education, health, and unemployment assistance) while the number of jobs decline precipitously. Frightened foreign investors fled rapidly and mercilessly– to use Friedman's (1999) 'electronic herd' metaphor. Domestic entrepreneurs saw their confidence shaken and encountered problems in raising new capital for investment. The newly emergent middle class (the segment widely viewed as the catalyst for bringing about a democratic polity) and non-agricultural labor force saw their savings and net value plummet as poverty also increased. The social and economic stress caused by the financial crisis portended political crises.

An estimated 40 million people lived on less than one U.S. dollar per day in the five affected countries before the crisis, primarily in Indonesia and the Philippines. The first year of the crisis witnessed those living in absolute poverty more than double in countries without elaborate social safety nets, with pockets of absolute poverty reappearing in South Korea and Thailand (Jackson, 1999a, 2).

Despite these problems, prior to the outbreak of the 1997 crisis, the Asian economies were praised as among the most successful LDCs. Their predominant development strategy– ELI with a focus on manufactured goods, promoted by a strong, autonomous and developmentally oriented state– nearly achieved the status of the new development orthodoxy.

Both the material fortune of these countries and the intellectual popularity of the model vanished quickly with the 'sudden', 'surprising', and dramatic collapse of their financial and property markets. As a sign that theorizing in international and comparative studies often gets unduly dictated by daily events and caught up in the fads of the moment, many unsophisticated accounts began to blame these countries' misery on, more or less, the identical factors that had contributed to these countries' earlier success. Was the developmental state model intellectually hypocritical to begin with? Did the model outlive its usefulness as national economies became increasingly enmeshed with one another through the activities of the global market? Answers to these key questions require an exploration into the causes of the Asian financial crisis.

Table 2.6 Asian Crisis: Shrinking Currency and Vanishing Wealth

Country	Thailand	Indonesia	Philippines	Malaysia	S. Korea
Exchange rate to US dollar	baht	rupiah	peso	ringgit	won
Jun 1997	24.5	2,380	26.3	2.5	850
Jul 1998	41.0	14,150	42.0	4.1	1,290
Aug 1999[a]	37.3	6,915	38.8	3.8	1,199
Sep 2000[a]	42.6	8,740	45.9	3.8	1,126
GNP (US billions dollars)[b]					
Jun 1997	170	205	75	90	430
Jul 1998	102	34	47	55	283
Aug 1999	103	71	51	59	318
Sep 2000	122	129	79	75	404
Growth rate (%)					
Jul 1998-Aug 1999	-8.0	1.8	1.2	-1.3	4.6
Sep 1999-Sep 2000	5.2	4.1	4.5	5.2	9.6

Notes: [a] Exchange rates obtained on 4 August, 1999 and 20 September, 2000 from *Yahoo! Currency Converter* (http://www.yahoo.com).
[b] All current dollars.
Source: Jackson (1999a, 2); *Asiaweek* (1999; 2000).

The Developmental State as Cause of the Asian Crisis?

Although no consensus exists regarding the precise cause of the Asian Crisis, general agreements exist. Although the precise causes in each country were slightly different, most analysts generally agree that the causes of the crisis included both external forces and internal weaknesses: (1) financial-sector weaknesses (corruption and nepotism, lack of credit-worthy criteria for lending, 'moral hazards', excessive speculative investments in real estate), (2) external-sector problems (overvalued currencies due to 'pegging', speculative buying and selling by international financiers, excessive borrowing abroad, and a substantial portion of short-term debt) and (3) the 'contagion effect' (Haggard, 2000; Pempel, 1999; Jackson, 1999b; and Goldstein, 1998).

Intellectual honesty requires that advocates of neoliberalism share some responsibility for the Asian financial crisis. The crisis qualifies as a case of unintended consequences of premature liberalization that 'back-fired'. Over the years, Western countries pressured Asian economies to globalize long before they possessed the technical expertise and political will to establish the requisite financial institutions to properly manage large amounts of capital in and out of their countries. Malaysian Prime Minister Mahatir's war of words with George Soros, the international financier, captures Asians' frustration and resentment toward the devastation caused by 'rational' currency traders: "All these countries have spent forty years to build up their economies and a moron like Soros comes along" (Loh, 1997).

At a deeper structural level, since most of these Asian countries embrace capitalism, can their collapse be attributed to some structural flaws within capitalism? Here Stephen Gill's differentiation between two different varieties of capitalism provides valuable clues (Gill 1998, 4-5). In the Anglo-American capital-market system (or 'fluid' capital system), the stock and bond markets provide a supply of capital to firms. The providers of capital, mainly shareholders and investors, expect a high level of accountability and adherence to profit projections. In return, corporate failure results in declining share value and bond ratings, the removal of the top executives of the firm, or in worse case scenario bankruptcy with all workers dismissed and assets liquidated.

In contrast, Gill describes the Japanese and East Asian financial systems as 'credit-based' or dedicated capital systems. Historically these tended to be bank-centered, highly concentrated, and state-directed systems. In a crisis, the government generally negotiates adjustments among affected groups ('stakeholders') within the society, including workers. In other words, the government, through informal workouts, works to socialize risk rather than privatize it. Based on this distinction, he criticizes the IMF bailout packages as 'socialization of private debts' and questions the class bias of the whole process.

> The IMF assured foreign investors and banks that their debt would be repaid, and it moved to roll over short-term into long-term debt, compelling various governments in effect to socialize private debts... [This] shows the limit of the commitment of pure free-market policies when the interests of Western capital are endangered (Gill, 1999, 6).

In other words, the West preaches the philosophy of free market capitalism, but when its own capital becomes jeopardized, the West practices socialization of private debts.

The financial crisis also contributed to full-fledged political crises or uncertain political transitions in several Asian countries. Authoritarian governments previously dominated many of these countries and they relied heavily on economic development for legitimacy. Consequently, economic crisis served to undermine the very political foundation of authoritarian governments. Not surprisingly, the economic crisis prompted severe regime instability and a change of political leadership in Indonesia, Thailand, the Philippines, and South Korea. (Suharto's downfall in Indonesia and his succession by three weak transitional figures, Habibie, Wahid, and Megawati, became *sin qua non* examples of evaporating legitimacy.) Only Malaysian Prime Minister Mahathir, who managed to hang on by turning against his reformist deputy, Anwar Ibrahim, increasing repression, rejecting IMF package, and limiting capital movement managed to remain in power. Whether his approach will ultimately be vindicated remains to be seen.

Without question, the Asian financial crisis dealt those affected serious political, economic, and social setbacks. At the same time, however, it also ushered in a promising new era of democratization. But do these harbinger the death of the developmental state? Does the prevalence of IMF bailout signify– to use Fukuyama's (1989) phrases– the 'unabashed triumph' of, and the 'exhaustion of viable alternatives' to, neoliberalism? Can that be interpreted as underscoring America's unparalleled power? Furthermore, was the Asian economic miracle merely an ephemeral fluke? Lastly, what kind of government (or governance) do Asian countries need in order to cope with the internal and external challenges posed by a new century characterized by globalization?

Concluding Remarks: Whither (or Wither?) the Developmental State?

Discussion of the future fate– of the often venerated and sometimes vilified developmental state in the new era of new globalization– requires a review of the logic and condition under which it excels should provide some answers. Table 2.7 compares the essential features of the developmental state (the Asian model) with the regulatory state (the Anglo-American model).

To summarize, the developmental state paradigm consists of three elements (or rather, observations or reification). First, the East Asian states place top priority on economic development, often operationalized in terms of growth, productivity, and competitiveness. Second, in order to achieve these broadly defined goals, the state actively intervenes in the market to guide, discipline, and coordinate the private sector through the strategic allocation of resources and the use of diverse policy instruments.

Table 2.7 Developmental State vs. Regulatory State

Characteristics	Regulatory State	Developmental State
Basis of Rationality	Market-Rational	Plan-Rational
Focus	Rules	Outcome
Main Goal	Regulation	Development
Criterion of Success	Efficiency	Effectiveness
Explicit Industrial Policy	No	Yes
Focal or Pilot Agency	No	Yes
Prerequisite for Success	No	National Consensus
Better at Coping With	Shocks	Routines
Locus of Decision Making	Parliament	(Elite) Bureaucracy
Main Actors	Economists and Lawyers	Bureaucrats and Nationalists
Examples	US and UK	Japan, S. Korea, and Taiwan

Third, competent bureaucrats, who insulate themselves from political and social pressures, increase the success of strategic state intervention in Asian economies. These insulated, interventionist states, contrary to neoclassical projections, have been relatively free from rent-seeking or predation (Moon and Prasad, 1998).

At the heart of the debate over the developmental vs. regulatory state is the central issue– and perennial scholarly controversy– of the relative importance of the state and the market in economic development (Putterman and Rueschemeyer, 1992). Today virtually no serious scholar completely dismisses *any* role for the state. Nor can corporations replace states for governing. Even the World Bank, the institutional embodiment of neoliberal ideology, recognized the importance of sound policy and good governance (World Bank, 1997, 1993).

Both the state and the market are key agents of economic development. Earlier theorizing on East Asia depicted an adversarial relationship between the two, but the precise formula, to a considerable extent, still depends on vogue. Current scholarship aspires to move beyond either state or market and toward a third-generation theory (Chan, Clark, and Lam, 1998; Rowen, 1998).

A brief recap serves to trace the evolution of scholarship (or vogue) in the field. The first-generation theory, espoused by neoclassical economists and the World Bank in the 1970s and early 1980s, attributes East Asia's dynamic development and economic success to the 'magic of the market'– *laissez faire* and open economy (Balassa, 1981). State intervention, if any, forces market conformity by aiming only to 'get the fundamentals right' (World Bank, 1993).

In contrast, the second-generation theory, emerging in the late 1980s and early 1990s and advocated mainly by political scientists, argues that the key to East Asia's success is the 'developmental state', an autonomous and strong political entity with a coherent corporate goal– development. State intervention in 'late industrializers' (LDCs) is pervasive, seeking to deliberately 'set the prices wrong' in order to create competitive advantage for the developing country (Amsden, 1989).

The popularity of the statist theory lasted until the outbreak of the Asian financial crisis. The once venerated East Asian model became discredited and scorned. While earlier admirers championed the East Asian developmental state as a model for other LDCs to emulate, today's critics disparage 'moral hazard' and other undesirable collusive practices, especially financial sector weakness (Kaminsky and Reinhart, 1998).

The swift shift in explanations leaves much to be desired. In reality, the developmental state probably never exercised omnipotent presence as many enthusiasts believed. At the same time, it certainly cannot be as guilty as detractors portray. For the foreseeable future, the Asian states are likely to maintain their exposure to the world markets, rather than turning inward. Globalization undeniably will pose special challenges to the developmental state. But the proper response for the Asian states is to reform, rather than jettison, their developmental state. Reasons for necessary reform abound.

First, the political milieu of most Asian countries today reflects quite different concerns and realities from that during the take-off phase. Most Asian developmental states made their transitions to democracy in the 1980s-90s and some are well under way toward consolidating their new democracies. In the aftermath of decades of suppression, civil society begins to reassert itself as distributional coalitions form and postmodern values (Inglehart, 1997) gradually take hold. These trends mean that an increasingly large portion of the population seek to benefit from economic development and will use the political process to obtain them. For example, more than three decades of pursuing single-minded growth, environmental degradation constituted a costly and irreversible price. Facing these new expectations and priorities, the developmental state will have to promote a form of development that is true to the meaning– that is, balancing growth and sustainability, quantitative expansion and qualitative improvement, production and consumption (welfare), and foreign markets and the domestic market. In other words, development in a democracy should aim at improving security and the physical quality of life, rather than a singular focus on quantitative macroeconomic expansion.

Walden Bello and Stephanie Rosenfeld, two long-time critics of the East Asian developmental state, prophetically proclaimed almost one decade ago, "The old strategy of high-speed, export-oriented growth will not get the NICs through the 1990s" (1992, 337). They called for a comprehensive and coherent vision of an alternative mode of development. They then went on to portray the contours of this new comprehensive alternative paradigm: democratic participation, the growth and consolidation of the domestic market, equity, sustainable development, a selective export policy, and the development of equitable regional associations (1992, 338-41). With corporations and NGOs undermining the authority of the state, it is increasingly doubtful whether a globalized world economy can afford a developmental state *par excellence* that pursues national interests in terms of maximizing its relative gains through the practice of neomercantilism.

Secondly, the operating principles of globalized economy juxtaposed against a developmental state consisting of competent technocrats insulated by authoritarian politicians without accountability to the public has become a practical impossibility and an anachronism in a world where information flows more freely. Increasingly, the need for political accountability reflects a popular theme among those calling for reforms in governance, whether on domestic or international level. Thus far, despite its evident benefits to a large number of people and states, globalization suffers from a paucity of democratic accountability. At the global level, many critics view the institutions and procedures as undemocratic and non-transparent and its impacts uneven or unjust. Tactics notwithstanding, the protesters at the World Trade Organization's Seattle meeting in 2000 and the Group of Eight summit meeting in 2001 legitimately demanded corrections to globalization's democratic deficits. Under this global context, a developmental state seeking to operate in secret and withhold information from its citizens cannot succeed in increasing its legitimacy. A fiasco like the Asian financial crisis actually provides a welcome wake-up call in the still unfolding historical process of globalization. We can learn from the crisis the importance of good governance.

Because of its emphasis on technology, globalization entails some potential (not guaranteed) to level the playing field between decision-makers and those that are affected by the decisions. For example, the computer and communication technology may enable the advent of 'electronic democracy'. It can empower the citizenry by making it easier and more meaningful for ordinary citizens to participate in politics and express their views. By facilitating more participation in our unfortunate but necessary republican form of government, it may enable efforts toward good governance without too much government dictate. It also contributes to the emergence of a vibrant civil society. Many writers (e.g., Barber, 1995) have always considered the civil society as the necessary (but missing) link and buffer between the state and the individual. In the global age, the civil society takes on new importance as the 'human face' between anonymous global forces and real individuals.

The third reason the developmental state needs reform rests in the realities of the internal dislocations caused globalization (i.e., to protect its citizens from the excesses of globalization). While globalization may bring material and political benefits directly to citizens by bypassing states that consistently censor information, it must also protect citizens from economic difficulties and the erosion of cultural values. For example, in China where the regime still strictly controls information and the media still primarily serves as a tool for government propaganda, the Internet allows more and more people to receive alternative information, allowing them to formulate political opinions outside those supported by the government. At the same time, does the global community have China's best interest at heart in terms of economic and social development? These are difficult questions that the Chinese state must address as it reforms its political system.

At the same time, globalization can also expose people more directly to both the beneficial and harmful forces beyond the control of the state. Whereas in the past all politics may well have been local, as the former Speaker of the House Tip O'Neil once said, in the globalized world in which we live today, arguably all politics are global. In this regard, the developmental state should not 'wither away', by abdicating its responsibility to the global market forces that are best at producing efficiency and profits. It is unrealistic to expect corporations to provide global public goods, such as democracy, cooperation, and solidarity. If these public goods are provided at all by global market forces, they are afterthoughts or unintended consequences. Such values are too important to be relegated totally to an invisible hand.

For the foreseeable future, good alternatives to the state, albeit an imperfect institution, will still be hard to find. Optimists who pin their hopes on 'corporate-like states' replacing states are remiss. The state exists to advance the interests of a group of people with a clear sense of destiny that resides on a geographically defined territory. The capacity for the state to take care of people during hard times is particularly important, as the Asian financial crisis sorely demonstrates. The true test of the state therefore lies in its ability to protect its citizens from the harms of globalization and to enable them to benefit from the advantages of globalization.

Unless and until the state-centered Westphalian system is fundamentally overhauled, the developmental state will likely retain its *raison d'être*, but it will have to become a 'kinder and gentler' (perhaps even slower) entity. Since extrication from the global economy is not a viable option for the Asian states, the developmental state must retool itself so as to cope with this still-unfolding process, known as globalization.

References

Agence France Presse (1999), 'Dissident Says Internet Becoming Weapon of Choice', *Inside China Today*, 1 September, [Online]; available from http://www.insidechina.com/news.php3?id=80096&html; accessed 1 September, 1999.

Amsden, A.H. (1989), *Asia's Next Giant: South Korea and Late Industrialization*, Oxford University Press, New York.

Asiaweek (2000), "The Bottom Line", 22 September, [Online]; available from http://www.cnn.com/ASIANOW/asiaweek/magazine/2000/0922/bottomline.html; accessed 20 September, 2000.

Asiaweek (1999), 'The Bottom Line', 6 August, [Online]; available from http://www.pathfinder.com/@@87bmuAQA4Wwb1LyE/ asiaweek /current/issue/bottom.html; accessed 6 August, 1999.

Balassa, B. (1981), *The Newly Industrializing Countries in the World Economy*, Pergamon Press, New York.

Barber, B.R. (1995), *Jihad vs. McWorld: How Globalism and Tribalism Are Shaping the World*, Ballantine Books, New York.

Barrett, R.E., and Chin, S. (1987), 'Export-oriented Industrializing States in the Capitalist World System: Similarities and Differences', in F.C. Deyo (ed.), *The Political Economy of the New Asian Industrialism*, Cornell University Press, Ithaca, pp. 11-22.

Bello, W., and Rosenfeld, S. (1992), *Dragons in Distress: Asia's Miracle Economies in Crisis*, The Institute for Food and Development Policy, San Francisco.

Berger, P. (1987), *The Capitalist Revolution*, Wildwood House, Aldershot.

Bernard, M. and Ravenhill, J. (1995), 'Beyond Product Cycles and Flying Geese: Regionalization, Hierarchy, and the Industrialization of East Asia', *World Politics*, vol. 47, pp. 171-209.

Burbach, R. and Robinson, W.I. (1999), 'The Fin De Siecle Debate: Globalization as Epochal Shift', *Science & Society*, vol. 63, pp. 10-39.

Cairncross, F. (1998), *The Death of Distance: How the Communications Revolution Will Change Our Lives*, Harvard Business School Press, Cambridge.

Cardoso, F.H., and Faletto, E. (1979), *Dependency and Development in Latin America*, University of California Press, Berkeley.

Chan, S., Clark, C. and Lam, D. (eds.), (1998), *Beyond the Developmental State: East Asia's Political Economies Reconsidered*, St. Martin's Press, New York.

Computer Industry Almanac, Inc. (1999), '150 Million Internet Users Worldwide Year-End 1998', [Online]; available from http://www.c-I-a.com/199904iu.htm.

Council for Economic Planning and Development (CEPD) (2000), *Taiwan Statistical Data Book, 2000*, CEPD, Taipei.

Council for Economic Planning and Development (CEPD) (1998), *Taiwan Statistical Data Book, 1998*, CEPD, Taipei.

Cumings, B. (1987), 'The Origins and Development of the Northeast Asian Political Economy: Industrial Sectors, Product Cycles, and Political Consequences', in F.C. Deyo (ed.), *The Political Economy of the New Asian Industrialism*, Cornell University Press, Ithaca, pp. 44-83.

Evans, P. (1987), 'Class, State, and Dependence in East Asia: Lessons for Latin Americanists', in F.C. Deyo (ed.), *The Political Economy of the New Asian Industrialism*, Cornell University Press, Ithaca, pp. 203-26.

Evans, P.B. (1995), *Embedded Autonomy: States and Industrial Transformation*, Princeton University Press, Princeton.
Evans. P. (1979), *Dependent Development: The Alliance of Multinational, State, and Local Capital in Brazil*, Princeton University Press, Princeton.
Fajnzylber, F. (1990), 'The United States and Japan as Models of Industrialization', in G. Gereffi, and D.L. Wyman (eds.), *Manufacturing Miracles: Paths of Industrialization in Latin America and East Asia*, Princeton University Press, Princeton, pp. 323-52.
Falk, R.A. (1998), *Law in an Emerging Global Village: A Post-Westphalian Perspective*, Transnational Publishers, New Brunswick.
Frieden, J.A. (1991), *Debt, Development, and Democracy: Modern Political Economy in Latin America, 1965-1985*, Princeton University Press, Princeton.
Friedman, T.L. (1999), *The Lexus and the Olive Tree*, Farrar, Straus, and Giroux, New York.
Fukuyama, F. (1989), 'The End of History?', *The National Interest*, vol. 16, pp. 3-16.
Gereffi, G. and Wyman, D.L, (eds.), (1990), *Manufacturing Miracles: Paths of Industrialization in Latin America and East Asia*, Princeton University Press, Princeton.
Gill, S. (1999), 'The Geopolitics of the Asian Crisis', *Monthly Review*, vol. 50, pp. 1-9.
Goldstein, M. (1998), *The Asian Financial Crisis: Causes, Cures, and Systemic Implications*, Institute for International Economics, Washington.
Haggard, S. (1999), *The Political Economy of the Asian Financial Crisis*, Institute for International Economics, Washington.
Haggard, S. (1990), *Pathways from the Periphery: The Politics of Growth in the Newly Industrializing Countries*, Cornell University Press, Ithaca.
Holm, H., and Sorensen, G. (eds.), (1995), *Whose World Order? Uneven Globalization and the End of the Cold War*, Westview, Boulder.
Hoogvelt, A. (1997), *Globalization and the Postcolonial World: The New Political Economy of Development*, Johns Hopkins University, Baltimore.
Inglehart, R. (1997), *Modernization and Postmodernization: Cultural, Economic, and Political Change in 43 Societies*, Princeton University Press, Princeton.
Jackson, K.D. (1999a), 'Introduction: The Roots of the Crisis', In K.D. Jackson (ed.), *Asian Contagion: The Causes and Consequences of a Financial Crisis*, Westview Press, Boulder, pp. 1-27.
Jackson, K.D. (ed.) (1999b), *Asian Contagion: The Causes and Consequences of a Financial Crisis*, Westview Press, Boulder.
Johnson, C. (1982), *MITI and the Japanese Miracle: The Growth of Industrial Policy*, Stanford University Press, Stanford.
Johnstone, B. and Kinoshita, J. (1993), 'Past Success Provides No Sure Guide to the Future', *Science*, 15 October, pp. 358-60.
Kaminsky, G., and Reinhart, C. (1998), 'Financial Crises in Asia and Latin America: Then and Now', *American Economic Review*, vol. 88, pp. 444-8.
Krugman, P. (1994), 'The Myth of Asia's Miracle', *Foreign Affairs*, vol. 73, pp. 62-78.
Laris, M. (1999), 'Beijing Turns the Internet on Its Enemies', *Washington Post*, 4 August, p. A01.
Lin, O.C.C. (1998), 'Science and Technology Policy and Its Influence on Economic Development in Taiwan', in H.S. Rowen (ed.), *Behind the East Asian Growth: The Political and Social Foundations of Prosperity*, Routledge, London, pp. 185-206.
Loh, H.Y. (1997), 'Mahathir Calls Soros 'Moron' in War of Words', *Business Times*, 25 August.
Luke, T.W. (1989), *Screens of Power: Ideology, Domination, and Resistance in Informational Society*, University of Illinois Press, Urbana.

MacIntyre, A. (ed.), (1994), *Business and Government in Industrializing Asia*, Cornell Univerisity Press, Ithaca.
'Measuring Globalization', (2001), *Foreign Policy*, no. 122, p. 56-65.
Moon, C., and Prasad, R. (1998), 'Networks, Politics, and Institutions', in S.Chan, C. Clark, and D. Lam (eds.), *Beyond the Developmental State: East Asia's Political Economies Reconsidered*, St. Martin's Press, New York, pp. 9-24.
NUA Internet Surveys (2001a), 'NUA Internet How Many Online', [Online]; available from http://www.nua.ie/surveys/how_many_online/index.html; accessed 27 June, 2001.
NUA Internet Surveys (2001b), 'NUA Internet How Many Online: Asia', [Online]; available from http://www.nua.ie/surveys/how_many_online/asia.html; accessed 27 June 2001.
NUA Internet Surveys (2001c), 'NUA Internet How Many Online: Europe', [Online]; available from http://www.nua.ie/surveys/how_many_online/europe.html; accessed 27 June, 2001.
NUA Internet Surveys (2001d), 'NUA Internet How Many Online: North America', [Online]; available from http://www.nua.ie/surveys/how_many_online/n_america.html; accessed 27 June, 2001.
NUA Internet Surveys (1999a), 'Newsbytes: Asia To Have 374m Internet Users By 2005', [Online]; available from http://www.nua.ie/surveys/?f=VS&art_id=905355236&rel=true; accessed 27 August, 1999.
NUA Internet Surveys (1999b), '37 Million Chinese Users Predicted by 2005', [Online]; available from http://www.nua.ie/surveys/?f=VS&art_id=905354685&rel=true; accessed 9 February, 1999.
NUA Internet Surveys (1998), 'Internet Users By Location, 1998', [Online]; available from http://www.nua.ie/surveys/analysis/graphs_charts/1998graphs/location.html; accessed 27 June, 2001.
NUA Internet Surveys (1997), 'Internet Users By Location, 1997', [Online]; available from http://www.nua.ie/surveys/analysis/graphs_charts/1997graphs/location.html; accessed 27 June, 2001.
Önis, Z. (1991), 'The Logic of the Developmental State', *Comparative Politics*, vol. 24, October, pp. 109-26.
Pempel, T.J. (ed.), (1999), *The Politics of the Asian Economic Crisis*, Cornell University Press, Ithaca.
Putterman, L., and Rueschemeyer, D. (eds.), (1992), *State and Market in Development: Synergy or Rivalry?*
Radelet, S. and Sachs, J. (1997), 'Asia's Reemergence', *Foreign Affairs*, vol. 76, November/December, pp. 44-59.
Romm, J. (1992), 'Japan's Flying Geese (Japanese Corporate Management of Overseas Operations in Asia)', *Forbes*, 23 November, pp. 108-11.
Rosecrance, R. (1996), 'The Rise of the Virtual State', *Foreign Affairs*, vol. 75, July/August, pp. 45-61.
Rothschild, E. (1999), 'Globalization and the Return of History', *Foreign Policy*, no. 115, Summer, pp. 106-16.
Rowen, H.S. (ed.), (1998), *Behind the East Asian Growth: The Political and Social Foundations of Prosperity*, Routledge, London and New York.
Shapiro, A. (1999), 'The Internet', *Foreign Policy*, no. 115, Summer, pp. 14-27.
Smith, P. (1999), 'Globalism's Pen Pal', *The Nation*, 14 June, pp. 28-34.
Snidal, D. (1991), 'International Cooperation Among Relative Gains Maximizers', *International Studies Quarterly*, vol. 35, pp. 387-402.
United Nations Development Programme (UNDP). (1999a), *Human Development Report, 1999*, Oxford University Press, New York.

United Nations Development Programme (UNDP). (1999b), 'Globalization with a Human Face', *Human Development Report, 1999*, [Online], available from http://www.undp.org/99.htm.
United Nations Development Programme (UNDP). (1998), *Human Development Report, 1998*, Oxford University Press, New York.
Wade, R. (1990), *Governing the Market: Economic Theory and the Role of Government in East Asian Industrialization*, Princeton University Press, Princeton.
Wallerstein, I. (1979), *The Capitalist World Economy*, Cambridge University Press, Cambridge.
Wang, V. W. (1995/96). 'Developing the Information Industry in Taiwan: Entrepreneurial State, Guerrilla Capitalists, and Accommodative Technologists', *Pacific Affairs*, vol. 68, Winter, pp. 551-76.
World Bank (2000), *World Development Report, 2000/2001: Attacking Poverty*, Oxford University Press, New York.
World Bank (1999), *World Development Report, 1998/99: Knowledge for Development*, Oxford University Press, New York.
World Bank (1997), *World Development Report, 1997: The State in a Changing World*, Oxford University Press, New York.
World Bank (1993), *The East Asian Miracle: Economic Growth and Public Policy*, Oxford University Press, New York.
World Technology Evaluation Center (1999), *Electronics Manufacturing in the Pacific Rim*, [Online], available from http://www.itri.loyola.edu/em/05_03.htm.

Chapter 3

Chinese Elite Conflict over Globalization

Lawrence C. Reardon

Introduction

Over time, Chinese elites developed a love-hate relationship with the international marketplace. Elites often viewed the international economy as a dangerous adversary, which only desires to reestablish the asymmetrical, colonial relationship of the 19th century to extract the lifeblood of the nation. At other times, Chinese elites regarded the international economy as the primary source of financial capital, advanced technology and management expertise that will aid the country's rise to power in the 21st century. While not unique, this paradoxical attitude produced four decades of dramatic development policy shifts unlike any experienced in East Asia.

Understanding the underlying causes for this development antinomy helps explain why these dramatic shifts occurred (Reardon, 2001; 1996). Using an opinion group approach, this study hypothesizes profound crisis causes elites to question the underlying assumptions of current policy. Seeking to find the most reliable policy to avoid chaos, elites do not have the luxury to sit back and ponder the nuances of policy options. Under pressure to find the best solution to the crisis, elites place more emphasis on their personal experience- such as those gained through living, studying or working- to guide them toward a correct policy path. While coalescing around similar basic attitudes to resolve crisis, opinion groups do not remain static over time. Elites not only learn from their past experiences, but also generate new groups when confronting a new crisis (Reardon, 1998).

This chapter analyzes Chinese opinion group formation by evaluating two cases of profound crisis: one following the Great Leap Forward (GLF) of the late 1950s and the less obvious crisis following the 1978 Third Plenum. The GLF crisis generated two major opinion groups promoting import substitution and autarchy in the 1960s and 1970s; the development crisis in the early 1980s resulted in opinion groups taking either a radical or conservative approach to export promotion. The ensuing struggle within the policy elite to implement a particular vision of development strategy thus has been the primary cause for Chinese development antinomy, which delayed China from following the globalization path chosen by the other major Asian economies.

Chinese Development in Comparative Perspective

The uniqueness of China's development path becomes obvious when comparing the Chinese and East Asian experiences. Despite differences in economic size, resource endowments and internal market organization, many similarities exist with Asian nations, in particular with the South Korean and Taiwanese economies. All three economies share similar 'Confucian' traditions and close geographic proximity. Furthermore, the relative insulation of the policy making processes resulting from state autonomy, rather than merely 'reflecting the demands or interests of social groups, classes, or society' attest to their 'strong state' orientation (Skocpol, 1985; Katzenstein, 1978). While a long tradition of a centralized decision-making structure characterizes China, Taiwan and South Korea inherited their centralized structures from their previous colonial masters— the Mainland Chinese and the Japanese. Both established non-democratic, authoritarian institutions in order to extract material resources and control aberrant societal forces (Grindle and Thomas, 1991; Cheng, 1991). Whether the Kuomintang Party in Taiwan or the various political and military regimes in control of South Korea, the successors to the colonial elites, in both cases, expanded control by co-opting business interests, organized labor and other societal interests. Unlike the liberal democracies and clientalist states of Latin America, these three economies remained less susceptible to pressures from distributional coalitions pursuing their self-interest (Cheng, 1991; Haggard, 1990; Johnson, 1987).

Similar to many countries in the developing world, the policy elites in the three economies used their policy autonomy to accelerate national economic growth (Rhee, 1994; Amsden, 1989). Such direct intervention went beyond guaranteeing macroeconomic stability and providing public goods (Wade, 1991). The state also played a larger role compared with marketplace, which was only comparatively 'free' in Hong Kong (Balassa, 1982; Freeman and Freeman, 1980; Chen, 1979). Instead, elites of the three economies adopted a neomercantalist approach of development by implementing at various times selective restrictions on imports, maintaining overvalued exchange rates and promoting selected industries through tax incentives, privileged access to development capital, etc. (Haggard and Cheng, 1987).

This 'pragmatic flexibility' originated from policy autonomy and neomercantalist philosophy, which enabled them to experiment with a variety of development regimes. Such flexibility became an extremely important variable to the Taiwan and South Korean success story, because it allowed policy elites to respond inventively to economic crisis brought about by the international and domestic environments. While switching from primary-product exports to various forms of import substitution during the 1950s and early 1960s, Taiwan and South Korea learned that the import substitution strategy led to economic inefficiency, the production of inferior commodities and other related social and economic problems (Sheahan, 1986; Little and et. al, 1970). A new group of development economists, especially in the World Bank, argued that an outwardly oriented regime promised greater long-term benefits. The greater economies of scale and efficient allocation of resources allowed a country to realize its comparative advantage, and produce products highly competitive on the world market. The country also could attract greater foreign investment and absorb foreign technology and management skills (Sheahan, 1986).

Unlike their counterparts in many Latin American states, South Korean and Taiwanese policy elites remained unpersuaded by the 'dependencia' view of world trade advocated by Raúl Prebisch (1950) and others during the 1950s (Singer, 1950; Myrdal, 1956; Emmanuel, 1972). Instead of blindly supporting import substitution development, the South Korean and Taiwanese policy elites 'pragmatically' gambled on a neomercantalist version of export promotion (Gilpin, 1975) whenever faced with a severe economic crisis. Whether it was the withdrawal of American aid during the early 1960s (Haggard and Pang, 1994; Cheng, 1991; Haggard, 1990; Haggard and Cheng 1987) or economic turmoil caused by mistaken macroeconomic policies, or the Arab oil embargoes (World Bank, 1993; Shive, 1991) the developmental state responded with greater integration with the global economy through exports. Much to the dismay of the neoclassical school, these policy elites did not adopt an orthodox form of outwardly oriented development, which would have entailed a 'neutral' trade and industrial policy (Balassa, 1982; Bhagwati, 1978; Krueger, 1978). Their neomercantalist approach to export promotion entailed a mixture of selective sectoral protection as well as limited import substitution in order to maximize the national good, even if it violated the norms of the global free trade regime. Yet, the neoclassical economists admit that the policy elites' 'pragmatic flexibility' enabled these economies to better withstand economic crisis caused by the oil embargoes of the 1970s and the global economic recession of the 1980s than their counterparts in Latin America (Balassa, 1980; World Bank, 1993). The success of the East Asian developmental state model resulted in over one-third (51) of the world's developing countries (144) adopting some variation of an outwardly oriented strategy by 1975 (Basile and Germidis, 1984).

Policy elites in Taiwan and South Korea thus enjoyed the autonomy and capacity to effect major changes in their development strategies, especially when confronted by economic crisis. After discovering the diminishing returns of primary export-led development and import substitution, they embarked upon the export promotion path. Inwardly oriented development represented a transitory phase; the next phase of outwardly oriented strategies ended discrimination against export sectors and allowed domestic market forces ('private initiative') to play a larger role in the country's development in the

1950s and 1960s (Balassa, 1982). While arguing the absence of a single prescription for their success, the World Bank cites the promotion of a rapid growth in exports and the guaranteeing of macroeconomic stability (maintenance of moderate to low inflation rates, a serviceable foreign and domestic debt, etc.) as two key catalysts for their high growth rates (World Bank, 1993). Thus, the 'pragmatic flexibility' exhibited by South Korean and Taiwanese policy elites guaranteed a sustained growth of exports, laying the foundation for the 'Asian Miracle'.

Like their counterparts in Taiwan and South Korea, Chinese policy elites enjoyed in the pre-1979 period the autonomy to formulate development policy and the capacity to implement specific policies. Furthermore, elites' decisions were predicated on their perception of the national good; when they perceived impeding economic crisis, elites called for dramatic changes in the development strategy. Encountering the increased tensions of the early Cold War, the three economies initially adopted an inwardly oriented development regime to reassert sovereignty over the national economic process and to achieve a high degree of self-reliance. The three economies thus protected domestic 'infant' industries by erecting high tariff barriers and other obstacles, which permitted little if any foreign competition for domestic producers. Supported by an overvalued currency, the state allowed domestic producers to import selectively key technology and equipment to substitute for imported goods. During their inwardly oriented phase, South Korea, Taiwan and the PRC thus actively discriminated against imports and only promoted exports in order to finance import substitution projects (Balassa, 1980).

Unlike Taiwan and South Korea, both charter members of the Asian 'miracle' economies, China continued to pursue inwardly oriented development for twenty more years. During this period, Chinese elites primarily disagreed over the correct inwardly oriented approach, which resulted in an antinomy of development strategies and delayed the experimentation of a more outwardly oriented approach. When Chinese elites finally learned the diminishing returns of inwardly oriented development by the late 1970s, elites subsequently differed over the degree of involvement with the global economy. These disagreements over globalization dominated the formation of Chinese foreign economic policy during the last half of the 20th century, and set the Chinese apart from their Asian cousins.

Elite Conflict and Opinion Groups

Understanding the delayed acceptance of outwardly oriented development, requires analysts to come to terms regarding the differing opinions of key Chinese policy elites. Grindle and Thomas point out that elites, especially from developing countries, are not pure utility maximizers. In addition to the international environment, various society-centric (social classes, interest groups) or state-centric (bureaucracies) variables influence elites' behavior. These variables establish barriers within which policy elites possess a wide degree of maneuverability. The primary variables affecting policy decisions include the 'prior experience in the problem or area, professional expertise in a particular discipline, personal values, ideology or study, debate, and discussion among a group of individuals concerned with similar issues' (Grindle and Thomas, 1991). To understand the policy formation process, Grindle and Thomas' emphasize the revealing of the 'embedded' preferences of individual decision-makers.

In the China field, the opinion group model has been influenced by Chinese polemics during the Cultural Revolution and Richard Lowenthal's work on the 'communist dilemma' (1985; 1970), both of which focused on the differing perceptions within the policy elite concerning the correct path of economic development. Building on previous opinion group models (Yan, 1995; Jacobson and Oksenberg, 1990; Van Ness and Raichur, 1989; Harding 1987; Solinger, 1984; Joseph, 1984; Eckstein, 1977; Ahn, 1976; Schurmann, 1968), this study analyzes the dynamics of opinion group formation and evolution. In the two cases examined, the divergent views on development to a large degree can be traced to the elites' previous experience with and understanding of the capitalist marketplace. Three opinion groups can be identified– Nativists, Internationalists and the Moderates. For forty years, their interactions created development antinomy.

The Nativists

Of the three opinion groups, the Nativists criticized the international marketplace more than the others. As a group, these policy elites had limited experience with the outside world, and possessed little knowledge of the economies in the advanced industrialized states or even other developing states. Their revolutionary experience in the Chinese countryside– especially in Yan'an during the 1930s and 1940s– taught them the importance of motivating 'communist man' as the primary means to develop China in an adversarial world (Sun, 1996; Schram 1991; Lieberthal, 1987). Based on their personal experiences, these policy elites believed their parochial approach to development was the purest, most genuine Chinese path to self-reliance; they condemned the economist's manipulation of financing and planning schedules because in reality they did not understand economics (Lieberthal, 1987).

Mao Zedong was by far the most prominent Nativist, who only ventured out of China for two short-term visits to the Soviet Union. Beginning in the mid-1950s, Mao Zedong moved away from market-based incentives of the early 1950s (Lardy, 1983) to embrace normative measures that mobilized the people's sense of nationalism and communist ideals. According to Eckstein (1977), Mao believed the key catalyst for economic change was the Chinese people, who could overcome any development obstacle through proper indoctrination. Policy elites could effect a change in attitudes not by simply offering material benefits such as those provided by market-oriented economies, but providing 'spiritual' rewards. The Communist Party could mobilize the people to pursue the national good and eschew all sense of self-interest. Nativists considered market-oriented incentives not only vestigial, but a dangerous economic tool that would act as a capitalist cancer infecting the socialist ethos.

China only needed to rely on the resourcefulness of her people, including those already trained in the Soviet Union and Eastern Europe, to achieve its production potential. With the conclusion of the First Five-Year Plan (FFYP), China possessed the tools to become self-reliant and no longer needed to rely solely on the Soviet technology or equipment, nor take advantage of greater access to western marketplace to enhance its development. In this new semi-autarchic form of inwardly oriented development, foreign trade played a minor role; the small amount of needed imports could be financed with exports achieved through normative/administrative measures, such as the reemphasis of meeting planning targets, institution of wide-spread campaigns and sloganeering. Advocates of this normative/administrative approach to development are somewhat similar to Lowenthal and Harding's 'Utopians', Joseph's 'Cultural Revolutionaries', Van Ness/Raichur's 'social mobilizers', Jacobson/Oksenberg's 'Nativists', Yan's 'Negators', as well as Oksenberg and Goldstein's 'Militant Fundamentalists' and 'Radical Conservatives' (Oksenberg and Goldstein, 1974).

The Internationalists

Unlike the Nativists, the Internationalists enjoyed a high degree of interaction with the international economy– whether through extensive experience of studying, traveling and/or working in the western capitalist economies. Although never questioning the need to build a strong, independent socialist China, they adopted a more utilitarian view of development. The productive potential of 'communist man' could be enhanced by normative exhortation, but would be more fully realized by using material incentives and foreign technology. To accelerate domestic development, Chinese leaders thus needed to use normative and remunerative tools of encouragement, as well as promote a greater interchange with the global economy.

Marilyn Levine (1993) and others documented the experiences of a generation of policy elites who went to Europe during the 1920s and became members of European branches of the Chinese Communist Organizations. Similar to the Chinese students who studied in Russia during the 1950s, and in the advanced industrialized economies since the early 1980s, the Chinese studying in Europe in the 1920s were part of a transitional generation who witnessed the failure of the previous political order. They searched for the one road of national salvation to establish a new China. Initially, they hoped western technology would lead to national salvation. After arriving in Europe, many discovered the political solution to China's new order– Marxism. Yet, the experience of studying and working in Europe undoubtedly made a lasting impression on communist political elites such as Zhou Enlai, Zhu De, Deng Xiaoping, Li Fuchun, Nie Rongzhen and Chen Yi. Not only did they form lasting bonds of friendship, but also understood from personal experience the political and economic situation outside China and the positive and negative aspects of the market economy.

In their search for supplementary tools of resource mobilization and allocation, Internationalists championed a combination of both the command economy's administrative tools of mobilization with the more market-oriented approach of remunerative measures (Eckstein, 1977). Remunerative measures are characterized by the use of material incentives– increases in wages, prices, privileged access to materials, and etc.– to achieve higher economic growth rates in the 1960s and 1970s. They encouraged the importation of foreign technology and equipment to achieve self-reliance (import substitution) and the use of market-oriented incentives to encourage fulfillment of state quotas.

Having learned by the late 1970s that inwardly oriented development would not produce high growth rates (Reardon, 2001), Internationalists argued for a more outwardly oriented strategy, whose bold experimentation would result in high growth rates. After 1979, Fewsmith (1994) argues that the Internationalists (Fewsmith's 'reformers') such as Deng Xiaoping wanted to replace the state planner and state industrial sector with the marketplace and individual entrepreneurs. By establishing various economic development zones and providing various policy incentives, Internationalists promoted a coastal economy more integrated with the international market that had few protections against imports and few restraints on foreign direct investment.

In contrast with the Nativists, the Internationalists willingly promoted greater interaction with the international economy. Their extensive experience of studying and working in a foreign capitalist environment made it easier for them to treat economics as a tool, not to be feared, but to be utilized to achieve a modern socialist state. These policy elites, to a qualified extent, are similar to Lowenthal's 'Technocratic Developmentalists,' Harding's 'Developmentalists and Liberals,' Joseph's 'Veteran Revolutionaries,' Van Ness/Rai-chur's 'Stalinists' and 'market socialists,' Jacobson/Oksenberg's 'Cosmopolitans,'

Yan's 'Affirmers' and 'Developers' as well as Oksenberg/Goldstein's 'Eclectic Modernizers' and 'Westernized Chinese'.

The Moderates

The final opinion elite group, the Moderates, appreciated the potentially beneficial role of the international market through study in the Soviet Union, or their work experiences in China's coastal areas or in Manchuria during the pre-1949 period. Liu Shaoqi during his student days at the Communist University of the Toilers of the East (Moscow) was leader of the 'practical workers,' who emphasized practice as opposed to those students who emphasized ideology and theory (Zhang, 1969; Dittmer, 1974). Elites such as Chen Yun gained extensive knowledge about the market economy from educational and work experiences in pre-Liberation Shanghai and about the Soviet planning system while in Manchuria (Li and Yao, 1995; Goncharov, Lewis and Xue, 1993). Among the current leadership generation, Li Peng represents the 1950s generation of policy elites trained in the Soviet Union. During the 1960s and 1970s, the Moderates, remained mainly silent and agreed with the Internationalists' remunerative or administrative approach and promoted an inwardly oriented development based on import substitution. They disagreed with the Nativist vision of growth, and had no cause to break stride with the Internationalists.

Yet, the Moderates transformed themselves into an active opinion group by the early 1980s. While studying in the Soviet Union or working in the economic planning bureaucracy, the Moderates were immersed in the socialist planned economy. While they realized the need for renewal and innovation, the Moderates disagreed with the Internationalists on abandoning the basic remunerative administration approach in the early 1980s. They deviated from the Internationalist's vision of the incorporation of China's coastal economy into the global economy. As Fewsmith argues, Moderates such as Chen Yun (i.e., Fewsmith's 'Conservatives') promoted the continuation of the socialist planned economy that avoided economic imbalances and inefficiencies rampant in the western market economies. They continued to champion the role of the central planners and administrative tools to foster balanced growth.

Although Fewsmith does not focus on foreign economic policy, it can be argued that Moderates welcomed an expansion of foreign trade and foreign investment, which were regarded as important engines of development. They understood that the basis of the Soviet Union's industrial might had been the New Economic Policy of the 1920s, and the utilization of foreign capital and technology. As a developing country, China enjoyed comparative advantage in labor and land resources, and needed to expand production of labor-intensive commodities for the domestic and export markets. Lacking capital and entrepreneurial ability, China could increase imports of capital-intensive products and programmatically lift certain protectionist barriers to foreign direct investment. In the long-term, China's planners could adopt a more equitable pricing system for production inputs, reduce artificially high currency exchange rates, and eliminate certain protectionist quotas and non-tariff barriers (Myint, 1979). Thus, Moderates argued that the international marketplace should be tapped to preserve and expand China's socialist economic system, not replace it.

Crisis as an Intervening Variable

Previous opinion group approaches can be criticized for lacking a sense of dynamism. Just because one studied in Paris in the 1920s or the Soviet Union in the 1950s does not mean that the same two elites arrive at identical perspectives. Furthermore, Chinese elites with different backgrounds also learn from previous mistakes and collaborate upon joint strategies. Such collaboration can be motivated by belief, or by political necessity. For instance, during the mid-1950s as Mao Zedong searched for a unique Chinese path of development, elites such as Deng Zihui, Chen Yun and Zhou Enlai vocally disagreed with Mao's vision of 'rash advance' (Chen Yun, 1996a; Lieberthal, 1987; Bachman, 1985; Lardy and Lieberthal, 1983). Yet, after Mao reasserted control of the Political Bureau during the first half of 1958, these policy elites endorsed Mao's normative approach to Chinese development during the Great Leap Forward (Reardon, 2001; Teiwes, 1999).

Yet, behind this facade of unity lurked division. There are always differences of opinion, even within a particular opinion group. However, a catalyst is needed to operationalize these differences, and to cause elites to coalesce into competing opinion groups. The fear of chaos is the missing ingredient. According to Grindle and Thomas, crises involve all the top policy elites, who are pressured to enact dramatic change to prevent total political or economic disorder. As a result, they often adopt innovative reforms that can change the basic direction of the state (Grindle and Thomas, 1991). In his pathbreaking book on Japanese politics, Calder (1988) argues that crisis serves as the primary catalyst for 'domestic, non-industrial innovation in Japan... rather than the routine lobbying of corporatist interest groups (either business federations or labor unions) or even the strategic planning of the state.' Psychologists and political scientists explain that crises frequently threaten the goals or values important to policy elites (Holsti, 1972; Hermann, 1963). According to experimentation findings, 'there is a narrowing of the cognitive organization at the moment; the individual loses broader perspective, he is no longer able to 'see' essential aspects of the situation and his behavior become, consequently, less adaptive'. According to Holsti (1972), people thus '[regress] to simpler and more primitive modes of response,' and lose a large degree of 'creativity, flexibility, [and] tolerance for ambiguity'. Jervis (1976) adds that elites under pressure process information based on pre-existing beliefs and without full information often leading to premature cognitive closure. As a result, more innovative solutions elude policy makers, and instead they adopt 'reliable' solutions, especially ones learned through firsthand experience.

Crisis thus acts as a catalyst to break apart previous opinion groups, and contributes to the evolution of new opinion groups. Crisis made the Nativists, the Internationalists and the Moderates rely on their pre-existing beliefs, which resulted in differing policy prescriptions. Crisis thus can destabilize the political status quo, but as Li Xiannian (1992a) argued in the early 1960s, 'through chaos order will be achieved [youluan daozhi]'. The opinion group that most effectively argues for stability is thus able to de-legitimate the former ruling elite coalition(s) and implement a policy prescription to achieve stability and growth.

Case Study: Mao Zedong's Search for a Chinese-style of Development

During the early 1950s, the ruling policy elites– or as Lieberthal referred to them, the Yan'an coalition (Lieberthal, 1987)– uniformly looked to the Soviet Union for guidance, technology and financial assistance to achieve an independent, self-reliant China. With the FFYP, China embarked upon one of the largest transfers of technology in modern time. China imported hundreds of turnkey plants and technology projects from the Soviet Union. Thousands of Chinese students and technicians visited the Soviet Union, learned and copied their methods, and returned to re-create the Soviet experience in China. Yet, this uniform support of the development strategy proved short-lived. Debating the correct path of development beginning in the mid-1950s, the Yan'an coalition eventually divided into two general opinion groups following the chaos of the Great Leap Forward. This division of opinion would remain until Mao Zedong's death in 1976.

Despite the successful transfer of technology during the FFYP, Mao rejected Stalin's path to economic development by the mid-1950s. Mao and the Chinese communist movement successfully developed a strong, innovative economy during the Yan'an period of the 1940s. By reviving the Yan'an model, Mao could promote a truly unique Chinese-style development mode from which the Soviets could learn (Bo, 1991). Starting in late 1955, Mao criticized Stalin's overemphasis of administrative tools at the expense of more normative methods– such as the mass line. By not involving the people and preventing the revival of the capitalist class, China could suffer the same fate as Hungary, whose socialist path was endangered by counterrevolutionaries in 1956 (Mao, 1986a). At the Party's Chengdu Conference of March 1958, Mao concluded that Chinese leaders copied the Soviet development experience too closely, especially in industrial and planning management. Many recognized the danger of such dogmatism; China needed 'to do away with blind faith, eliminate old thinking, and bring into play their creative spirit' (Bo, 1991). During the FFYP, China already imported a sufficient number of industrial plants from the Soviet Union. While some new imports might be necessary, the future of China's development did not lay in copying the Soviet industrial structure. Mao would 'advance recklessly' by advocating an alternate, distinctively Chinese path toward development– the GLF. Mao's accelerated approach relied on the indomitable strengths of the 'communist man', who possessed the ability 'to walk on two legs' to achieve self-reliance (Riskin, 1987; Eckstein, 1977).

With the local communist elite motivating the peasantry and workers, China could become self-sufficient in grain and steel, whose production eventually would surpass the British and Americans. Some elites adopting Mao's Nativist view of development concurrently promoted an extreme form of self-reliance or autarchy by arguing that China did not have need of any imports from abroad. As a result, a conflict arose over the signing of the US$ 1.25b technical aid agreement with the Soviet Union that had been included within the 2nd Five-Year Plan (Li, 1992b).

The GLF thus would become the shining example of a unique Chinese path of development (Bo, 1991). Such results not only would impress Khrushchev– who also did not believe China could achieve such growth– but also increase China's standing within the world communist movement. Unfortunately for Mao, this 'rash advance' approach to economic development would result with the death of tens of millions of Chinese people in 1959, 1960 and 1961 (Yang, 1996).

Chaos and the Emergence of the Internationalist Opinion Group

Since the mid-1950s, Mao differed with other policy elites, in particular Zhou Enlai and Chen Yun, about the necessity of promoting "rash advance". During the Nanning Conference of 1958, Mao (1974) described the previous policy making situation as:

> Like the United Nations of Dulles, the Political Bureau has become a voting machine. You give it a perfect document and it has to be passed. Like the opera, you have to go on stage and perform since the show has been announced. The document itself does not go into textual research and essence, and it also has foreign words. I do have a method, and that is passive resistance. I will not read it. For two years, I have not read your documents and I do not expect to read them this year either.

In early 1958, Mao effectively dissolved the Yan'an coalition by severely admonishing Zhou Enlai, Chen Yun and others for criticizing Mao's strategy of 'rash advance'. Zhou Enlai even tendered his resignation as Prime Minister (Zhonggong, 1997). For the next several months, Mao and his intimidated cohorts on the Political Bureau praised the glorious work of the Great Leap, with its communal kitchens and backyard furnaces. Yet, by November 1958, Mao and Chinese policy elites foresaw the impeding economic chaos resulting from the 'rash advance' strategy of the Great Leap Forward (Lardy, 1987). Producers failed to meet agricultural production quotas with the onset of a series of natural and man-made disasters. Looking for a convenient scapegoat, Mao now criticized the other policy elites for using 'adventurist' and 'rash' development policies that imperiled China's well being (Bo, 1991; MacFarquhar et. al, 1989).

Unwilling to continue in the front line of Chinese leadership, Mao decided to retire to the 'second line' of leadership in spring 1959 (MacFarquhar, 1983). As he demonstrated during the Lushan Conference, Mao with the support of Liu Shaoqi, Zhou Enlai, Deng Xiaoping and Ye Jianying continued to defend his control of the Party. Mao reviewed all documents issued in the name of the Central Committee. However, he gradually ceded influence in the economic development policy sphere to Liu Shaoqi and Zhou Enlai, who completely readjusted the GLF development strategy by 1961. In his extensive analysis of the GLF period, MacFarquhar (1983) concludes that Mao's semi-retirement resulted in 'the swift diminution [after Lushan] in the number and size of Mao's speeches and writings on current domestic policy.' Although Mao's ultimate authority was never challenged, the chaos of the GLF and the purge of Peng Dehuai 'combined to unravel the political consensus that had held the Yan'an leadership together...' (Lieberthal, 1987). These disaffected elites thus sought a new alliance coalescing around a shared view of China's correct path of economic development. The chaos arising from the failure of the Nativist's approach to development served as the catalyst for the formation of the post-GLF elite leadership who promoted a more Internationalist agenda.

Liu Shaoqi, Zhou Enlai and the post-GLF elite leadership faced the largest economic dislocation since 'Liberation' that endangered the lives of the Chinese people, its ability to repay its financial debts to the Soviet Union, and most importantly the Party's legitimacy. With Mao temporarily out of the policy game, the new governing elite coalition coalesced around a more flexible approach to economic development– one that accepted remunerative incentives and foreign technology to revive the Chinese economy. They thus rejected Mao Zedong's proto-experiment with autarchy embodied by the Great Leap Forward, and would gradually seek help from abroad, but this time from the advanced industrialized economies.

By readjusting the development strategy to a more remunerative approach in the agricultural, industrial and commercial sectors, the new coalition eventually revived the domestic economy after 1962, and readopted an import substitution strategy, whose reduced scale reflected China's weakened economy. Chinese leaders such as Chen Yun (1981) and Li Xiannian still viewed the import substitution strategy as a long-term solution to improving the economic infrastructure. In August 1963, Li Xiannian (1992b) argued that the importation of grains and raw materials for light industrial production was 'a temporary measure which the state will gradually change following the recovery and improvement of domestic agricultural production.' By September 1963, Li Xiannian (1992c) revealed, 'China's [policy] direction is to import more industrial equipment. Originally, we imported turnkey plants and equipment from socialist countries. Now, we must import them from capitalist countries...'

These projects would become the foundation for Zhou Enlai's Four Modernization strategy, which envisioned a thoroughly modernized agricultural, industrial, military and technology sector by the end of the century (Zhonggong, 1997). Beginning in June 1963, China initialed an agreement with Japan to import a Vinylon factory to increase textile production, which included a long-term Japanese loan to finance China's imports (Sun, 1996). Between 1963 and 1966, China imported 51 complete plant and equipment projects from Western countries. Of these '14 were industrial machine-building projects, 13 were metallurgical equipment projects, 13 were chemical industry projects, three oil equipment projects, two each for construction material processing equipment projects, light industrial projects, geological survey equipment projects, and one each for electrical equipment projects and printing projects' (Long, 1985). China also signed 33 other technology exchange accords with the west for a grand total of 84 import substitution projects (Sun, 1996).

Thus, the antinomy of Chinese development during the 1959-76 period resulted from the fundamental disagreement among policy elites as to the best approach to achieve a self-reliant, strong state. Reacting to a slowdown in Chinese development growth and the upheavals in Eastern Europe in the mid-1950s, Mao invoked a strong Nativist model that saw the international economy as inhibiting Chinese initiative and inherent strengths. The chaos of the GLF inspired the post-GLF political elites to coalesce around a more Internationalist agenda that saw the global marketplace as an invaluable source of technology and finance. In both cases, the perception of chaos was the primary catalyst to sharpen differences within the policy elites. Elites relied on their personal experiences– whether in the interior of China or the Paris factories– to determine the general direction of development strategy.

Unfortunately, this difference of opinion resulted in a cycling of two inwardly oriented strategies: import substitution development and semiautarchy during the 1960s and 1970s. After overcoming serious economic dislocation, the post-GLF coalition used the remunerative/administrative policies to finance a continuation of a limited import substitution strategy. Up to the mid-1960s, Mao refused to give up on his proto-experiment in autarchy. With the support of Jiang Qing and Lin Biao, Mao overthrew the post-GLF coalition and their Internationalist agenda, and revived his Natvist approach toward development, which evolved into a more autarchic approach during the Cultural Revolution and a brief period in the middle 1970s. By the early 1970s, Zhou Enlai revived the Internationalist's program of import substitution, which was expanded by Hua Guofeng in middle to late 1970s. Such cycling prevented China's adoption of an outwardly oriented development regime such as those implemented by Taiwan, South Korea and the other Asian 'miracle economies' during the same time period.

Case Study: Deng Xiaoping and Outwardly-Oriented Development

After 6 October 1976, China underwent a process of exorcising the ghosts of the Nativists. Hua Guofeng, Mao Zedong's appointed successor, joined the Internationalists in condemning the Nativist policies of the Cultural Revolution. Hua then set about realizing Zhou Enlai's Four Modernization development strategy first enunciated in the mid-1960s. His new 'Ten-Year Plan' included a very substantial import substitution program far exceeding Zhou's import programs of the early 1960s and 1970s. However, Deng Xiaoping, Chen Yun and other Internationalists began to question the efficacy of the inwardly oriented development regime. Not only was Hua Guofeng's 'Ten Year Plan' extremely expensive, but also the import substitution projects that had come on line in the mid-1970s were oftentimes inefficient and expensive to operate. With the effective ouster of Hua Guofeng prior to the Third Plenum of 1978, the Internationalists not only readjusted Hua's grandiose schemes of large-scale import substitution development. The Internationalists also initiated the transformation from inwardly oriented to outwardly oriented development similar to many other East Asian developing economies (Fei et. al, 1985).

With the reduction in import and export restraints beginning in the late 1970s, Chinese production units were encouraged to look to the international marketplace as a possible source of new revenue. To facilitate this transition, the state began the long process of devaluing the RMB, which had been kept unrealistically high during the previous decades to enhance the import substitution strategy. The new regulations for compensation trade and the approval of joint ventures allowed private international capital from non-Chinese sources to re-enter the Chinese market. Acceptance of buyers credit and accession to the IMF and the World Bank opened to China a new source of development capital, but also opened China to the scrutiny and intervention of these key international economic organizations. Finally, the successful experimentation with decentralization in Guangdong, Fujian and their Special Economic Zones (SEZs) resulted in the gradual implementation nationwide beginning in the mid-1980s.

The Chaos of the Early 1980s: Macroeconomic Impact

By 1982, China was the 18th largest exporter in the world, rising 10 places over its 1980 position and 16 places over its 1976 position (Zhongguo, 1984). While impressive, these statistics mask the difficulties faced by Beijing authorities in controlling Chinese exports and imports. The state was unable to fulfill the export procurement plan because of increased domestic competition to procure export goods. There also was an alarming growth in Chinese imports, which threatened native industries and the implementation of the domestic development strategy. This occurred despite the 1979 general readjustment of the national economy and the concurrent reduction in scale of import substitution strategy.

The Chinese described foreign trade during 1980-1982 as 'chaotic' (Davie and Carver, 1982). In a series of questions and answers first published in 1982 by the major military paper, *Jiefang junbao*, the authors succinctly stated

> the reasons for the 'chaotic' situation are very complicated. Sometimes experience was lacking. Many [administrators] were like green recruits brought up to the front; a large amount of problems occurred since the appropriate management measures had failed to keep up with structural changes; in addition, there were some people who only cared about their area or department in procuring foreign exchange. They ignored the general situation, did not calculate the costs involved and exacerbated the chaos in procurement, exports and imports, etc. (Liu and Zou, 1983).

When expanding foreign trade inexperience and bureaucratic bottlenecks stymie short-term growth. A reforming command economy compounds these problems on political, economic, and social fronts. As the reforms deepen, a concurrent aggravation of the contradiction between the needs of the state plan and the demands of the market place develops. Xu Dixin, Director of the CASS Institute of Economics and later appointed President of Shantou University, analyzed the problem of fulfilling the state plan in 1981. According to Xu (1982),

> every province, especially every SEZ, will consider their develoment needs; like 'the Eight Immortals crossing the sea, each showing their special prowess,' [they will consider only themselves,] even at the expense of national sovereignty or the unitary nature of

the planned economy. This occurred during the winter of 1979 when many provinces reduced the selling price of Chinese medicines on the Hong Kong market and during the 1980 Spring Guangzhou Trade Fair.

The sudden lessening of foreign trade controls beginning in 1979 encouraged localities to increase exports, regardless of the dictates of the state export plan. With the increased amount of retained foreign exchange, these localities in turn imported expensive durable goods through legal and illegal channels.

The increased domestic demand for procuring goods for export was one of the major problems caused by the decentralization measures. The command economy could not accommodate this new infusion of market-style competition. As more units obtained exporting privileges, they increasingly competed between themselves and the state to procure export items. This affected not only state procurement quotas, but also created dramatic price fluctuations. Competition between buyers caused commodity prices to rise. The state thus was unable to procure goods at the inflated price. The inflationary price for fresh water pearls in the early 1980s illustrates this phenomenon. Suzhou, a major producer of the highly profitable fresh water pearls, exported them through Shanghai prior to 1979. However, starting in 1980, areas and ports outside the region could procure and export the pearls. Competition drove up the procurement price, which increased from a 1979 average of RMB 406 to over RMB 900 for a half kilogram. As a result, the Suzhou Prefecture Foreign Trade Department failed to procure them at this higher price (Guoji, 1983).

This rise in export product procurement prices also exacerbated inflationary tendencies present in the national economy. In 1979, the State Council raised the procurement price of primary agricultural products, the sales price of agricultural side products, and the salaries and bonuses of staff and workers (Wang and Zhu, 1987; Dangdai, 1986). By April 1980, the Central Committee (1983a) complained that:

> some localities, departments and enterprise units have violated pricing policy and pricing discipline without regard for the general good. To increase their profits and issue more bonuses, they indiscriminately enlarged the numbers of commodities whose prices were to be readjusted, arbitrarily raised the rate of readjustment; some adopted improper methods to raise prices such as changing labels, mixing low quality and fake goods with regular goods, employing shoddy methods to produce inferior goods, selling seconds at regular prices, and selling less than the quantity specified; some indiscriminately reduced the number of set price goods and replaced them with goods with a negotiated price. To raise material prices, some units even procured goods at the regular set price and sold them at a negotiated price; some arbitrarily raised the number of public utilities and services requiring fees and raised the fee rates.

Throughout 1980 and 1981, the State Council thus adopted various measures to control inflation, including the strengthening of price management, readjustment of the negotiated price system, and imposing stricter controls of certain important industrial goods.

Secondly, the chaos in foreign trade threatened domestic industrial growth. In general, Chinese 'people believe that foreign goods are excellent in quality' (State Council, 1986b). Units and individuals thus preferred to purchase imported goods, than similar goods produced on the domestic market. Hu Yaobang (1982), the new General Secretary of the Chinese Communist Party, criticized this attitude during his speech to the Central Committee Secretariat on 14 January 1982, stating:

> In my opinion, except those uniformly arranged by the state, no department or locality should be allowed to import consumer goods on an unauthorized basis. Those areas and departments that are currently importing consumer goods for themselves are in reality harming national industry. This is disgraceful behavior and the greatest profiteering [crime]. This is not the importation of advanced technology. This is harmful to the nation and the people.

Finally, the chaos in foreign trade adversely effected the implementation of the domestic development strategy. According to the readjusted import substitution development strategy, units and localities financed technical renovation of their industrial structure with retained foreign exchange. Instead, provinces used these funds to import consumer goods. Hu Yaobang (1982) cited the case of Gansu, a very poor province located in western China. In 1981, Gansu earned:

> local foreign exchange [totaling] US$ 15m and retained an amount [totaling] over US$ 6m. Yet, this amount of foreign exchange was not used effectively. Except a minority of areas and cities that imported badly needed equipment and medical equipment, the majority blindly imported things such as watches, bicycles, and sewing machines. These materials were of poor quality and they were cheated! Beside what has been reported, it is unknown what things have been imported. Look, they don't know that this hard earned foreign exchange is to be used to import needed equipment, technology and raw materials, to increase production and earn even more foreign exchange. Instead, they waste it on importing low quality consumer goods and let the foreigners again leave with profits.

By diverting foreign exchange funds to consumer imports, local planners were unable to finance the development of their locality. This in turn adversely affected the national development strategy. If such chaos in foreign trade had been allowed to continue, the readjusted import substitution strategy and other economic reforms adopted in the late 1970s would have been in danger.

The Chaos of the Early 1980s: The SEZs

During his speech to the Central Committee Secretariat on 14 January 1982, Hu Yaobang (1982) criticized the excessive importation of durable goods that occurred in the early 1980s. He was aware that Chinese units considered foreign goods more prestigious and higher in quality than domestically produced items. He was especially concerned that such attitudes would reduce demand for domestically produced goods. This would cause a drop in domestic production, which would lead to unemployment and to higher government outlays for domestic production support.

The leadership felt that most imports were funneled through Guangdong and Fujian provinces and their SEZs. Leaders granted these export processing zones extraordinary powers of importation, which allowed them to import many goods duty-free or at reduced tariff rates. According to Central Committee document 80.41,

> machines, equipment, spare parts, raw materials and other production materials should be allowed to be imported duty-free; in principle, the goods used in daily life should for the most part be supplied by the domestic economy. Those necessary items used in daily life, which the domestic economy truly has difficulty supplying, can be imported upon approval and customs duties levied. Some of items can be imported on a reduced or duty-free basis (Central Committee, 1994a).

The government designed duty-free importation originally to reduce SEZ construction costs. Rules stipulated SEZ consumption of imported goods and denied re-exportation into the interior economy, without special provisions. According to Central Committee document 81.27, regular import duties would be levied on those goods that were permitted to be re-exported to the interior (Central Committee, 1994b). However, with high domestic demand for such durable goods and the high cost of SEZ construction, large-scale re-exportation to the domestic economy occurred. Entrepôt trade was the fastest growing economic activity of the SEZs– especially Shenzhen– and the major source of financing between 1979 and 1982. With ready access to Hong Kong and the interior, the Shenzhen SEZ earned extraordinarily high profits from entrepôt activities. SEZ enterprises and individuals could earn various transaction fees in both RMB and foreign exchange; the entrepôt trade did not require a developed infrastructure or many skilled personnel. The situation was similar to the Klondike gold rush: everyone rushed to Shenzhen to discover his pot of gold.

SEZ units and the representative offices of domestic units primarily carried out the entrepôt trade. According to document 81.27,

> under the guidance of the unified state policy, the SEZs can engage in foreign trade. The SEZs can act as an agent for every province, municipality and SAR and carry out approved export and import operations, yet not be under the uniform management of the Ministry of

Foreign Trade... upon approval, some departments and areas [to] station a few people in Shenzhen to investigate the business situation in Hong Kong, Macao and abroad as well as make contacts with them.

Provinces and ministerial departments were authorized to establish representative offices in Shenzhen in the early 1980s ostensibly to expand exports to ong Kong and abroad. Yet, many offices acted as procurement agents for durable goods demanded by domestic units.

One very lucrative import item, the foreign automobile became a prestige item, given the poor quality and low quantity of domestic sources. Chinese units had been very unhappy with domestic car production based on Soviet technology of the 1950s (Harwit, 1995). After production units and localities were granted greater decision-making rights in 1979, they bought more automobiles, especially imported models from abroad. By 1980, domestic automobile production exceeded the state production plan by 77.4%; with over 20,000 vehicles imported from outside the plan (State Planning Commission et. al., 1985). According to a State Council Office Circular of 20 March 1982, 'Between January 1980 and June 1981, every area illegally purchased over 10,000 vehicles of different types. Most were bought from Guangdong at a high price' (State Council Office, 1986). One State Planning Commission report issued in 1981 stated that Guangdong imported 'several tens of thousands of automobiles' (State Council Office, 1982).

Legal and illegal methods were used to import vehicles and other durable goods. Some Overseas Chinese willingly brought or mailed durable goods to relatives living in China; others were 'intimidated and bribed'. The units or individual subsequently sold the goods at local black markets. Central Military Commission/State Council document 80.184 (1994), which is a fascinating, detailed report on smuggling activities in Guangdong and Shenzhen between 1979 and 1980, states that the Shantou customs office recorded the importation of:

> 250,000 televisions, over 480,000 radio-tape recorders, 1,160,000 hand-held calculators and 180,000 wristwatches. In fact, these amounts are growing monthly. In May of last year [1979], the Shantou Customs counted over 6,000 hand-held calculators sent through the mails. In November 1979, the number had increased to 38,000... Since the sale of foreign goods potentially is profitable, many Overseas Chinese and Hong Kong/Macao Compatriots are sending materials instead of currency. This has seriously affected Overseas Chinese remittances.

In some cases, the SEZ unit or representative office procured imported material for personal use or to be re-exported to the interior. According to document 80.184:

purchasing agents, sent by the Parts and Accessories Department of the Second Ministry of Machinery's Sixth Bureau, linked up with commune members from Chao yang County and Xiacuo Brigade members from Pinggong Commune to sign a false contract. Under the pretext of procuring weaved rubberized tape, they used over RMB 64,800 to purchase 548 electronic calculators and 2 radio-tape recorders.

Another method consisted of establishing joint ventures to import the durable good. On 23 August 1983, the *People's Daily* reported that:

> Harper Motors wanted to use the preferential treatment provided by the Zone to raise car competitiveness in the domestic market. Shenzhen agreed with this and let it come. Subsequently it wanted to dump its cars and invade our domestic market. We could not agree with this, because our country's car industry has had a certain foundation and we cannot give up our car market to foreign countries. In the end, Harper Motors pulled out. In this way, we protected our own car industry.

Yet, smuggling became the most widespread method to import goods into the country. This was not a new occupation for southern Chinese, especially for fishermen from Guangdong, Fujian and Taiwan. The 'opening' policy and the more relaxed atmosphere of 1979 allowed smuggling to flourish (Shenzhen Municipal Revolutionary Committee, 1986). According to document 80.184 (Central Military Commission/State Council, 1994), the state uncovered 13,423 cases of smuggling involving an estimated RMB 7.31m of goods in 1979. Compared to 1978, the number of cases increased by 40% and the value of goods confiscated doubled. In Guangzhou alone, the number of smuggling cases quadrupled the 1978 number.

> During the last half of 1979, over 200 Taiwanese fishing vessels entered the areas around Guangdong Province's Shanwei and Haimenzhen alone, smuggling 200,000 watches... From December 1979 to January 1980, Guangdong's Haimenzhen port investigated 12 Taiwanese fishing trawlers. They discovered over 210 liang of smuggled gold, 322 jin of silverware, over 2,490 pieces of silver yuan, 72 radio-tape recorders, 36 pocket calculators, and 18,650 Taiwanese watches. In January 1980, Shaoguan Municipality uncovered smuggling, profiteering and speculation cases involving over 150 people covering 10 provinces. They seized 124 liang of gold, 39,900 silver yuan, 130 jin of musk, over 500 jin of other expensive medical supplies, 2 jin of agate, and RMB 18,300 in cash.

The Chinese thus took advantage of the high international price of gold, silver, Chinese medicine and musk to purchase durables such as televisions, radios and calculators. They were all attracted by the high profit, since the sale price of smuggled goods was '2-10 times the purchase price.' Yet, there was a high demand for these goods. Black market traders would sell at a price lower than the state retail price; naturally, the traders would not demand prior purchase approval from the buyer's units. Document 80.184 (Central Military Commission/State Council, 1994) states:

Cai Jiancheng and three others of Fujian's Anxi County purchased 173 pocket electronic calculators in Fujian at RMB 70 to 90 a piece. On average, they sold them in Sichuan for RMB 250 a piece... When converted from the Hong Kong price, a 20' Japanese Lesheng color television set is worth RMB 623. The procurement price for state-run commercial enterprises, including the levied customs duty, is RMB 1,660. The retail cost is RMB 3,020. Purchased from an individual, the price is around RMB 2,200.

Larger units, such as 'state-owned commercial enterprises, cooperative enterprises' and smaller dealers, such as 'communes, streets [jiedao] and individual entrepreneurs,' were involved in the domestic trading of smuggled goods. In one village near Shantou, two hundred people from an agricultural production team decided to quit the land and trade in foreign goods. Besides local peasants and workers, military personnel, 'Party and Youth League members as well as sons and daughters of high officials' trafficked in smuggled goods. Units ranging from universities to state enterprises 'used all means possible to penetrate Overseas Chinese areas and rush to purchase foreign goods'. Smuggled goods could be bought easily at black markets established 'in Guangzhou, Shantou, Foshan, Shenzhen, Haimen, Shanwei and Fujian Province's Qingyang, Shishi, Changle. Often there are over 1,000 people gathered at these places.' These 'visitors' to the Guangdong and Fujian black markets formed the conduit that 'link[ed] the coastal areas and interior areas covering all the provinces'.

One of the most active purchasing organizations was the People's Liberation Army. Document 80.184 (Central Military Commission/State Council, 1994) states:

> To purchase the 'three machines' (television, radio-tape recorders, hand-held calculators), some military units have sent people on special vehicles to purchase the goods; some have used helicopters to transfer the goods; some have exchanged military lumber supplies for the goods; to avoid inspection, some have sealed containers with strips declaring they were 'defense materiel'; some even intimidated and bribed their Overseas Chinese relatives who were not willing to buy foreign goods. The PLA unit stationed in Guangdong's Haimenzhen numbers over 400 people. Since last July, they have received on average RMB 6,000 in remittances per day to purchase foreign goods. This town has a black market in foreign goods. On average, four or five military vehicles would arrive to buy foreign goods.

Central policy elites were apprehensive about the involvement of Party and government cadre in smuggling, profiteering and speculating activities. 'Peoples' ideas [were being] corrupted,' resulting in the recurrence of 'gambling, itinerant performers and prostitutes'. Between 1979 and 1982, the central leadership attempted to rectify the problems encountered in foreign trade and SEZ development. This 'chaos' increasingly threatened the stability of the Chinese nation, resulting in the emergence of the Moderate opinion group.

Chaos and the Emergence of the Moderate Opinion Group

While Fewsmith (1994) argues that the division between the two opinion groups was 'clearly marked' by the introduction of urban reforms at the 12th Party Congress of 1984, this study argued that the parting of ways became clear by late 1981/early 1982. By December 1981, Chen Yun attacked the Internationalist's development strategy, arguing that the 1979 reform strategy– especially the SEZs– was disrupting the state plan's targets in agriculture, basic construction, and foreign trade (Chen Yun, 1982). During a meeting of the Party Standing Committee on 11 January 1982, Chen Yun submitted a brief of a Discipline and Inspection Committee report on the 'criminal economic activities' in the SEZs and other regions in China. According to the Emergency Circular issued by the Standing Committee in 11 January 1982, the brief summarized 'the extremely serious criminal smuggling activities by some cadre. Some of them occupied responsible leadership positions' (CCP Standing Committee, 1994).

The contents of the Discipline and Inspection brief and the positions adopted by the leadership can only be hypothesized. It is highly probable that the brief described the 'Case of the Shenzhen Branch', which involved Zhou Zhirong, the 'temporary' Secretary of the Shenzhen Party Committee. According to the *Shenzhen Tequbao* of 29 November 1982, Zhou's large-scale smuggling operation was uncovered in fall of 1981 and officially reported to the Central Committee on 11 January 1982. The Standing Committee also discussed the serious economic crimes committed by 'some cadre and responsible cadre in other Provinces, Cities, Special Administrative Regions and Central Government departments' (Si, 1982). The Directive specifically mentioned Guangdong, Fujian, Zhejiang, and Yunnan.

As for the positions adopted by the leadership during the 11 January 1982 Standing Committee meeting, there is no doubt that they all strongly criticized the criminal activities. Yet, disagreement on the methods to suppress these activities existed. Chen Yun lobbied for a strong response; he continued to fear the effect of decentralization on Party discipline and the state plan. In a talk on 25 January 1982, Chen Yun (1982b) stated:

> Currently planning is not welcomed! So in the beginning of this year I am talking to a few of the responsible comrades of the State Planning Commission about this matter. Should the SPC indulge in idle boasting? Or should it be earnest and down to earth? Should we forget past experiences?

In his December 1981 speech, Chen Yun (1982a) specifically called for a review of the SEZ policy by stating, 'We must summarize the experiences of the SEZs in Guangdong and Fujian and the foreign economic activities of every province. Currently we haven't summarized them well.' It appears that many senior Beijing officials supported Chen Yun's position. Hu Yaobang concurred with the need to summarize experiences. In his major speech on foreign trade delivered Central Party Secretariat on 14 January, Hu (1982) stated:

> From 1978 to 1980, our foreign economic relations truly made great strides forward unlike those of the past. Yet, there also arose several errors in certain [areas]. In view of this, we must summarize our experience, and steadily carry out measures. In addition, we do not want any mistaken views, even the idea of shrinking back and never again dare to develop foreign economic relations... How can we shrink back because of a small amount of problems.

The leadership coalition complied with Chen Yun's (1982a) demand to impose a moratorium on the establishment of new SEZs and to implement a general policy review. The review, held during the Guangdong, Fujian Conference of February 1982, resulted in the rectification of 303 local branches of the Shenzhen Communist Party, severe restrictions on the importation of 17 major durable goods, and the authorization of a 108.77 km long barbed wire fence completely separating Shenzhen from the interior economy (the 'Second Line'). To strengthen macro-management of the four SEZs, the State Council established the Office of the SEZs in June 1982, directed by Gu Mu (Central Committee, 1994c). Thus, the Beijing leadership redirected the SEZs to be more like China's traditional EPZs and promote national development first and regional economic development second.

Yet, Deng's chosen leaders and the newest members of the Internationalist opinion group– Hu Yaobang and Zhao Ziyang– countered Chen Yun's 1981 criticisms of the decentralized foreign trade system and the SEZ experiment by arguing for a more outwardly oriented development strategy. As a result, they persuaded Deng Xiaoping to begin a systematic process of greater integration with the international economy and treat foreign trade and investment as 'engines' for domestic development. Eventually by January 1988, Zhao Ziyang formally designated the new approach as the Coastal Development Strategy (State Council, 1992; Tzeng, 1991; Fewsmith, 1994).

Simply stated, this outwardly oriented development strategy required the richer coastal regions to be transformed into major foreign economic trade centers that were partially integrated with the international economy. According to the Nine Coastal Provinces, Cities and Special Administrative Regions Conference Summary approved by the Central Committee in January 1982 (Central Committee, 1994d), the state:

> must greatly develop economic associations [jingji lianhe] and technological cooperation between the coast and the interior. Based on mutual benefit, we must carry out well economic association. Coastal areas, especially large and medium cities, must transfer production technology in a planned way to the interior. This includes production technology; production instructions; technological secrets; and the dispatch of skilled technicians to provide instruction [as well as] provide advanced equipment. There must be a logical division of sales

between the foreign and domestic markets, with each having its own particular emphasis. Beijing, Tianjin, Shanghai and the important coastal cities must provide goods for foreign sales. Interior factories for the most part will fulfill the needs of the domestic market.

Coastal regions would become more integrated into the international market by absorbing foreign investment, and producing goods for the international market. The Central Committee, most importantly, envisioned the creation of 'practical laboratories' experimenting with foreign technology and management techniques. Protected from international competition, the interior regions would concentrate production on domestic consumption and carry out technical and management renovations based on the coastal experience. Throughout the 1980s and 1990s, Chen Yun and the Moderates opposed the de-emphasis of the planned socialist economy. Chen criticized the SEZs, the coastal development strategy and any attempt to establish a market socialist economy. He neither objected to the 'opening', nor the use of foreign direct investment. After all, he supported storngly the remunerative/administrative approach since the 1950s. However, Chen Yun feared that the onslaught of international market forces would endanger the Communist Party and the economic stability of the nation. In contrast to Chen Yun, Deng Xiaoping remained an adamant supporter of high growth and gradual integration of the coastal areas with the global economy.

Conclusion

When policy elites perceive that a crisis has the potential of evolving into general chaos, elites must take drastic policy actions. Support for past policy initiatives and allegiances become unimportant as elites lack the time to carry out an in-depth review or rationally discuss alternative policy options among themselves. Frankly stated, they lack the luxury of learning from past mistakes. Such learning can and does take place among elites, but not during periods of profound crisis. Elites realize that legitimacy of their rule and their control over the state is endangered if elites cannot deal with problems promptly and efficiently. They thus have a greater tendency to rely on their past experiences to choose strategies that will most promptly resolve the crisis.

In the mid-1950s, Chinese elites discussed the benefits and costs of implementing Mao Zedong's 'rash advance' policy. This was not a period of profound crisis, but one in which Mao and the other elites increasingly realized that they supported fundamentally different solutions to achieve a strong, independent China. During this first round of debates, Mao eventually prevailed by 1958. However, his Nativist approach to development embodied by the Great Leap Forward resulted in dramatic economic dislocation. As Chen Yun observed at the time, nothing was more dangerous than to have a people without food in their stomachs. If the debates over development strategy in the mid-1950s had endangered the Yan'an coalition, the profound chaos resulting from the GLF permanently broke the previous alliance.

Liu Shaochi, Zhou Enlai, Zhu De, Chen Yun and others never thought to attempt a challenge to Mao's authority. Nonetheless, they strongly rejected Mao's Nativist approach to economic development that had resulted in millions of Chinese deaths. As long as Mao stayed on the sidelines, these Internationalists enacted policies promoting a remunerative/administrative approach to economic development. Their experiences overseas and in pre-1949 Shanghai had proven to them that normative exhortations needed to be supplemented by economic remuneration. Furthermore, the Internationalists knew that the semi-autarchic strategy embodied in the GLF could not bring about an industrialized state. They personally witnessed the advanced industrialized societies in Western Europe and Japan, as well as the tremendous industrial growth of Stalinist Russia. They understood that the Chinese people would need the advanced technology from the Soviet Union and the West in order to build China into a strong, independent state. In the early 1960s, Zhou Enlai thus revived the import substitution strategy to build China's infrastructure– although this time he relied on Western European and Japanese technology. Zhou Enlai's Four Modernization program, formally announced in the early 1960s, was designed to make China an industrialized state by the end of the century. Foreign technology was the key to the program's success.

The Internationalists evolved as an opinion group. By the late 1970s, they had learned of the diminishing effectiveness of the inwardly oriented strategies (Reardon, 2001). Having consolidated their power by the Third Plenum, the Internationalists thus began to experiment with outwardly oriented development and opening their economy to the outside world. While taking over twenty years to follow the rest of East Asia down the road of export promotion, China would become just as successful in accelerating domestic development by harnessing foreign capital, technology and management expertise.

Yet, just as the chaos of the Great Leap broke apart the Yan'an coalition, the chaos of the early 1980s broke apart the Internationalists. Millions of Chinese had not died as they did twenty years beforehand. However, after reading the Emergency Circular of January 1982, certain members of the Central Committee considered the illegal smuggling activities to represent a more profound threat to Party integrity and control of China. No matter how useful the international economy, the Moderates wanted to maintain centralized control and the predominance of the planning system. While equally concerned about the insidious nature of criminal activities, the Internationalists would advocate experimentation and reform, and eventually created a new, socialist market economy.

This difference in opinion between the Moderates and the Internationalists continues to impact domestic and foreign economic policy today. Although delayed by Moderate criticisms from elites like Li Peng, the Internationalists have succeeded in adopting more market-oriented reforms, including the opening China's coastal areas to the outside world. Yet, with China's recent accession to the World Trade Organization (WTO), a similar debate has become more fervent within China. Moderates are concerned that WTO would totally disrupt the state's ability to manipulate and protect the domestic economy; Internationalists hope the process of joining the WTO will result in the dismantling of inefficient state-owned enterprises (SOEs), thus making China a more efficient economy. Only time will tell whether the WTO accession will cause dramatic economic and political dislocation. If such dislocation endangers the Chinese state, there is a chance that such chaos could change elite opinion on the sagacity of globalization.

References

Aberbach, J.D., Dollar, D. and Sokoloff, K. L. (eds.) (1994), *The Role of the State in Taiwan's Development*, M.E. Sharpe, Armonk.
Ahn, B.J. (1976), *Chinese Politics and the Cultural Revolution*, University of Washington Press, Seattle.
Amsden, A. (1989), *Asia's Next Giant: South Korea and Late Industrialization*, Oxford University Press, New York.
Bachman, D.M. (1985), *Chen Yun and the Chinese Political System*, Institute of East Asian Studies, University of California, Berkeley.
Balassa, B. (1980), *The Process of Industrial Development and Alternative Development Strategies*, Essays in International Finance, No. 141, Princeton University Press, Princeton.
Basile, A. and Germidis, D. (1984), *Investing in Free Export Processing Zones*, OECD, Paris.
Belassa, B. (1982), *Development Strategies in Semi-Industrializing Economies*, The Johns Hopkins University Press, Baltimore.
Bhagwati, J.N. (1978), *Foreign Trade Regimes and Economic Development: Anatomy and Consequences of Exchange Control Regimes*, Ballinger, Cambridge.
Bianji Weiyuanhui, *Shenzhen jingji tequ nianjian, 1985* [Shenzhen Special Economic Zone Yearbook, 1985], Xianggang Jingji Daobao Chubanshe, Hong Kong.
Bo Yibo (1991), *Ruogan zhongda juece yu shijian de huigu* [Looking Back on Certain Important Decisions and Events], Zhonggong Zhongyang Dangxiao Chubanshe, Beijing.
Calder, K.E. (1988), *Crisis and Compensation*, Princeton University Press, Princeton.
CCP Standing Committee (1994), 'Zhonggong Zhongyang jinji tongzhi' [Emergency Circular from the Standing Committee], in Lawrence C. Reardon (ed.), 'China's Coastal Development Strategy, 1979-1984 (II)' *Chinese Law and Government*, vol. 27, pp. 21-23.
Central Committee (1994a), 'Guangdong, Fujian liangsheng huiyi jiyao de pishi' [Comment on the Summary of the Conference on Guangdong and Fujian Provinces], in Lawrence C. Reardon

(ed.), 'China's Coastal Development Strategy, 1979-1984 (I)', *Chinese Law and Government*, vol. 27, pp. 45-58.

Central Committee (1994b), 'Guangdong, Fujian liangsheng he jingji tequ gongzuo huiyi jiyao'[Summary of the Work Conference on Guangdong, Fujian and Special Economic Zones], in Lawrence C. Reardon (ed.), 'China's Coastal Development Strategy, 1979-1984 (I)', *Chinese Law and Government*, vol. 27, pp. 59-79.

Central Committee (1994c), 'Guanyu pizhuan Guangdong, Fujian liangsheng zuotanhui jiyao de tongzhi' [Circular Promulgating the Summary of the Guangdong, Fujian Provincial Conference], in Lawrence C. Reardon (ed.), 'China's Coastal Development Strategy, 1979-1984 (I)', *Chinese Law and Government*, vol. 27, pp. 81-95.

Central Committee (1994d), 'Yanhai jiusheng, shi, zizhiqu duiwai jingji maoyi gongzuo zuotanhui jiyao'[Summary of the Conference of 9 Provinces, Cities and SARs on Foreign Economic Trade Work], in Lawrence C. Reardon (ed.), 'China's Coastal Development Strategy, 1979-1984 (II)', *Chinese Law and Government*, vol. 27, pp. 45-8.

Central Committee (1983), 'Guanyu jiaqiang wujia guanli, jianjue zhizhi luanzhangjia he bianxiang zhangjia de tongzhi' [Circular on Strengthening Price Management, and Firmly Preventing Indiscriminate Price Inflation and Covert Inflation], in Zhongguo Shehui Kexueyuan, Faxue Yanjiusuo (ed.), *Zhonghua Renmin Gongheguo jingji fagui xuanbian, 1979.10-1981.12* [Collection of Economic Laws and Regulations of the People's Republic of China, October 1979-December 1981], Zhongguo Caizheng Jingji Chubanshe, Beijing.

Central Military Commission/State Council (1994), 'Guanyu jiaqiang dui huaqiao, Gang'ao, Taiwan tongbao jinkou wupin guanli he daji zouzi, touji daoba huodong de baogao'[Report on Strengthening Management of Imported Materials from Overseas Chinese, Hong Kong, Macao and Taiwan Compatriots and attacking Smuggling, Engaging in Speculation and Profiteering Activities], in Lawrence C. Reardon (ed.), 'China's Coastal Development Strategy, 1979-1984 (II)', *Chinese Law and Government*, vol. 27, pp. 11-19.

Chang, K.Y. (ed.) (1985), *Perspectives on Development in Mainland China*, Westview, Boulder.

Chen Yun (1996), 'Shehui zhuyi gaizao jiben wancheng yihou de xin wenti' [The New Problems Proceeding the Basic Completion of Socialist Transformation], in *Chen Yun wenxuan, 1956-1985* [Chen Yun's Selected Works, 1956-1985], Renmin Chubanshe, Beijing, pp.1-27.

Chen Yun (1982a), 'Dui jingji gongzuo de jidian yijian' [Some Views on Economic Work], in Zhonggong Zhongyang Wenxian Yanjiushi (ed.), *Sanzhong quanhui yilai zhongyao wenxian xuanbian* [Selected Important Documents Issued Since the Third Plenum], Renmin Chubanshe, Beijing, pp. 1057-60.

Chen Yun (1982b), 'Jiaqiang jihua jingji' [Strengthen the Planned Economy], in Zhonggong Zhongyang Wenxian Yanjiushi (ed.), *Sanzhong quanhui yilai zhongyao wenxian xuanbian* [Selected Important Documents Issued Since the Third Plenum], Renmin Chubanshe, Beijing, pp. 1132-34.

Chen Yun (1981), 'Jiasu fazhan danfei gongye' [Accelerate the Development of the Nitrogenous Fertilizer Industry], in *Chen Yun tongzhi wengao xuanbian, 1956-1962* [Selections of Comrade Chen Yun's Manuscripts, (1956-1962)], Renmin Chubanshe, Beijing.

Chen, E.K.Y. (1979), *Hypergrowth in Asian Economies: A Comparative Survey of Hong Kong, Japan, Korea, Singapore and Taiwan*, Macmillan, London.

Cheng C.Y. (1964), *Economic Relations Between Peking and Moscow: 1949-63*, Praeger, New York.

Cheng Tun-jeng (1991), 'Political Regimes and Development Strategies: South Korea and Taiwan', in G. Gereffi and D. Wyman (eds), *Manufacturing Miracles*, Princeton University Press, Princeton, pp. 139-78.

Davie, J.L. and Carver, D.W. (1982) 'China's International Trade And Finance', in U.S. Congress. Joint Economic Committee, *China Under the Four Modernizations*, 97th Cong., 2nd Session, GPO, Washington, D.C., pp. 19-47.

Deyo, F.C. (ed.) (1987), *The Political Economy of the New Asian Industrialism*, Cornell University Press, Ithaca.
Dittmer, L. (1974), *Liu Shaoqi and the Chinese Cultural Revolution*, University of California Press, Berkeley.
Eckstein, A. (1977), *China's Economic Revolution*, Cambridge University Press, Cambridge.
Emmanuel, A. (1972), *Unequal Exchange: A Study of the Imperialism of Trade*, Monthly Review Press, New York.
Evans, P., Rueschemeyer, D. and Skocpol, T. (eds.) (1985), *Bringing the State Back In*, Cambridge University Press, New York.
Fei, J.C.H., Ohkawa, K.and Ranis, G. (1985) 'Economic Development in Historical Perspective: Japan, Korea, and Taiwan', in K. Ohkawa, G. Ranis, and L. Meissner (eds.), *Japan and the Developing Countries*, Basil Blackwell, New York, pp. 35-64.
Fewsmith, J. (1994), *Dilemmas of Reform in China*, ME Sharpe, Armonk.
Friedman, M. and Freeman, R. (1980), *Free to Choose*, Harcourt Brace Jovanovich, New York.
Gereffi, G. and Wyman, D. (eds.) (1991), *Manufacturing Miracles*, Princeton University Press, Princeton.
Gilpin, R. (1975), 'Three Models of the Future', *International Organization*, vol. 29, pp. 37-60.
Goncharov, S.N., Lewis, J.W. and Xue Litai (1993), Uncertain Partners: Stalin, Mao and the Korean War, Stanford University Press, Stanford.
Grindle, M. and Thomas, J. (1991), Public Choices and Policy Change: The Political Economy of Reform in Developing Countries, The Johns Hopkins University Press, Baltimore.
Guoji Maoyi Wenti Bianjibu (ed.) (1983), *Zhongguo duiwai maoyi wenti yanjiu* [Research on the Problems of China's Foreign Trade], Zhongguo Duiwai Jingji Maoyi Chubanshe, Beijing.
Haggard, S. (1990), *Pathways From the Periphery*, Cornell University Press, Ithaca.
Haggard, S. and Cheng, T.J. (1987),'State and Foreign Capital in the East Asian NICs,' in F.C. Deyo (ed.), *The Political Economy of the New Asian Industrialism*, Cornell University Press, Ithaca, pp. 84-135.
Haggard S. and Pang, C. K. (1994), 'The Transition to Export-Led Growth in Taiwan,' in J.D. Aberbach, D. Dollar and K. L. Sokoloff (eds), *The Role of the State in Taiwan's Development*, M.E. Sharpe, Armonk, pp. 47-89.
Harding, H. (1987), *China's Second Revolution*, Brookings, Washington, DC.
Harwit, E. (1995), *China's Automobile Industry: Policies, Problems and Prospects*. M. E. Sharpe, Armonk.
Hermann, C.F. (1963), 'Some Consequences of Crisis which Limit the Viability of Organizations', *Administrative Science Quarterly*, vol.8, pp. 61-82.
Holsti, O. (1972), *Crisis Escalation War*, McGill-Queen's University Press, Montreal, pp. 9-11.
Hu Yaobang (1982), 'Guanyu duiwai jingji guanxi wenti' [Problems Concerning Foreign Economic Relations], in Zhonggong Zhongyang Wenxian Yanjiushi (ed.), *Sanzhong quanhui yilai zhongyao wenxian xuanbian* [Selected Important Documents Issued Since the Third Plenum], Renmin Chubanshe, Beijing.
Jacobson, H.K.and Oksenberg, M. (1990), *China's Participation in the IMF, the World Bank and GATT*, University of Michigan Press, Ann Arbor.
Jervis, R. (1976), *Perception and Misperception in International Politics*, Princeton University Press, Princeton.
Johnson, C. (1987), 'Political institutions and economic performance: the government-business relationship in Japan, South Korea, and Taiwan', in F.C. Deyo (ed.), *The Political Economy of the New Asian Industrialism*, Cornell University Press, Ithaca, pp. 136-64.
Johnson, C. (ed.) (1970), *Change in Communist Systems*, Stanford University Press, Stanford.
Joseph, W.A. (1984), *The Critique of Ultra-Leftism in China, 1958-1981*, Stanford University Press, Stanford.

Katzenstein, P. (ed.) (1978), *Between Power and Plenty: Foreign Economic Policies of Advanced Industrial States*, University of Wisconsin Press, Madison.
Katzenstein, P. (1978), 'Introduction: Domestic and International Forces and Strategies of Foreign Economic Policy', in P. Katzenstein (ed.), *Between Power and Plenty: Foreign Economic Policies of Advanced Industrial States*, University of Wisconsin Press, Madison, pp. 3-22.
Kau, Y.M. and Leung, J.K. (eds) (1986), The Writings of Mao Zedong, 1949-1976, vol. 2, M.E. Sharpe, Armonk.
Krueger, A. (1978), Foreign Trade Regimes and Economic Development: Liberalization Attempts and Consequences, Ballinger, Cambridge.
Lardy, N. (1996), 'The Chinese Economy under Stress, 1958-1965', in R. MacFarquhar and J. Fairbank (eds), *The Cambridge History of China*, vol. 14, Cambridge University Press, Cambridge, pp. 360-97.
Lardy, N.L. and Lieberthal, K. (1983), Chen Yun's Strategy for China's Development: A Non-Maoist Alternative, M.E. Sharpe, Armonk.
Lardy, N.R. (1983), *Agriculture in China's Modern Economic Development*, Cambridge University Press, Cambridge.
Levine, M.A. (1993), The Found Generation: Chinese Communists in Europe during the Twenties, University of Washington Press, Seattle.
Li Ruizhen and Yao Yuanyang (1995), 'Chen Yun zaoqi geming huodong shulüe' [A Short Account of Chen Yun's Activities During the Early Revolutionary Period], in Zhu Jiamu (ed.), *Chen Yun he ta de shiye* [Chen Yun and His Career], Zhongyang Wenxian Chubanshe, Beijing., pp. 977-87.
Li Xiannian (1992a), 'Zuohao wuzi tongyi guanli gongzuo'[Do a Good Job in Unifying Management over Goods and Materials], in Li Xiannian, *Li Xiannian lun caizheng jinrong maoyi, 1950-1991*[Li Xiannian's Discussions on Finance and Trade, 1950-1991], Zhongguo Caizheng Jingji Chubanshe, Beijing.
Li Xiannian (1992b), 'Liangnian yilai guomin jingji tiaozheng gongzuo qude juda chengjiu' [In Two Years the Readjustment of the National Economy Has Achieved an Enormous Success], in *Li Xiannian lun caizheng jinrong maoyi, 1950-1991*[Li Xiannian's Discussions on Finance and Trade, 1950-1991], Zhongguo Cai-zheng Jingji Chubanshe, Beijing.
Li Xiannian (1992c), 'Yiju xinqingquang zuohao waimao gongzuo'[Do a Good Job in Foreign Trade Work According to the New Situation], in *Li Xiannian lun caizheng jinrong maoyi, 1950-1991*[Li Xiannian's Discussions on Finance and Trade, 1950-1991], Zhongguo Caizheng Jingji Chubanshe, Beijing.
Liao Gailong (ed.) (1991), *Zhongguo Gongchandang lishi dacidian, shehui zhuyi shiqi* [The Historical Encyclopedia of China's Communist Party, Socialist Period], Zhonggong Zhongyang Dangxiao Chubanshe, Beijing.
Lieberthal, K. (1987), 'The Great Leap Forward and the split in the Yan'an leadership', in R. MacFarquhar and J. Fairbank (eds), *The Cambridge History of China*, vol. 14, Cambridge University Press, Cambridge, pp. 293-359.
Lieberthal, K. and Oksenberg, M. (1988), *Policy Making in China*, Princeton University Press, Princeton.
Little, I. and et. al (1970), *Industry and Trade in Some Developing Countries*, Oxford University Press for the OECD, London.
Liu Yuji and Zou Yinghao (eds) (1983), *Duiwai kaifang zhengce wenda* [Questions and Answers on the 'Opening' Policy], Falü Chubanshe, Beijing.
Long Chucai (ed.) (1985), *Liyong waizi gailun* [An Introduction to the Use of Foreign Capital], Zhongguo Duiwai Jingji Maoyi Chubanshe, Beijing.
Lowenthal, R. (1970), 'Development vs. Utopia in Communist Policy,' in C. Johnson (ed.), *Change in Communist Systems*, Stanford University Press, Stanford, pp. 33-116.

Lowenthal, R. (1985), 'The Postrevolutionary Phase in China and the Soviet Union,' in K.Y. Chang (ed.), *Perspectives on Development in Mainland China*, Westview, Boulder, pp. 1-14.
MacFarquhar, R. (1983), *The Origins of the Cultural Revolution, 2: The Great Leap Forward 1958-1960*, Columbia University Press, New York.
MacFarquhar, R. and Fairbank, J. (eds.) (1991), *The Cambridge History of China*, vol. 15, Cambridge University Press, Cambridge.
MacFarquhar, R. and Fairbank J. (eds.) (1987), *The Cambridge History of China*, vol. 14, Cambridge University Press, Cambridge.
MacFarquhar, R., Cheek, T. and Wu, E. (eds.) (1989), *The Secret Speeches of Chairman Mao*, Harvard University Press, Cambridge.
Mao Zedong (1986), 'Speech to a Symposium of Delegates to the First Meeting of the Second National Committee of the ACFIC', in Y.M. Kau and J.K. Leung (eds.), *The Writings of Mao Zedong, 1949-1976*, vol. 2, M.E. Sharpe, Armonk.
Mao Zedong, (1974), 'Talks at the Nan-ning Conference", in *Miscellany of Mao Tse-tung Thought (1949-1968)*, 2 vols., 61269-1, 61269-2, Joint Publications Research Service, Arlington, VA.
Myint, H. (1979), *Exports and Economic Development of Less Developed Countries*, Macmillan Press, London.
Myrdal, G. (1956), *An International Economy*, Harper, New York.
Ohkawa, K.and Ranis, G. and Meissner, L. (eds) (1985), *Japan and the Developing Countries*, Basil Blackwell, New York.
Oksenberg, M. and Goldstein, S. (1974), 'The Chinese Political Spectrum,' *Issues of Communism*, vol. 23, pp. 1-13.
Prebisch, R. (1950), *The Economic Development of Latin America and Its Principal Problems*, The United Nations, New York.
Reardon, L.C. (1996), 'The Rise and Decline of China's Export Processing Zones', *The Journal of Contemporary China*, vol. 5, pp. 281-303.
Reardon, L.C. (1998), 'Learning How to Open the Door: A Reassessment of China's 'Opening' Strategy', *China Quarterly*, vol. 155, pp. 479-511.
Reardon, L.C. (2001), *The Reluctant Dragon: the Impact of Crisis Cycles on Chinese Foreign Economic Policy*, University of Washington Press, Seattle.
Rhee, Y.W. (1994) 'Managing Entry into International Markets: Lessons from the East Asian Experience', in S.C. Yang (ed.), *Manufactured Exports of East Asian Industrializing Economies*, M.E. Sharpe, Armonk, pp. 53-83.
Riskin, C. (1987), *China's Political Economy*, Oxford University Press, Oxford.
Schram, S. (ed.) (1974), *Chairman Mao Talks to the People*, Pantheon, New York.
Schram, S.R. (1991), 'Mao Tse-tung's Thought from 1949-1976,' in R. MacFarquhar and J. Fairbank (eds), *The Cambridge History of China*, vol. 15, Cambridge University Press, Cambridge, pp. 1-104.
Schurmann, F. (1968), *Ideology and Organization in Communist China*, 2 ed., University of California Press, Berkeley.
Sheahan, J.B. (1986) *Alternative International Economic Strategies and Their Relevance for China*, World Bank Staff Working Papers, No. 759, Washington, D.C.
Shenzhen Municipal Revolutionary Committee (1986), 'Guanyu zhizhi zai duiwai jingji huodongzhong wuzhang huodong de tongzhi' [Circular on Restricting Activities That Break Rules and Regulations in Foreign Economic Activities], in Shenzhen Jingji Tequ Nianjian
Shive, C. (1991),'The Next Stage of Industrialization in Taiwan and South Korea,' in G. Gereffi and D. Wyman (eds), *Manufacturing Miracles*, Princeton University Press, Princeton, pp. 267-91.
Si Fu (ed.) (1982), *Guoneiwai dashiji, 1981* [The Major Foreign and Domestic Events of 1981], Renmin Chubanshe, Beijing.

Singer, H.W. (1950), 'The Distribution of Trade between Investing and Borrowing Countries', *American Economic Review*, v. 40, pp. 473-85.

Skocpol, T. (1985), 'Bringing the State Back In: Strategies of Analysis in Current Research', in P. Evans, D. Rueschemeyer and T. Skocpol (eds) *Bringing the State Back In*, Cambridge University Press, New York, pp. 3-37.

Solinger, D. (1984), *Chinese Business Under Socialism*, University of California, Berkeley.

State Council (1986a), 'Guanyu jiaqiang chaye gongzuo de tongzhi' [Circular on Strengthening Tea Work], in Dangdai Zhongguo De Jingji Guanli Bianjibu (ed.), *Zhonghua Renmin Gongheguo jingji guanli dashiji* [A Chronology of the Major Events in the PRC's Economy and Management], Zhongguo Jingji Chubanshe, Beijing.

State Council (1986b), 'Guanyu dangqian duiwai jingji maoyi ruhe wei guomin jingji tiaozheng fuwu de baogao' [Report on How the Current Foreign Economic Trade Serves the National Economic Readjustment], in Dangdai Zhongguo De Jingji Guanli Bianjibu (ed.), *Zhonghua Renmin Gongheguo jingji guanli dashiji* [A Chronology of the Major Events in the PRC's Economy and Management], Zhongguo Jingji Chubanshe, Beijing.

State Council (1992), 'Guanyu yanhai diqu fazhan waixiangxing jingji de ruogan buchong guiding' [Several Supplementary Regulations Regarding the Development of an Outwardly-Oriented Economy in the Coastal Areas], in Quanguo Renda Changweihui Fazhi Gongzuo Weiyuanhui, *Yanhai yanjiang yanbian kaifang falü fagui ji guifanxing wenjian huibian*, Falü Chubanshe, Beijing.

State Council Office (1982), 'Guanyu jinkou xiaoqiche de chuli he zuojia wenti de baogao de tongzhi'[Circular on the Report on Handling the Imported Car Problem and Its Pricing], in Zhonghua Renmin Gongheguo Cai-zhengbu Bangongshi (ed.), *Caizheng guizhang zhidu xuanbian, 1981* [A Selection of Financial Rules and Regulations, 1981], Zhongguo Caizheng Jingji Chubanshe, Beijing.

State Council Office (1986), 'Guanyu jixu shehui jituan goumaili de baogao' [Report on Continuing to Restrict Institutional Purchases], in Dangdai Zhongguo De Jingji Guanli Bianjibu (ed.), *Zhonghua Renmin Gongheguo jingji guanli dashiji* [A Chronology of the Major Events in the PRC's Economy and Management], Zhongguo Jingji Chubanshe, Beijing.

State Planning Commission, et. al. (1985), 'Guanyu kongzhi qiche shengchan, jinkou he gaijin fenpei banfa de zhanxing guiding'[Temporary Regulations on Restricting Automobile Production and Importation and Improve Methods of Distribution], in Zhejiangsheng Sifating, Zhejiangsheng Duiwai Jingji Maoyiting, ed., *Duiwai jingji falü zhengce huibian* [A Selection of Foreign Economic Laws and Policies], no page numbers.

Sun Yeli (1996), 'Wenge houqi Chen Yun guanyu dui ziben zhuyi guojia maoyi wenti de jidian sikao' [Some of Chen Yun's Reflections During the Latter Period of the Cultural Revolution on the Problem of Trade with Capitalist Countries], in Zhu Jiamu (ed.), *Chen Yun he tade shiye* [Chen Yun and His Career], Zhongyang Wenxian Chubanshe, Beijing, pp. 1080-91.

Teiwes, F. C. (1999), *China's Road to Disaster*, M.E. Sharpe, Armonk.

Tzeng, F.W. (1991), 'The Political Economy of China's Coastal Development Strategy', *Asian Survey*, vol. 31.

Van Ness, P. (ed.) (1989), *Market Reform in Socialist Countries*, Rienner, Boulder.

Van Ness, P. and Raichur, S. (1989), 'Dilemmas of Socialist Development: an Analysis of Strategic Lines in China', in P. Van Ness (ed.), *Market Reform in Socialist Countries*, Rienner, Boulder, pp. 143-69.

Wade, R. (1991), 'Industrial Policy in East Asia: Does It Lead or Follow the Market', in G. Gereffi and D. Wyman (eds), *Manufacturing Miracles*, Princeton University Press, Princeton, pp. 231-266.

Wang Zhiye and Zhu Yuanzhen (eds.) (1987), *Jingji tizhi gaige shouce* [Handbook on Economic Structural Reforms], Jingji Ribao Chubanshe, Beijing.

World Bank (1993), *The East Asian Miracle: Economic Growth and Public Policy*, Oxford University Press, New York.

Xu Dixin (1982), *Zhongguo shehui zhuyi jingji kaizhanzhong de wenti* [Problems in Developing China's Socialist Economy], Zhongguo Shehui Kexue Chubanshe, Beijing.

Yan, S. (1995), *The Chinese Reassessment of Socialism, 1976-1992*, Princeton University Press, Princeton.

Yang, D.L. (1996), *Calamity and Reform in China*, Stanford University Press, Stanford.

Yang, S.C. (ed.) (1994), *Manufactured Exports of East Asian Industrializing Economies*, M.E.Sharpe, Armonk.

Zhang Guotao (1969), 'Introduction', in Union Research Institute (ed.), *Collected Works of Liu Shao-ch'i Before 1944*, Union Research Institute, Hong Kong.

Zhonggong Zhongyang Wenxian Yanjiushi (ed.) (1997), *Zhou Enlai nianpu (1949-1976)* [A Chronicle of Zhou Enlai Life, 1949-1976], Zhongyang Wenxian Chubanshe, Beijing.

Zhongguo Duiwai Jingji Maoyi Nianjian Bianji Weiyuanhui (ed.) (1984), *Zhongguo duiwai jingji maoyi nianjian* [The Chinese Foreign Economic Trade Yearbook], Zhongguo Duiwai Jingji Maoyi Chubanshe, Beijing.

Zhu Jiamu (ed.) (1996), *Chen Yun he tade shiye* [Chen Yun and His Career], Zhongyang Wenxian Chubanshe, Beijing.

Chapter 4

Political Culture as a Source of Japanese Immobilism in the New World Order

Robert W. Compton, Jr.

Introduction: The Problem of Japan

Two periods of rapid Japanese economic development, one following the Meiji Restoration and the other after defeat in World War II, suggested that a unique combination of political and business leadership coupled with a culture suited for economic development could propel countries into the ranks of highly developed nations. In the 1980s, Japan's economic might led to a resurgence of confidence in Japan and even throughout all of East Asia. Furthermore, the 1980s and early 1990s witnessed the emergence of a vast array of literature on the developmental state, which suggest an Asian model of development (Haggard and Moon, 1993; Wade, 1990; Amsden, 1989; Deyo, 1987; Johnson, 1982). However, during the 1990s, Japan experienced unprecedented economic decline and the economic strategy that promoted economic growth seemed no longer as effective. In fact, throughout East Asia, the developmental state became synonymous with 'Asian Crony capitalism' (Haggard, 2000; and Riess and Starr, 2000; Henderson, 1998).

The tremendous economic dislocation resulted in declining political legitimacy throughout the Asian region as governments that traditional derived legitimacy by promoting economic growth lost public faith. Political turmoil ensued in virtually all East and Southeast Asian countries, including South Korea, Taiwan, the Philippines, Thailand, Indonesia, Malaysia, and Japan. In the cases of South Korea, Taiwan, Indonesia, and Japan, long dominant political parties lost electoral control. Japan in particular became embroiled in political instability and a breakdown of electoral politics. As late as 1993, some observers predicted the demise of the Japan's ruling party, the Liberal Democratic Party. The changes that took place in the 1990s transformed researchers' views about the linkages between culture, politics, and economy and the evaluation continues to this day. Much of the accepted theories of the developmental state need reworking and assumptions about the 'guided economy' through the 'visible hand' (Amsden, 1989) appear anachronistic in this age of globalization.

Several vexing questions pertaining to Japan's relative decline need exploring. The particularly strong Japanese economy of the 1980s led to a plethora of work about Japan's superior economic system (Johnson, 1995; Prestowitz, 1993; Kearns, 1992; Fallows, 1989; van Wolferen, 1989). One article in *Foreign Affairs* spoke of a 'Pax Nipponica' (Vogel, 1986). Meanwhile the value of the yen continued to soar and its trade surpluses grew, apparently immune from exchange rate mechanisms, leading to protectionist sentiments throughout the world. Japan became the world's largest creditor nation and its leaders, including nationalists Nakasone and Ishihara suggested that the American economic system and even its society was experiencing terminal decline. A popularized version of this argument appeared from Asian 'values' leaders (Zakaria, 1994; Ishihara 1994) with Singaporeans Lee Kuan Yew and Kishore Mahbubani suggesting that 'Asian values' contributed to rapid economic growth and political stability.

By 2000, the discussion of Japan's economic superiority vanished and the country and the entire region, save PR China, remained mired in economic depression. What went wrong with Japan? Can Japan escape from the myriad of problems it currently experiences and lead Asia in a 'Pacific Century'? Unlike most of the research that focuses on the economic explanation for Japan's problems, this chapter suggests that Japan's problems have a socio-cultural basis rather than a socio-economic one. Furthermore, Japan's unique cultural construction together with the global changes taking place create conditions which inhibits the development of Japan's future leadership role in the region and world. In other words, the very bases of Japanese society prevent it from becoming an effective economic, political, and culture force for the foreseeable future. This paper explores why Japan's cultural construction prevents it from actualizing economic and political leadership in a globalized world. It concludes by suggesting that the synergistic effects of Japan's cultural construction with its impact on domestic politics and economics coupled with the integrative nature of globalization create conditions antithetical to Japan's future success. At the same time, Japan, for cultural reasons, cannot alter its basic and fundamental orientation significantly, because such abrupt or dramatic change would lead to the loss of its cultural identity.

Cultural Nature of Power

Many scholars, including Alexis de Tocqueville noted the culture of fundamental equality which the United States possessed from its inception (Tocqueville, [1956]). With manifest destiny and the opening up of a western frontier, notions of self-sufficiency, independence, and controlling the environment thrived in contradistinction to Japan and older societies, where more rigid class structures and a sense of hierarchy permeated life.

Unlike continental Europe or Japan, fundamental social hierarchy based on feudalism and re-enforced by industrialization simply did not exist. As a result, strong socialist ideological leanings failed to develop in the United States. In Japan, too, socialist ideological attachment remains weak, but for very different reasons involving the inculcation of traditional communitarian values. Two societies, both eschewing socialist ideologies, came to their respective positions for very different reasons. The answers for such differences lay in the conceptualization and practice of community and its formation in Japan.

According to early historical folklore and nationalistic accounts the Japanese descended from the sun-god Amaterasu while others suggest that the Japanese really came from the Korean peninsula via China (Hong, 1994). Japanese society, unlike Western Europe or the United States experienced industrialization much later and traditional values remained much more salient. When Japan experienced rapid industrialization after the Meiji Restoration, notions of community became inculcated into the national ethos (Pye, 1985, 168-70). This closed society ethos according to anthropologists explained the behavior of the Japanese toward in and out groups (Benedict, [1989]) and why the Japanese behave in singularly dedicated and focused manner when it comes to national conquest as noted by Lee Kuan Yew (Zakaria, 1994). In order to address the social dislocations created by modernization, the Japanese political elite created a sense of nation-state that endures to this day. The concept of nation-state, often discussed in the concept of political anthropology and social reflect the core notions of state construction. According to Benedict Anderson (1991, 7),

> it is the imagined as a *community*, because, regardless of the actual inequality and exploitation that may prevail in each, the nation is always conceived as deep, horizontal comradeship. Ultimately, it is this fraternity that makes it possible, over the past two centuries, for so many millions of people, not so much to kill, as willingly to die for such limited imaginings.

Chie Nakane (1970), a Japanese social anthropologist, discusses the role of frames in structuring Japanese society whereas Takie Sugiyama

Lebra (1976) explores the relationship between hierarchy and social order in Japan. The success of the modernizing elite in imposing a modern system based on traditional hierarchical notions and frames provided organizing mechanisms for creating a modern Japan. Simultaneously, these traditional symbols recreated and recast for modern state building appears to limit Japan's ability to adapt to rapid post-Cold War globalization.

Unlike the United States, Japan today remains a closed society created to function in a zero-sum international order. The zero-sum mentality derived from years of nation building in the Sakoku period of isolation (Anderson, 97) and the subsequent Meiji era. During the Meiji era, the new modernizing elite paid close attention to inculcating Confucian and Shinto values into the population (Hardacre, 1991). Thus, universal manhood education resulted in an educational curriculum emphasizing service for the nation and state. Because Japan needed to industrialize rapidly in a hostile environment of imperialism progressing throughout Asia in the 19th century, the citizens needed mobilization and the modernizing elite needed to emphasize the 'us' versus 'them' mentality. The Dutch missions abroad, often led by Fukuzawa Yukichi assisted Japan in two ways. First, it provided Japan an avenue to emulate and adapt European and American social and technological systems (Giddens, 1984, 253) in line with state building. Second, more importantly, the mission allowed state builders to create cultural meanings that clearly demarcated the Japanese from the outside world. In other words, the creation of the modern Japanese state relied on notions of *Gemeinschaft* and 'us' versus 'them' Weltanschauung. Thus Lucian Pye surmises that the Japanese maintained a traditional personal outlook in the private sphere but easily adopted modernity for the public sphere (Pye, 1985, 177). Edwin Reischauer (1983, 374-85) asserts that Japan is not Westernized but nonetheless modernized.

During the 1950s to 1980s, the Cold War environment, based on what Friedman calls the 'dammed up' and 'walled up' world (Friedman, 2000) that facilitated the Asian developmental states' rapid economic growth. Relying upon a unique international environment based on bipolarity, Japan, South Korea, Taiwan, Singapore, and Indonesia benefited from the Cold War environment. Hostile neighbors in the form of the USSR, PR China, North Korea created a national security environment that fed the 'us' versus 'them' distinction and strengthened the *Gemeinschaft* orientation within these societies. In addition, American military and economic hegemony in the West allowed these countries to 'catch-up' without paying their fair share of maintaining a system of embedded liberalism. Japan, too derived value from this type of international system by heightening anti-leftistism and destroying independent unions and by promoting a sense of vulnerability of an island nation devoid of natural resources barely surviving in a hostile world. Thus, each country could 'internationalize' their economies while maintaining significant national control over domestic economic practices, the movement of citizens, and cultural values. Asian countries harnessed their communitarian strengths and mobilized their citizenry out of fear.

In the type of world based extensively on the nation-state, such psychological devices differentiated 'us' and 'them' and proved very useful in allowing the Japanese to carve out their niche in the international political economy. However as discussed later, a closed psychological system makes adjusting to globalization without borders– *a la* Thomas Friedman in *The Lexus and the Olive Tree*– virtually impossible. The new globalization, involving the need for open systems, assumes the importance of an open cultural system, willing to accept immigrants, the destruction of national stereotypes, and a more limited role for government in economic planning. All Asian state lacks these characteristics.

Culture and Economy

Many scholars suggest that the developmental state's successes result from specific policies involving the 'guided economy' (Wade, 1990; Amsden, 1989; Johnson, 1987). In essence this line of argument suggests that economic statecraft and the adoption of industry specific policies and general government promotion of savings and investment, domestic infant industry protection, and subsidies for export-oriented companies differentiate the developmental state from American and European political economy systems.

Other scholars suggest that culture accounts for the economic miracle in Japan and East Asia. Hofeinz and Calder (1982), Durlabhji and Marks (1993) state that Confucianism and the functional equivalent it possesses with the Weberian Protestant work ethic account for the economic growth and disciplined and harmonious society. Lee Kuan Yew, in an interview with Fareed Zakaria (1994) stated that Confucianism and traditional values form the core foundation for East Asia's economic growth over the years. The political quiescence that results for the Confucian system allows governments to focus on economic growth. Economic growth, in turn serves as the major source of legitimacy in developmental states (Compton 2000b).

Finally, a third group of scholars suggests that East Asia's economic rise correlates with 'embedded liberalism' and associated economic principles, including comparative advantage and international division of labor (Balassa, 1982). Instead of explaining East Asia's rise primarily on institutionally crafted policies or on culture, the primary reason for the region's rise relates to the expansion of world trade and the role of East Asia in that context. The availability of cheap labor coupled with political stability, created an environment conducive for foreign direct investment (FDI) into East Asia and allowed these countries to utilized 'export oriented' growth strategy.

Yet despite these varied interpretations regarding the rise of the entire region, regional and country specific evidence suggest that all three factors played a role (Compton 2000a; 2000b). Culture provided the foundation and the catalyst for Japan and other East Asian nations to be able to take advantage of international trade through the use of specific governmental policies. In other words, political and economic institutions in East Asia, in general, and in Japan specifically, developed from cultural construction. Elements of life-time employment, the role of the bureaucracy in policy formation, the *keiretsu* system derive from culture. The statecraft exercised by these countries relied upon congruence with culturally established norms of *Gemeinschaft*.

Japanese Cultural Foundations of Political Economy

During the period following the Meiji Resotration, the Japanese modernizing elite sought to adapt and adopt Western technology in what was known as Dutch learning missions. Prior to the Meiji Restoration, Japan experienced a period of 'Sakoku' or isolation during which time, the foundations of Japanese society developed. When the Satsuma and Choshu clan came into power, they merely adapted the Tokugawa system for modernization by relying on traditional culture and recasting the samurai class within the bureaucracy and the corporate world.

The most important element of continuity that persists until now– the close cooperation between businesses and government– began during the Meiji era. During the 1880s, the Japanese government privatized industry and developed a governmental contracting system that supported the large zaibatsu. In fact, when the Japanese military expanded its political influence, after the successful wars with China and Russia, a close partnership among the military, the bureaucracy, and corporations emerged.

After Japan's defeat in World War II, the occupation failed to alter the basis premises of Japan's politics and economy. As noted by others (Compton 2000a; Johnson, 1982), the occupation failed to reform the bureaucracy and the Reverse Course, which followed an initial period of democratization, resulted in the re-instatement of pre-WWII political elite, including Prime Minister Yoshida Shigeru. Upon the ascendancy of Ikeda

Hayato to the premiership, a new slogan, 'Double Your Income' propelled the Japanese to new heights. Numerous slogans during the 1950s and 1960s reflected the heavy hand of Japanese bureaucracy through the use of traditional cultural symbols for social control and social construction purposes (Garon, 1997, 161-73).

What were the key cultural elements of the post-World War II that allowed the Japanese leadership to mobilize its citizens? Three primary characteristics can be identified. First, the Japanese political elite possessed the capacity to create a sense of organic society in which collective goods received priority over individual goods. Thus, Japanese citizens tolerated agricultural subsidies, inefficiencies in distribution, and low levels of welfare spending. LDP electoral alliances and constituency politics account for only part of the explanation. Instead, the LDPs success at manipulating traditional symbols perpetuated the system with the Japanese paying exorbitant prices for produce, rice, and meat. Only gradual external pressure for the US and other countries led to increased imports. This occurred slowly and with great recalcitrance as evidenced in the case of the rice market liberalization (Tilton, 1998; Itoh, 1994).

Second, the LDP successfully manipulated materialist values and a feeling of vulnerability among the citizenry. After the defeat of Japan, the relatively scarcity of food and security faced by the Japanese led to an embracement of LDPs economic growth policies. Because Japan possessed few natural resources, the citizens tolerated long hours at low wages, because without these sacrifices Japan could not re-industrialize (Gluck, 75-7). This logic was exercised even before the Meiji Restoration whereby officials extolled peasants to work hard and sacrifice more (Garon, 1997, 28). In the postwar era, perceived crisis– 'oil shocks' of 1974 and 1979– the government "structured public opinion polls" and contributed to "manufacturing this [environment of scarcity and the need for deferred gratification] consciousness" (Garon, 174).

Lastly, the ruling elite successfully took the traditional notion of family and village and expanded them to urban and industrial life. Much of these 'values' originated from Confucianism and found their way into the modern curricula of Japanese education. Here multiple layers of 'in' and 'out' groups operate as social control devices, working to solicit cooperation in the corporate world and simultaneously being less willing to deal with the outside world by cloaking activities and personal relations from outsiders. Issues of 'life-time employment', 'group promotion', and 'unit productivity' also resulted from traditional values. Rohlen (1974) explores traditional values in white-collar Japanese corporate organizations and life and demonstrated the pervasiveness of the 'in' and 'out' group notion.

Anatomy of Japan's Problems in the 1990s

Japan's strategy relied on shielding itself from a hostile Cold War environment by taking advantage of the US nuclear umbrella. With a foreign policy dependent on the US, Japan national security policy meant a concerted focus on economic growth. A record of marginal relations with South Korea, Russia, and China could be sidelined in such a bipolar world.

With the collapse of the Soviet Union and the 'new world order' based on a more globalized economy, some expected Japan to perform better than other Organization for Economic Cooperation and Development (OECD) nations because a significant amount of Japanese prosperity derived from exports. At the same time, a decline of global and regional Cold War hostilities should have opened up more opportunities for Japanese corporations abroad. For example, excluding the 'oil shocks' of the 1970s, the Japanese economy outperformed its OECD counterparts and its budget and trade surplus became the envy of other industrialized nations. The end of the Cold War should have, in theory, propelled Japanese economy toward exponential growth. Many scholars suggested that the future of global economic leadership and growth would come from Germany and Japan. For example, Bruce Cumings (1993, 63) observed,

> as the Asian 'Berlin walls' crumble, Japan will be poised to pursue a German option, that is, to deepen its market position in socialist China, Korea, and Vietnam. In other words, the twenty-first century may well be one driven by Germany and Japan

Instead, Japan's economy barely grew in the 1990s.

Most of Japan's economic stagnation resulted from years of internal inefficiency coupled with greater pressure for barrier free trade. Unfortunately, in addition to years of rapid ecomic growth, the developmental state policies and the LDP's bizarre electoral constituency make-up created the necessity to compensate various interests (Calder, 1988). As a result, glaring domestic economic inefficiencies resulted. For example, in 1963, the Japanese government enacted Small and Medium Enterprises Basic Law to subsidize 'mom and pop' stores. Furthermore, the Large Scale Retail Store Law of 1973 curtailed and controlled the expansion of large retailers into many markets by imposing zoning requirements (Michisada, 1981). During the 1960s, given Japan's labor-intensive economic nature, it made sense to protect these businesses, however, they have become a major problem in the distribution of goods through Japan in recent years (Nihon Seisan Honbu, 1993). The antiquated distribution system reflects gross domestic inefficiencies in Japan's market.

Richard Katz (1998) referred to the severe discrepancies between the export and domestic sectors of the economy as a 'dual economy' and the problems associated with declining productivity and profitability of the domestic economy as chronic. Overall the economy, according to him, suffered from 'anorexia' induced by domestic inefficiency and the super-efficiency of the export sector.

The three primary problems faced by Japan in the 1990s include declining economic productivity, increasing public and private debt– which resulted in a banking crisis, and the lack of political will to adopt reform. All three of these problems are deeply rooted in Japan's political culture developed over the past two centuries. Thus the root of the problem exists at the nexus of economic and political practices and understandings that developed in the Japanese cultural framework.

The cultural construction of the Japanese economy, which resulted in lifetime employment, 'seniority-based' promotion, and 'group-based' promotion prevents the economy from shifting into the information age in two ways. First as productivity of large domestic firms– in particular those in manufacturing, construction, banking, and retail– lagged, the companies resorted to borrowing and inertia rather than drastic cuts. Laying off employees would break the existing social contract. While companies in other countries laid off large number of employees, Japanese firms have, to date, resisted this. Thus official unemployment figures remain at 4.7% (Labour Force Survey Statistics Bureau & Statistics Center, 2001), a 125% percent increase from 1990. Many experts expect that the rate of unemployment should exceed 10% to counter the redundancy and deadwood present in these industries and the most recent figures show that the unemployment rate 5.0% (Japan Times, 2001b). Yet, most continue to depend on pork-barrel projects or government sanctioned loans to survive. As a result, anemic growth and deflation characterize the Japanese economy. From 1990 to 1999, real economic growth rates averaged 1.66% (International Department, Bank of Japan, 2000).

From 1990 to 2001, the Japanese national government's budgetary picture dramatically shifted toward alarming levels of continuous deficit. Because the Japanese government's legitimacy derives largely from economic growth and the ruling party's ability to provide a cushion from market forces, the government launched an unprecedented level of deficit spending to prime the economy. Currently, the deficit borrowing as a percentage of the budget stands at 20%-25% over the past three years (Ministry of Finance Statistics, 2001) putting Japan's deficit spending at one of OECD's highest.

The social contract that exists between the Japanese government and its people coupled with the corporate and banking sector's tangled alliances resulted in massive bad debt in the private sector and also forces the government to increase budgetary expenditures, which accounts for the massive borrowing. Cultural orientations and the lack of reliance on *Gesellschaft* arrangements involving contracts and transparent accounting practices heightened moral hazard as bank after bank continued to provide loans to failing firms. The inefficiencies of Japan's domestic economy caused both deficit spending and interest rate cuts to have no significant effect on the economy. The table below demonstrates the lack of positive effect of increased spending and interest rate reductions on Japan's GDP growth rates.

Table 4.1 Interest Rates, Deficit Spending, and Economic Growth

Year	Deficit Spending	Interest Rate Change	Growth Rate
1990	21.6	1.75	5.1
1991	22.8	-1.5	3.8
1992	22.8	-1.25	1.0
1993	21.3	-1.50	0.3
1994	19.6	0.0	0.6
1995	18.6	-1.25	1.5
1996	21.8	0.0	5.0
1997	21.7	0.0	1.6
1998	22.2	0.0	-2.5
1999	24.2	0.0	0.2
2000	25.8	-0.0	1.0

Notes: Deficit Spending equals bonds issued as a percentage of the National Budget; Interest Rate equals Bank of Japan Official Discount rate (change from previous year at year end); and Growth Rate equals Real Economic Growth Rate. Base interest rate was 4.25% in 1989 and was 0.25% in 2001.

Source: Ministry of Finance Statistics Monthly (May, 2001), Policy Research Institute, Ministry of Finance; Comparative Economic and Financial Statistics: Japan and Other Major Countries (2000), International Department, Bank of Japan; and Official Discount Rates (2001), Public Information Division, Public Relations Department, Bank of Japan.

Finally, the lack of political will represents the most alarming aspect about Japan's current economic malaise. While many analysts and scholars criticized Japan for its lack of leadership in the past, the current situation requires leadership. Since 1990 ten prime ministers rotated their positions without significant impact. Coupled with paralysis involving executive and bureaucratic stalwarts, initiatives for reform rarely materialize (Carlile and Tilton, 1998). Japan not only failed to provide leadership during the Asian Economic Crisis in 1997 and 1998, but showed ineptness by remaining haunted by issues from the Cold War era, including unresolved issues with South Korea, PR China, and Russia. Japan's economic health continued to remain dependent on exports to the Asia region, just as the region sought to export more to Japan. In fact, the Japanese continue to defend domestic political constituents as evidenced by the recent imposition of tariffs on tatami mats and shitake mushrooms from China.

Domestically, the collapse of the LDP in 1993 and the appearance of opposition led-government appeared to harbinger significant reforms. Unfortunately, significant reforms, save the 'Big Bang,' failed to materialize. When the Socialists entered into a coalition with the LDP, reforms stalled with the LDP seeking to regain and maintain power. Thus, the LDP could not fathom the tough economic measures. Ironically, had Japan been a developing nation along the lines of South Korea and without a hard currency, it would have ultimately gone to the International Monetary Fund (IMF). The IMF's austerity program surely would have resulted in significant economic hardships. As the world's second largest economy, it escaped these measures but failed to have the necessary external pressures for economic restructuring. Recently, Junichiro Koizumi, the current prime-minister promised reform, stating, "A rise in unemployment is inevitable in the process of reform. I believe now is the time to brace ourselves to endure the pain" (Japan Times, 2001a). Despite the calls for hard times and his unprecedented popularity, it remains to be seen if he can alter the behavior of rank-and-file LDPers, the powerful bureaucracy, and vested constituents. Recently, Koizumi's popularity plummeted in reaction to stalled reforms and persistent weakness in the economy.

Why Japan Cannot Excel in the Future

Despite the discussion about a Japanese threat to US economic security in the 1980s and 1990s, including a coming war with Japan (Friedman and Lebard, 1991) and alarm about a Pax Nipponica, the weaknesses of Japan became manifest in the past ten years. As discussed throughout this chapter, the primary problems Japan currently experiences traces its origin to culture and the social construction of the Japanese nation-state. The nature of the Japanese social construction of nation-state precludes its ability to excel in an increasingly globalized world. Precisely, what is Japan missing in order to become a global leader?

Japan developed its economy and modernized over the past 100 years based on insular notions embodied on the principles of *Gemeinschaft*. As such, most Japanese look at themselves as significantly different from other nationals. Despite the rhetoric of 'kokusaika' or internationalization, Japan remains a very closed and insular nation, culturally and economically. In fact, immigration to Japan among OECD states remains the lowest (Coppel and et. al, 2001, 6-10). While Japan hosts many temporary guest workers, few seek to remain in Japan. Many complain that Japanese society does not seek to embrace any element of multiculturalism. The strict citizenship laws in Japan, based not on (blood) *jus sanguis* or matrilineal relationships but on patriarchal lineage and virtually impossible naturalization rules make Japan unattractive to many guest workers. Recently, DNA tests resulted in the revocation of Japanese citizenship from a young boy based on false registration of a Japanese father (Kyodo News Service, 2000). Even most South Koreans residing in Japan are denied citizenship, face economic and social discrimination, and are forced assimilate into Japanese society. Discussions about the need to replenish the country's aging workforce produce no legislative reform for any sizeable increase in immigration.

The immigration issue reflects a microcosm of Japan's insular reality. Virtually every critical policy area, whether domestic or foreign, the current policy orientation seeks to maintain, conserve, and preserve the past system rather than innovate toward a new and dynamic system. Examples of societal immobilism exist in all significant policy areas, including but not limited to educational policy, governmental and administrative reform initiatives, social security and pension issues, financial and banking sector stabilization, small-scale retail laws, immigration issues, agricultural policy, and all aspects of foreign policy. Simply stated, policy innovation in Japan ceased to exist. The private sector also experiences this atrophic reality with many corporations refusing to adjust to international pressures.

Japan's insular nature already accounts for its difficulty in dealing with the post-developmental state and post-Cold War reality. Countries likely to excel in the future need to become much more open to absorbing multicultural attributes. For example, the United States, a country composed of immigrants created its identity, in part, on being a country of multiple cultures. As of 1999, only 920,000 non-Korean foreign residents reside in Japan (Immigration Bureau, Ministry of Justice, 2000). Despite the criticisms of the 'melting pot' analogy or the nativism that existed throughout American history, the United States continues to incorporate multiple cultures into its national identity. Incidentally, according to the US Immigration and Naturalization Service, 900,000 immigrants legally enter the country annually (Immigration and Naturalization Service, 1999). Ironically, Japan's cultural identity cannot allow for the absorption of large numbers of non-ethnic Japanese into its society without its very essence collapsing. Thus, any attempt at 'internationalization' means dealing with the world on its own terms, in a way that its culture can be preserved and insulated from the rest of the world. With increased global human and capital mobility and the deconstruction of nation-states currently taking place in Europe and along the American border, Japan appears an anachronism and fails to benefit from many aspects of globalization but reaps its primary disadvantages.

Conclusion: The Future of Japan

Given the unfavorable analysis of Japan's reality presented in the paper, what can be expected regarding Japanese future? What are some primary concerns that affect other Asian states, European nations, and the United States?

Japan's power peaked in the late 1980s when its citizens enjoyed the fruits of years of developmental state success. Granted, many Japanese believed that they were poor and unable to match the living standards of the West, in terms of housing and daily amenities but compared to previous generations, the Japanese today experience a much higher quality of life. The current problems assaulting Japan reflect not short-term cyclical dislocations, but are long range and protracted far beyond resolution by fiscal or monetary manipulation or legislative tinkering. Japan's current leadership fails to come to terms with these issues. While new leadership could invigorate Japanese society over many decades, these changes may not be enough to counter the continued atrophying of Japanese society and the intensification of globalization. In particular, any leadership faces extraordinary difficulties in altering the cultural and social construction of an entire nation-state without promoting a rapid decline as witnessed by Gorbachev's Soviet Union.

At best, Japan will continue to experience marginal growth and ultimately become a regional player weaker than China and perhaps even a United Republic of Korea. In light of this, both the United States and the European Union (EU) need to come to terms with Japan's relative long-term decline. The United States, in particular, needs to address whether the long-term maintenance of bases in Japan serves to strengthen its security over the long term. As China and Korea become more important players in Asia, the United States needs to adapt and shift its policy to account for Japan's decline.

References

Amsden, A. (1989), *Asia's Next Giant: South Korea and Late Industrialization*, Oxford University Press, New York.
Balassa, B. and et al. (1982), *Development Strategies in Semi-Industrial Economies*, Johns Hopkins University Press, Baltimore.
Benedict, R. (1946), *The Chrysanthemum and the Sword: Patterns of Japanese Culture*, Houghton, Mifflin, Boston.
Calder, K. (1988), *Crisis and Compensation: Public Policy and Political Stability in Japan, 1949-1986*, Princeton University Press, Princeton.
Carlile, L. and Mark T. (1998), 'Is Japan Really Changing?,' Lonny Carlile and Mark Tilton, (eds.), *Is Japan Really Changing Its Ways?*, Brookings Institution, Washington, DC, pp. 197-218.
Comparative Economic and Financial Statistics: Japan and Other Major Countries (2000), International Department, Bank of Japan, Tokyo.
Compton, R. (2000a). *East Asian Democratization: Impact of Globalization, Culture, and Economy*. Praeger, Westport.
Compton, R. (2000b). 'Reconstructing Political Legitimacy in Asia: Globalization and Political Development', *International Journal on World Peace*, vol. 17, 19-39.
Coppel, J. and et al. (2001). 'Trends in Immigration and Economic Consequences', Economics Department, Organization for Economic Cooperation and Development (OECD), Working Paper No. 284.
Cumings, B. (1993), 'Japan in the World System' in Andrew Gordon, (ed.), *Postwar Japan as History*, University of California Press, Berkeley, pp.34-63.
Deyo, F. (1987), *The Political Economy of the New Asian Industrialism*, Cornell University Press, Ithaca.
Durlabhji, S. and Marks, N., (eds.), (1993), *Japanese Business: Cultural Perspectives*, SUNY Press, Albany.
Fallows, J. (1989), 'Containing Japan', *Atlantic Monthly*, May 1989, p. 40-54.
Friedman, T. (2000), *The Lexus and Olive Tree*, Farrar Straus & Giroux, New York.
Friedman, G. and Lebard, M. (1991), *The Coming War With Japan*, New York, NY: St. Martin's Press.
Garon, S. (1997), *Molding Japanese Minds: The State in Everyday Life*. Princeton University Press, Princeton.
Giddens, A. (1984), *The Constitution of Society: Outline of the Theory of Structuration*, Polity Press, Cambridge.
Gluck, C. (1993), 'The Past in the Present', in Andrew Gordon, (ed.), *Postwar Japan as History*, University of California Press, Berkeley, pp.64-95.
Haggard, S. (2000), *The Political Economy of the Asian Financial Crisis*, Institute for International Economics, Washington, D.C.
Haggard, S. and Moon, Chung-in (1993), 'The State, Politics, and Economic Development in Postwar South Korea", in Hagen Koo, (ed.), *State and Society in Contemporary Korea*, Cornell University Press, Ithaca, pp. 51-93.
Hardacre, H. (1991), *Shinto and the State, 1868-1988*, Princeton University Press, Princeton.
Henderson, C. (1998), *Asia Falling*, McGraw-Hill, New York.
Hofheinz, R. and Calder K. (1982), *The Eastasia Edge*, Basic Books, New York.
Hong, W. (1994), *Paekche of Korea and the Origin of Yamato Japan*, Kudara International, Seoul.
Ishihara, S. (1989), *The Japan That Can Say No*, Simon and Schuster, New York.
Itoh, M. (1994), 'Kome Kaikoku and Japanese Internationalization', *Asian Survey*, vol.34, pp.991-1001.

Japan Times (2001a), 'Job Losses Sure to Increase: Koizumi', August 24.
Japan Times (2001b), 'Unemployment rate for July seen hitting 5%', August 24.
Johnson, C. (1995), *Japan: Who Governs?*, W.W. Norton, New York.
Johnson, C. (1982), *MITI and the Japanese Miracle*, University of California Press, Berkeley.
Katz, R. (1998), *Japan: The System That Soured*. M.E. Sharpe, Armonk.
Kearns, R. (1992), *Zaibatsu America: How Japanese Firms Are Colonizing Vital U.S. Industries*, Free Press, New York.
Kyodo News Service (2000), 'Fukuoka Bureau Revokes Boy's Japan Citizenship After DNA Tests', Kyodo News Service, November 8.
Labour Force Survey (2001), Statistics Bureau & Statistics Center, Ministry of Public Management, Home Affairs, Posts and Telecommunications, Tokyo.
Lebra, T. S. (1976), *Japanese Patterns of Behavior*, University of Hawaii Press, Honolulu.
Michisada, H. (1981), *Hojokin to Seikento* [Government Subsidies and Political Processes], Asahi Shinbunsha, Tokyo.
Ministry of Finance Statistics (2001), Monthly Policy Research Institute, Ministry of Finance, Tokyo.
Nakane, Chie (1970), *Japanese Society*, Berkeley, CA: University of California Press.
Nihon Seisan Honbu [Nippon Production Headquarters] (1993*), Wagakuni no Ryutsu no Genjo to Kadai* [The Present and Future Situation of Our Country's Distributive System], Nihon Seisansei Honbu, Tokyo.
Prestowitz, C. (1993), *Trading Places: How We Are Giving Our Future to Japan and How to Reclaim It*, Basic Books, New York.
Pye, L. W. (1985), *Asian Power and Politics*, Belknap Press, Cambridge.
Reischauer, E. (1983), 'Not Westernization But Modernization', H. Wray annd H. Conroy, (eds.), in *Japan Examined: Perspectives on Modern Japanese History*, University of Hawaii Press, Honolulu.
Riess, P. [Peter Starr, trans.] (2000), *Asian Storm: The Economic Crisis Examined*, Charles E Tuttle Co, Boston.
Rohlen, T. (1974), *For Harmony and Strength: Japanese White-Collar Organization in Anthropological Perspective*, University of California Press, Berkeley.
Statistics on Foreign Residents (2000), Immigration Bureau, Ministry of Justice, Tokyo.
Tilton, M. (1998), 'Regulatory Reform and Market Opening in Japan', in L. Carlile and M. Tilton, *Is Japan Really Changing Its Ways?: Regulatory Reform and the Japanese Economy*, Brookings Institution, Washington, D.C., pp. 163-96.
Tocqueville, A. [1956], R.D. Hefner, (ed.), *Democracy in America*, Mentor Books, New York.
US Department of Justice (1999), *The Triennial Comprehensive Report on Immigration*, Immigration and Naturalization Service, Washington, D.C.
Vogel, E. (1986), *Japan as Number One: Lessons for America*, Harvard University Press, Cambridge.
Wade, R. (1990), *Governing the Market: Economic Theory and the Role of Government in East Asian Industrialization*, Princeton University Press, Princeton.
Wolferen, K. van (1993), *The Enigma of Japanese Power*, Alfred A. Knopf, New York.
Zakaria, F. (1994), 'Culture is Destiny: A Conversation With Lee Kuan Yew', *Foreign Affairs*, vol. 73, pp. 9-26.

Chapter 5

Globalization, Asian Political Culture and State Control

Kunihiko Imai

Introduction

Many scholars of international political economy argue that the internationalization of national economies dismantled the barriers that previously separated countries from each other. Countries trade more freely than ever before, resulting in greater interdependence. As a result, the pace of economic and political convergence increased dramatically over the past few decades as states appear increasingly similar in terms of their political structures and values and economic functions. Further, many believe that globalization of economy weakened the political elites' control over politics and policies within their societies; thus, globalization promotes civil liberties and democracy. Regardless of various religious or cultural differences between states, according to these scholars, the integration of national economies into the global market place serves as a catalyst to the states' democratization. Globalization loosens the grip of political elites over popular freedom by allowing citizens to participate in the decision-making processes concerning vital political and economic issues facing the country.

Other scholars of international politics, however, reject the claim regarding the universal effect of economic globalization on politics. They contend that cultural influences on politics mitigate globalization influences. Therefore, the effects of globalization differ from the rest of the world. Cultural arguments stress the influence of Confucianism on peoples' attitudes and the uniquely Asian brand of rampant 'crony capitalism'. Over the years, collusion between business and government that perpetuates the existing power structure within the society emerged and became institutionalized. As a result, the political elites' control over its citizens remains stronger in Asia than in other regions of the world, thus thwarting the impact of the economic globalization.

The validity of either argument remains unresolved. Confucian influence on interpersonal relations and the existence of government and business collusion in Asia seem undeniable. However, the extent of the effect of such political culture remains an empirical question. As part of the broader discussion on globalization and its impact on Asian politics, this chapter tries to shed some light on the myth and reality of the Asian 'uniqueness'.

Globalization of Economy

The volume of international commercial transactions increased dramatically after World War II and consequently many countries' economies became internationalized with an increase percentage of GNP attributable to trade related economic activities. The internationalization of economy caused what we now call globalization, which 'refers broadly to the process whereby power is located in global social formations and expressed through global networks rather than through territorially-based states' (Thomas, 1997, 6). Subsequently, the effects of globalization on national economy and state's control over its society became the focus of attention among scholars.

Increasing economic integration among nations, some scholars argue, dramatically reduced the barriers between national economies, undermining the autonomy of national governments (Rodrik, 1997; Slaughter, 1997; Thomas, 1997; Bryant, 1994; Ohmae, 1993). As the countries' economies become more internationalized, the governments become less able to control or manipulate their economy, and the states' political control over their society lessens. Many point out that globalization erodes the authority of states because:

- the states' 'power to implement national regulations within [their] boundaries declines both because people can easily flee their jurisdiction and because the flows of capital, pollution, pathogens, and weapons are too great and sudden for any [states] to control' (Slaughter, 192), and;
- various other transnational capitalist actors including transnational and international bodies such as the World Bank and the IMF supersede 'the states in determining entitlement on a now global scale' (Thomas, 15),

Complicating the matter that international actors erode sovereignty, subnational actors (communities, local governments, and regions within nations) also increasingly assert their claims to cultural and political autonomy (Sachs, 1998). In other words, increased globalization narrowed the menu of choices available to national political elites in maintaining strong centralized control.

The casual observer of global politics might equate the onslaught of globalization with the government's diminished state autonomy and capacity to control their own society, and that private interests, including the general public, increase its power. However, the subtle realities paint a complicated and a multi-faceted situation. Globalization, for example, supposedly increases interdependence of national economies, but national economies may not be as interdependent or universally interdependent as one may expect. As a result, differing degrees of interdependence and integration with the global economies exist. Some 'national economies retain a considerable degree of isolation from each other, and [their] national policymakers enjoy more autonomy than is assumed by most recent writings on the erosion of national sovereignty'

(Rodrik, 1997, 21). Moreover, the same degree of integration into the global economic system may have a different effect on industrialized countries than on developing countries. For example, the governments in the advanced industrialized countries may retain more autonomy in regulating their economies due to their greater access to resources than those in the less industrialized countries. In addition, developed countries tend to posses greater control over their monetary and fiscal policies than less developed nations.

One could also argue that 'a gain in power by non-state actors does not necessarily translate into a loss of power for the state' (Slaughter, 1997, 184). Globalization enhances the opportunities for those capable of competing in the world markets. At the same time, it leaves those who less competitive vulnerable to external competition. They become susceptible to the negative effects of economic liberalization such as reduced social insurance, job security, and diminished social welfare. Employers, who previously provided such benefits, now experience increased competition from both domestic and foreign sources and therefore, must curtail such costs. Greater demand for wage increases and employee benefits in the more developed labor markets force them to become more internationally mobile. As a result, national governments frequently must address a greater public need for unemployment compensation, job-force retraining, and social insurance for those at greater risk.

Globalization increases demands for social security programs, which may suggest the increased responsibility, thus sustained power, for the states. The increased demands placed on national governments strengthen the power of states that possess the capacity to meet them. The increased mobility of capital, for example, reduces a significant portion of a state's tax base and decreases the capacity to sustain social safety nets. The impact of the globalization of the economy on the state's control over its society is not a simple, all-or-nothing proposition. It is a much more complex issue. Although globalization may generally erode national boundaries and, possibly, the political elites' control over the society, the extent of its impact may vary greatly between states depending on their economic conditions. Against these backdrops, this chapter examines the specific case of Asian states and examines whether Asian states experience the effects of globalization differently than non-Asian states. This chapter also examines differences in the ability of Asian and non-Asian states to maintain control over society during the era of rapid globalization.

Asian Uniqueness?

As Asian economies become increasingly integrated into the global market place, people increasingly inquire whether Asian states exhibit immunity to the impact of the globalization because of the 'unique' cultural characteristics.

Unlike many nations that experienced democracy and multiparty competition, authoritarianism only gradually withered away. Only in the 1980s did South Korea, the Philippines, Taiwan, and Thailand experience sustained democratic consolidation.

Lee Kuan Yew, Singapore's former prime-minister emphasized the need for an Asian alternative to Western-style democracy because of Asia's unique Confucian cultural traditions (Zakaria, 1994). Accordingly, Lee developed a so-called 'soft' authoritarian regime, which 'combined capitalism with an authoritarian political system that suppressed freedom of speech and political dissent while intervening, often intrusively, in its citizens' personal lives' (Fukuyama, 1995, 24). He noted that this style of political management reflects East Asia's Confucian cultural traditions better than the Western 'democratic' model (Zakaria, 1994, 109-26).

Given the Confucianist orientation toward governance and leaders who adapt it for authoritarian purposes, the primary contention suggests that Asian countries lack the appropriate historical and cultural background to support democracy and therefore, experience an inability to transition to Western style democracy. The democratization question often explores the power relationship between state and its civil society. Democracy means, among other things, the primacy of individual freedom. It also connotes 'the state's increased responsiveness to societal pressures, and the emerging political diversity in turn reflects the increased pluralism in civil society' (Brown and Jones, 1995, 104). These developments failed to develop in East Asian countries because of the strong, deep-rooted influence of Confucianism. One of the most important reasons for incompatibility between Confucianism and democracy according to Samuel Huntingtion (1991, 24) is that "Confucianism merged society and the state and provided no legitimacy for autonomous social institutions at the national level".

Indeed, some Confucian traits seem incompatible with democratic ideals. Mostly importantly, Confucianism emphasizes harmony, order, and respect for hierarchy at the expense of individual liberty. In fact, traditional Confucian societies lacked any tradition of emphasizing human rights, particularly, rights against the state (i.e., the right to question, or request changes in, the policies made by the state). 'To the extent that individual rights did exist, they were created [and regulated] by the state)' (Huntington, 24). Further, traditional Confucianism stresses an automatic, superior-inferior relationship between the husband and his wife, the older and younger brothers, the ruler and the ruled, and so forth. In line with this paradigm, the subordinate follows the superior without questioning the legitimacy of his authority. This certainly contradicts the Western notion of democracy, which makes in principle, the people sovereign and above the elected officials. Similarly, in a Confucian society, 'harmony is to be prized, not legalistic bickering or competition' (Tamney,

1991, 402). This, too, delegitimizes the institutionalization of opposition, an important part of democracy. Confucianism accommodates neither a popular right of resistance nor any indefeasible individual right. 'There is no room for politics as an essentially pluralistic activity, or for the notion that government reflects a popular will.' (Jones, 1995, 75) Therefore, Confucian values and principles represent a paradigm antithetical to democratization.

In addition to fundamental differences in the conception of human rights and democracy between Asia and the West, some people argue, 'there is a general discontent throughout the [Asian] region with a purely Western interpretation of human rights' (Kausikan, 1993, 26). Thus, Asian societies possess a set of core values that unite elites with the masses with the political elites eschewing the universal application of the Western model of economic, political, and social development (Dupont, 1996, 16). Due to the unique type of social contract engrained in these political systems, the effects of economic internationalization on democratization may be attenuated in Asian societies compared to many parts of the world that experienced a Westernization of their core culture.

Another view about the impact of Confucian culture on Asian democratic development suggests that these obstacles may not necessarily prevent countries from becoming democratic (Huntington, 1991, 29-30). Despite a lack of support for individualism or a transcendent law that would 'provide the ground for individual conscience as the ultimate source of authority,' empirical evidence suggesting a causal link between the lack of democratization and Confucian societies remains unclear (Fukuyama, 1995, 25). Their principle argument suggests that much of the cultural argumentation exaggerates Asian uniqueness (Dupont, 1996, Fukuyama, 1995; Tai, 1993; Scalapino, 1989). 'The obstacles posed by Confucian culture do not seem any greater than those posed by other culture; indeed, when compared to those of Hinduism or Islam, they appear to be much smaller' (Fukuyama, 30). He notes (27):

- the traditional Confucian examination system was a meritocratic mechanism with potentially egalitarian implications;
- Confucianism emphasizes education (in practice, a society's general level of education provides an important underpinning of democratic institutions) and;
- Confucianism is relatively tolerant (in the past, Confucianism coexisted with other religions, notably Buddhism and Christianity).

Moreover, Confucian values assist 'governments and political elites to establish or maintain control of their people by creating new ideological orthodoxies, based on a contrived notion of a pan-Asian culture and value system' (Dupont, 25). Of course, Asian leaders share the need to legitimate their rule just like leaders in other countries. Throughout the world, political elites often use similar tactics in order to justify and reinforce their rule.

Therefore given the limited influence of Asian values, these scholars conclude that internationalization of national economy influences Asian states similarly to other states.

Yet another group of scholars argue that the effects of globalization may manifest themselves differently in Asian states than in non-Asian states not because of Confucianism but because of the heavy domination of their markets by state power. According to them, attributing the remarkable economic success of Asian states in the 1980s to their common Confucian heritage is 'a rather simplistic *post facto* rationalization' (Tai, 1993, 54). Instead, they emphasize the 'highly exclusionary corporatist or clientelistic relationship between state and capital' (Haggard, 131). While internationalization influences politics in all countries, Asian countries experience difference effects because 'markets are so heavily dominated by state power [in East Asia] that there exists no basis for the emergence of a capitalist class autonomous of the state' (Haggard, 133). As a result, globalization does not necessarily increase civil liberty to the same extent as in states outside the Asian region. Globalization reduces the control by political elites but liberalization still fails to take place. The internationalization of economy necessitates political elites to introduce limited economic reform (i.e., liberalization of market) thus reducing their autonomous power. However, such liberalization does not lead to democratization but simply increases the strength of private capital within the state *vis-a-vis* the political elites. In other words, globalization fails to change the balance of power between the state and society in Asian nations but merely shifts the locus of power from the political elites to private capital. Consequently, 'political change represents, not a move towards liberal democracy, but rather, a shift towards a more polycentric corporatism' (Haggard, 131). According to this scenario, the economic structure and behavior of Asian states differ from those in other regions and, therefore, result in less of an impact on democratization.

The following sections of this chapter test empirically the question of 'Asian uniqueness' by developing statistical measurements for concepts. The data form the basis for a statistical test utilizing multivariate analysis.

Measures of Internationalization

Testing the effects of the 'internationalization of national economy' on the 'state's control over its society' require the operationalization of these two concepts. Such complex concepts require a multiplicity of measures to capture adequately and thus must rely on several indicators. Several economic indices allow us to capture the totality of the concept involving trade, finance, and production as suggested by Jeffrey Sachs (1998). The most salient index of economic internationalization, trade, reflects the dramatic growth of the transnational transfer of goods. After World War II, international trade grew dramatically as a liberal trade regime spread throughout the world. In fact, most countries experienced a faster increase of trade with the outside world than their production, and, as a result, the share of exports and imports as a part of their GDP continues to increase (World Bank 2000). The 'volume of trade as percentage of GDP' captures an important aspect of the globalization of economy.

Second, during the past two decades, international financial flows expanded exponentially. In particular, foreign direct investment (FDI), through which foreign capital gains a controlling interest in a cross-border enterprise, experienced phenomenal growth. Consequently, FDI captures the degree to which a country's economy became internationalized. The FDI measure provides the second source of critical data on globalization.

To measure production within a state, most researchers use the Gross Domestic Products (GDP). The GDP represents the size of a country's market and reflect the degree to which it can attract FDI and trade. As a country's economy expands through globalization, the change in the market size may affect the state's control over the society by increasing the involvement of private interests in the country's economies. Therefore GDP, the third index of internationalization of national economy measure the size of the economy and its ability to attract FDI and trade.

Internationalization of a country's economy to a certain degree depends on economic health, especially robust demand within its market sustained by the public's purchasing power. As such, the sale of goods and services at home and abroad maintains economic health with domestic and international demand supporting and stimulating each other. Whenever a country's economy expands through its internationalization, the purchasing power of local consumers subsequently increases. GDP per capita measures a significant part of purchasing power, despite limitations involving cost-of-living differences. Furthermore, changes in GDP per capita will affect the state's ability to control the society because, *ceteris paribus*, the greater the number of private actors involved in the economy the more economic and political influence they obtain. Thus, increased economic and political power makes state control much more difficult.

In the early stages of economic development, countries often rely heavily on foreign economic aid. In fact, the majority of the countries in the world receive such aid. To a large extent, success of their economic development depends heavily upon the availability of capital. For many of these countries, foreign economic aid provides a vital pipeline to accessing convertible currency. Without enough aid, some of these economies may never achieve economic development and successfully become integrated into the global market. The disbursement of foreign aid, either bilateral or multilateral, often requires adherence to specific conditions, often forcing countries to liberalize and rationalize their economies. The amount of economic aid received impacts the level of internationalization.

Two measures of foreign economic aid exist. One examines the impact of aid on the country's overall economy by using 'aid as percentage of the GDP'. The other relates to its impact at the individual level, measured by using 'Aid Per Capita'. Either way, foreign economic aid facilitates internationalization and diminishes the state's control over society. Accordingly, foreign economic aid and aid per capita are used as the fifth and sixth indices of the internationalization.

In addition to FDI and foreign economic aid, a country's domestic investors and financial institutions also contribute to economic development and internationalization. As a country's economy develops, new industries expand more rapidly and yield profits. Some of these profits require reinvestment into capital goods and capital markets so that future growth takes place. Gross domestic investment impacts a country's ability to compete internationally and to integrate itself into the global economy. GDI is the seventh index used to measure the internationalization of national economies.

Urbanization rates reflect the displacement of agricultural production with manufacturing. With increased investment, existing industries that expand and new ones established will utilize workers and services in urban areas. As the excess capacity in urban areas diminish, greater migrations occur, as rural residents perceive increased economic opportunities in cities. The Urbanization of Population, therefore, is an indicator of economic development and the internationalization.

Measures of States' Counter Efforts at Controlling Society

When analyzing internationalization of national economies and its impact on state, the state's efforts to maintain its power and control over the society also exists in tandem. The political elites in primarily democratic countries attempt to maintain their power and control over the society by keeping some of their powerful clients especially big businesses and the general public satisfied with the status quo.

For corporations, states frequently provide credits with more attractive terms than private financial institutions can provide. For the general public, states provide all sorts of social programs to improve or maintain a high quality of life. In particular, almost all states emphasize the improvement of education for their citizens. Governments improve access to education and its quality to create a work force capable of engaging itself in higher value added production.

When the businesses and the citizens support the policies of government, can expect to stay in power and maintain their control over the society. If economic internationalization erodes political control elites can launch counter-measures to increase acceptance. Thus, governmental credits to private sector, spending on all social programs, and spending on education work to enhance acceptance. Therefore, these three variables are also included as the ninth, tenth, and eleventh independent variables.

Measuring the Dependent Variable: State's Control over Society

State's control over the society is indexed by using Freedom House's 'Freedom Country Ratings'. Since 1972, Freedom House's *Freedom in the World* survey provides an annual evaluation of political and civil liberties throughout the world. The survey rates the rights and freedoms enjoyed by individuals in each country by asking questions such as if the people are free from domination by the military, foreign powers, totalitarian parties, religious hierarchies, economic oligarchies, or any other powerful group. It also checks to see if the people have freedom of expression, association and organization, legal guarantee of basic human rights, and if they have personal autonomy, including the free from indoctrination and excessive dependency on the state, and economic rights such as to establish private businesses without undue influence by government officials or the security forces, and etc. It is an ideal index to measure state's control over society: that is, the state's, or the political elites', effort to maintain its power and authority over politics and policies of the country at the expense of, or at least in competition with, civil liberties of the citizens. Therefore, the dependent variable, *Civil Liberties*, is measured by using the Freedom Country Ratings on a 1 to 7 scale, with 1 representing the highest degree of freedom and seven the lowest. Countries and territories that receive a rating of 1 come closest to the ideal of an open, free, and democratic society where the citizens enjoy virtually complete political rights and civil liberties. A rating of 7 indicates the virtual absence of freedom. An overwhelming and justified fear of repression characterizes these societies.

Econometric Specification

In order to test the relationship between the independent variables, representing the internationalization of national economy and the state's counter efforts, and the dependent variable, *Civil Liberties*, representing the degree of state's control over their society, a pooled time-series multiple regression is used.

Pooled time-series models require special statistical considerations. The Ordinary Least Squares (OLS) model is not automatically applicable to pooled time-series analyses because it ignores the pooled structure of the data. It assumes that each case is independent of all others, not as part of a set of related observations. However, when the cases are systematically related to each other, OLS is not an appropriate technique to use, and some statistical controls are required.

Two particular violations are likely to accompany pooled data. First, the cases may not be independent along the time dimension within units, in which case autocorrelation would bias the statistical findings. Second, a form of heteroscedasticity is likely to be present in pooled data, since for a variety of reasons, some units (states) are more variable than others at all times (e.g., all years for one geographical region).

In this study, many of the independent variables are controlled for the GDP. In the case of the *Urban Population*, it is controlled for the 'total population' of the country for each year. So the first violation, autocorrelation, would not be a problem. Any variations in these independent variables would be independent of systematic, time-serial biases. For the other variables, the introduction of another independent variable, *Year* minimizes possible autocorrelational bias.

Even after taking care of the possible time-serial biases, the contaminant effects of the cross-sections– that is, some 'unit-specific (or state-specific) effects'– may still be present and so, further statistical controls are required. "One of the best ways to manage non-constant variance in a pool is by introducing a fixed value that represents the variance unique to the cross-section and conditional on the sample" (Sayrs, 1989). In this model, this is accomplished by using dummy variables representing each of the countries included in this study.

Data

The period of this study is between 1980 and 1998. Although, by the early 1980s, some countries such as Japan were industrialized and became more fully integrated into the international marketplace, most of the other Asian economies did not start their internationalization until the 1980s. For example, the People's Republic of China had declared its new Open Door policy only in 1979 and the modernization of its economy did not start in full force until the late 1980s. Hence, 1980 is chosen as the starting point of this data analysis. The data ends in 1998.

The number of the countries included in this study is, first of all, dictated by the availability of data. Among the Asian countries, eleven countries– 'the People's Republic of China (PRC), India, Indonesia, Japan, South Korea, Malaysia, Pakistan, Philippines, Singapore, Sri Lanka, and Thailand– are included in this study. These countries possess a sufficient number of data for the period, listed in the World Bank's *World Development Indicators 2000*

CDROM. For the other Asian countries, data measuring the independent variable was not available in sufficient quantity.

The non-Asian countries are also limited by the availability of data. In addition, countries engaged in war for most of the period are excluded because of the virtually impossibility in gauging the impact of the internationalization under such conditions. Moreover, former Communist block countries are excluded because of the unreliability of their data as well as the unique nature of their societies before the fall of Communism of 1989. Furthermore, all the industrialized countries (except for Japan) are excluded. By 1980, they were already fully integrated into the global marketplace. In fact, they comprised the marketplace and already granted virtually political and civil liberties to their citizens. As such, they are not appropriate to be included in the data in order to examine the effect of internationalization of their national economies upon their societies. As a result, twenty-six non-Asian countries– Argentina, Brazil, Cameroon, Chile, Colombia, Costa Rica, Cyprus, Ecuador, Egypt, Ghana, Greece, Guatemala, Kenya, Mali, Mexico, Mozambique, Nigeria, Paraguay, Peru, South Africa, Tunisia, Turkey, Venezuela, Zambia, and Zimbabwe– are included in this analysis.

Overall, internationalization of a country's economy has clearly influenced the degree of control the state has over its citizenry. Most of the indices of internationalization of national economy– except for *Trade* and *Aid*– show a statistically significant effect on *Civil Liberties*. The Asian political culture, which is considered to be fraught with crony capitalism and is often argued to be uniquely resilient to the outside influence, does not seem to be impervious to the effects of the internationalization of their economy. The negative coefficient of the dummy variable, *Asia*, (-1.82) clearly indicates that, during this period, Asian nations have actually become more politically transparent than many non-Asian nations. To the extent that the Asian states have become economically globalized, they have improved their civil liberties more than non-Asian states.

The data show that, on average, more than ninety percent of the Asian states' Gross Domestic Product (GDP) came from external trade while the rest of the world was less heavily dependent on trade.

These two facts– the heavier dependence by Asian states on international trade and the greater civil liberties among Asian states– suggest that, regardless of cultural differences, the more a country's economy becomes integrated into the global economy, the less able the state becomes to continue to restrict civil liberties.

However, interesting enough, the sheer volume of trade does not seem to affect the state's control over its citizenry. *Trade* had no statistically significant impact on *Civil Liberties*. This, together with the overall findings, shows that internationalization of national economies cannot be measured by looking at the states' trade alone. It has to be measured by incorporating all relevant indices.

Table 5.1. Globalization and Civil Liberties: A Pooled Time-Series Analysis

Independent Variable	Coefficient and Significance	Error
Intercept	-81.72	29.57
Year	.045	.015
Asian States	-1.82	.44
Trade	.000	.003
DI Net Inflow	-.026	.013
GDP	.007	.0
GDP Per Capita	-.002	.0
Aid	.015	.015
Aid Per Capita	-0.17	.0
GDI	-.034	.010
Urban Population	-.044	.018
Credit Private Sector	.009	.003
Education Spending	-.032	.051
Govt. Spending	-.016	.018

Notes: For parsimony of presentation, the dummy variables, included in the model to control for possible autocorrelational and heteroschedastic biases are not listed above. *Asian States* represents the dummy variable used to test for the systematic difference between Asian and non-Asian states in terms of the influence of internationalization of national economy upon the degree of control the state has over its society. *Trade* stands for each country's total volume of trade per year, measured as % of its Gross Domestic Products (GDP). *GDP* stands for each state's annual GDP, measured in billions of current US$. *GDP Per Capita* stands for each state's annual per capita GDP in current US$. *FDI Net Inflow* stands for each state's annual net receipt of foreign direct investments, measured in billions of current US$. *Aid* stands for annual net foreign economic aid, as % of GDP. *Aid Per Capita* stands for the annual net per capita foreign economic aid each country received, measured in current US$. *Urban Population* stands for the country's urban population as % of its total. *GDI* stands for the net annual Gross Domestic Investments in each country, measured as % of its GDP. *Credit Private Sector* stands for the annual government credit to private sector as % of the GDP. *Govt. Spending on Education* represents the annual government spending on education, measured as % of its GDP. *Govt. Spending* stands for the annual government spending on all social programs, measured as % of its GDP.

The following independent variables were significant at 0.05 or less: Year, Asian States, FDI Net Inflow, GDP, GDP Per Capita, Aid Per Capita, GDI, Urban Population, and Credit Private Sector.

$R^2 = .772$; Adj. $R^2 = .749$; and F-ratio= 34.81 and N=532.

Foreign Direct Investment, which is one of the indices of internationalization of national economy, proved to be another contributing factor toward greater civil liberties and less state control. The coefficient for *FDI Net Inflow*, -.0262, indicates that the more a country opened its market for foreign investors, the more open the society became, thus making it harder for the state to maintain its rigid control over it. Although the political elites may not like this effect of increased inflow of foreign direct investments, once they open their market and allow their economy to be integrated into the global market place, they may not have much choice but to continue with the globalization of their economy. After all, increasing investments, foreign or domestic, is one of the most fundamental rules of stimulating and sustaining a healthy economic growth. In order to satisfy the powerful private economic interests such as big businesses and to stay in power, the political elites simply may have to allow this economic internationalization, even though it may simultaneously undermine the control that the political elites wish to maintain over the society.

Since the market size (GDP) and the purchasing power of local consumers (GDP per capita) expected a positive relationship to the probability of foreign direct investment (FDI). As such both coefficients for *GDP* and *GDP Per Capita* should have a negative notation, indicating a positive influence on *Civil Liberties*. The greater the size of the economy, *ceteris paribus*, the greater the amount of FDI the country would attract, thus leading to less state control over the market. Similarly, the greater the purchasing power of local consumers, the more private economic activities in the country exist. This too, promotes less state control. The regression coefficient for *GDP Per Capita*, -.0002, indeed has a negative notation, indicating that increased purchasing power of consumers serves to increase *Civil Liberties*. *GDP*, however, has a positive coefficient, .0007, which indicates that, *ceteris paribus*, the greater the market size of a country, the less civil liberties the citizens have and the more state control they experience. This may be because a larger economy requires a greater degree of involvement by the state in regulating the economy (i.e., through regulatory agencies) thus, increasing the size of the government as well. Conversely, in a smaller economy, the size of the government will also be smaller and, once economic liberalization starts, it may be easier for private capital to gain greater influence *vis-a-vis* political elites. Hence, other things being equal, the market size is inversely related to the degree of civil liberties enjoyed by the general public.

Although the annual net foreign economic aid measured as percentage of GDP (*Aid*) did not show any impact, *Aid Per Capita* had a statistically significant effect on *Civil Liberties*. The regression coefficient of -.0165 indicates that, *ceteris paribus*, the more foreign economic aid a country receives per person, the harder it gets for the state to maintain tight control over the society. This happens because of the effect of economic aid on the economic development of the recipient country. As the country receives more aid per person, it may experience increased economic development. Subsequently, to the extent the economy develops and becomes more internationalized, it seems to make it harder for the state to continue to limit *Civil Liberties*.

As a country's economy develops and becomes more integrated into the global market, the country will have to continue to expand its economy by increasing domestic investments. The increased domestic investments, in turn, will have the same effect as the other variables mentioned above. The regression coefficient for *GDI* (% of GDP), -.0337, illustrates that the internationalization of a nation's economy, facilitated by increased domestic investments, fosters further liberalization of the society. Therefore, the state is caught in a dilemma. Although the political elites may desire to perpetuate their own power and control over the society by tightly regulating commercial activities, they would have to promote the economic development through market liberalization so that the continued economic success of the nation would sustain them in power. As long as they live within the capitalist market system, and as long as they utilize the nation's economic success to maintain the masses in control, the political elites will have no other choice but to continue on the current path. Ironically, market liberalization weakens the political elites' control over the society.

Economic development and globalization is closely related to the urbanization of population. As a country's economy develops from one stage to the next, the market activities expand, requiring a greater pool of labor. Enticed by greater opportunities for profit, workers in rural areas, engaged in traditional sectors of the economy such as agriculture, begin to migrate into the urban areas, thus causing the urbanization of the population. As the urbanization of population increases and the scope and magnitude of the country's economy expands through increased internationalization, the state again seems to lose some of its control over the society to the increased interests and power of the private citizens. The coefficient of -.0444 demonstrates that the increased *Urban Population* (as a % of the total population) positively contributes to the increased *Civil Liberties*, thus decreasing the state control.

The state or political elites, attempt always try to maintain its control over its society. Within the more or less democratic, capitalist nations examined in this chapter, one frequently applied method of achieving this objective is to satisfy the needs and wants of the more powerful private interests, such as big businesses, and the general public. Public finances provide one mechanism for maintaining control. In order to assist private businesses in meeting their financial needs, the state often provides businesses with financial assistance in the form of credits and loans. In return, corporate support for the government increases. However, such financing often comes with various conditions attached. Moreover, in addition to the officially stated terms of agreement, secretive behind-the-scene arrangements and understandings exist. Thus, the state's credit to private sector may serve to help maintain its control over the society. The empirical finding for *Credit to Private Sector* (as % of GDP) supports this argument. The coefficient, .0088, demonstrates that the greater state provision of credit and loans to the private sector, the more it is able to continue to limit *Civil Liberties*, thus limiting the effect of globalization.

States also attempt to maintain control over the public by providing essential public services such as education and health care as well as keeping the public happy through stable economic growth. As states spend more on public services (of course, within a reasonable limit), the public is supposed to remain content with the regime and support their policies. As long as the public is happy, the argument goes, the states will be able to perpetuate their status quo power and control over the society. The empirical findings, however, do not support this argument. Neither *Government Spending on Education* (as % of GDP) nor *Government Spending* (as % of GDP) shows any statistically significant effect on *Civil Liberties*. Once economic liberalization begins through the internationalization, political elites seem to have only a limited number of ways to delay political liberalization.

Conclusion

This chapter examined whether Asian states are uniquely different from other states. Specifically, it examined whether or not Asian states are less affected by the internationalization of their economies than other states. Further, it analyzed if there is any systematic difference between Asian and non-Asian states in terms of the way they are affected by their economic globalization.

Despite some scholars' claim that Asian states' unique political culture based on Confucian influences and 'crony capitalism' limits the influences of globalization, the empirical data show the contrary. The global market and economic integration into the global market affect both Asian and non-Asian states. In fact, as the variable '*Asian States*' demonstrated, Asian states are politically liberalized more, not less, than other comparable states. This negates the argument that Asian states are uniquely resistant to external pressures for change. It clearly shows that the 'unique' political culture in Asia does not prevent globalization of national economy from affecting the degree of state control over society. There seems to be a systematic difference between Asian and non-Asian states in terms of the degree of civil liberties in their societies. However, the difference does not originate in the 'Asian political culture,' purported to negatively influence democracy. Although determining the causes of this difference is an important inquiry, it is beyond the scope of this chapter and has to be pursued in future research.

It is a common knowledge that crony capitalism– the notorious collusion between political elites and businesses– remains an entrenched practice throughout Asia. As part of the effort to satisfy powerful private capitalists and retain their support, the political elites provides them with credits and loans. As the findings of Table 1 show, such an effort does seem to help in reducing the impact of internationalization of national economy upon democratization of the society. It may not negate the impact of globalization but it slows the process of political liberalization. However, not all such efforts bear fruit. The political elites' attempt to keep the public happy by increasing government spending on education and other social programs does not seem to help maintain their control over civil liberties. Together these findings seem to suggest that the degree of democratization of a society depends on the improvement of the standard of living of the general public and the subsequent popular involvement in the economic and, eventually, political decision making within the society. To the extent that political elites and a small number of private capitalists control a country's economic and political life, democratization stagnates.

Globalization of national economy is a complex issue. As explained before, it involves multiple layers of interactions between states, multinational corporations, international organizations, international investors, and banks. Naturally, its impact on civil liberties within states is also as complex an issue. This chapter has shown that, as elements of economic globalization, foreign direct investments, economic aid, domestic investments, and urbanization all have a positive impact on democratization of a society and that the claim of Asian cultural uniqueness is not warranted. Although *trade* failed to show any effect on *civil liberties*, it does not negate the assumption that it is one of the indices of economic globalization. Moreover, the fact that the increased volume of trade alone did not translate into increased civil liberties may not mean that trade has no bearing on democratization. It may turn out to be a contributing factor if matched with some of the other elements of economic globalization. An examination of such synergistic effects would further deepen our understanding of the relationship between globalization and democracy and would be a logical next step in this inquiry.

References

Bell, D.A., Brown D., Jayasuriya, K., and Jones, D.M. (1995), *Towards Illiberal Democracy in Pacific Asia*, St. Martin's Press, New York.

Brown, D. and Jones, D.M. (1995), 'Democratization and the Myth of the Liberalizing Middle Classes', in D.A. Bell and et. al, *Towards Illiberal Democracy in Pacific Asia*, pp.78-106.

Bryant, R.C. (1994), 'Global Change: Increasing Economic Integration and Eroding Political Sovereignty', *The Brookings Review*, vol.12, pp.42-45.

Ceglowski, J. (1998), 'Has Globalization Created a Borderless World?', *Federal Reserve Bank of Philadelphia Business Review*, pp.17-27.

Cotton, J. (1991), 'The Limits to Liberalization in Industrializing Asia: Three Views of the State', *Pacific Affairs*, vol.64, pp.311-27.

Dupont, A. (1996), 'Is There An 'Asian Way'?' *Survival*, vol.38, pp.13-33.

Freedom House (2000), *Annual Survey of Freedom Country Ratings: 1972-73 to 1999-00*, Washington, D.C.: Freedom House.

Fukuyama, F. (1995), 'Confucianism and Democracy', *Journal of Democracy*, vol.6, pp.20-33.

Funabashi, Y. (1993), 'The Asianization of Asia', *Foreign Affairs*, vol.72, pp.75-85.

Geriffi, G. and Wyman, D.L. (eds.) (1990), *Manufacturing Miracles: Paths of Industrialization in Latin America and East Asia*, Princeton University, Princeton.

Gyawali, D. (1997), 'Foreign Aid and the Erosion of Local Institutions: An Autopsy of Arun-3 from Inception to Abortion', in C. Thomas and P. Wilkin (eds.), *Globalization and the South*, pp.184-212.

Haggard, S. (1990), *Pathways for the Periphery: the Politics of Growth of the Newly Industrializing Countries*, Cornell University, Ithaca.

Hamilton, N. and Kim, E.U. (1993) 'Liberalization in South Korea and Mexico', *Third World Quarterly*, vol.14, pp.109-36.

Huntington, S. P. (1991), 'Democracy's Third Wave' *Journal of Democracy*, vol. 2, pp.12-34.

Jayasuriya, K. (1995), 'The Political Economy of Democratization', in D.A. Bell and et. al, *Towards Illiberal Democracy in Pacific Asia*, pp.107-33.

Jones, D. M. (1995), 'Democracy and Identity: The Paradoxical Character of Political Development', in D.A. Bell and et. al, *Towards Illiberal Democracy in Pacific Asia*, pp.41-77.

Kausikan, B. (1993), 'Asia's Different Standard', *Foreign Policy*, vol.32, pp.24-41.

Mahbubani, K. (1995), 'The Pacific Way', *Foreign Affairs*, vol.74, pp.100-11.

Ohmae, K. (1993), 'The Rise of the Region State', *Foreign Affairs*, vol.72, pp.78-87.

Rodrik, D. (1997), 'Sense and Nonsense in the Globalization Debate', *Foreign Policy*, vol.76, pp.19-37.

Rostow, W. W. (1990), *The Stages of Economic Growth*, Cambridge University Press, New York.

Sachs, J. (1998), 'International Economics: Unlocking the Mysteries of Globalization', *Foreign Policy*, vol.77, pp.97-111.

Sayrs, L. W. (1989), *Pooled Time Series Analysis: A SAGE University Paper, Series 70*, Sage, Beverly Hills.

Scalapino, R. A. (1989), *The Politics of Development: Perspectives on Twentieth-Century Asia*, Harvard University Press, Cambridge.

Slaughter, A. (1997), 'The Real New World Order', *Foreign Affairs*, vol.76, pp.183-97.

Smarzynska, B. K. and Wei, Shang-Jin (1999), *Corruption and Composition of Foreign Direct Investment: Firm-Level Evidence*, World Bank Policy Research Working Paper 2360.

Stimson, J. A. (1985), 'Regression in Space and Time: A Statistical Essay', *American Journal of Political Science*, vol.29, 914-47.

Tai, Kuo-hui (1993), 'Confucianism and Japanese Modernization: A Study of Shibusawa Eiichi', in S. Durlabjhi, and N.E. Marks, *Japanese Business: Cultural Perspectives*, State University of New York Press, Albany, pp.43-56.

Tamney, J. B. (1991), 'Confucianism and Democracy', *Asian Profile*, vol.19, pp.399-411.

Thomas, C. (1997), 'Globalization and the South', in C. Caroline and P. Wilken, (eds.), *Globalization and the South*, St. Martin's Press, New York, pp.1-17.

Wei-ming, T. (1984), *Confucian Ethics Today: The Singapore Challenge*, Curriculum Development Institute of Singapore, Singapore.

Zakaria, Fareed (1994), 'Culture is Destiny', *Foreign Affairs*, vol.73, pp.109-26.

Chapter 6

South Korea as a Middle Power: The Growing Globalization of South Korean Foreign Policy in the 1990s

Dlynn Armstrong-Williams

Introduction

The confluence of the post-Cold War era and South Korea's meteoric economic rise contributed to a diversification of its foreign policy. The multipolarity evidenced by the collapse of the Soviet Union and the increased globalization of economic activities and transnational issues place middle-powers in a unique position to contribute to global peace and stability. In the case of South Korea, the post-World War II era witnessed the transformation of its foreign policy. A clientelistic foreign policy, one in which South Korea depended on foreign aid to survive and thrive, shifted toward one of providing overseas development assistance (ODA). With this new diplomatic tool, its foreign policy tone changed from emphasizing unanimity with the United States to one of greater independence.

This chapter investigates the transformation of South Korean foreign policy, in the context of 'middle power theory', resulting from greater globalization and South Korea's new economic power. It looks at the extent to which South Korea works actively within the auspices of the United Nations in the area of multilateral and bilateral development assistance and peacekeeping support. Furthermore, this chapter examines the change in vision among South Korean diplomats and examines how this newfound activism benefits the emerging democratic South Korea.

The Logic of South Korean Foreign Policy: Middle Power Theory

South Korean foreign policy exists at the cusp of globalization. Economic globalization, in the form of expanding trade, benefited the East Asian nations by promoting economic development and bringing about unprecedented modernization. Beginning with the 1970s, Japan's foreign policy underwent a dramatic transition as its economy grew. Interdependence and globalization remain at the core of Japan's responses. As in the case of Japan, middle powers find motivation to alter their foreign policies out of enlightened self-interest. In addition to regional and global image concerns, foreign investments by South Korean firms into China, Southeast Asia, and the developing world in general reflects new opportunities and threats to South Korean diplomatic success. Like Taiwan, Singapore, Australia, and New Zealand, South Korea adopted a new strategy toward foreign policy as a result of domestic and international considerations.

Middle power theory provides insight into the foreign policy of newly industrialized countries (NICs) such as South Korea. Middle power theory contends that middle powers will actively participate in international organizations, act as a first follower of the hegemon, and will support international norms of behavior due to their desire for international stability (Wood 1988; Hobraad 1984; DeWitt and Kirton 1983; Holmes 1982, 1979). The principle characteristics of middle powers are summarized as follows:

- Active involvement in multinational organizations especially the United Nations (UN) and regional organizations;
- Increased involvement in (Official Development Assistance) ODA through the UN, regional institutions, and bilateral aid;
- Participation, but not leadership, in peacekeeping missions, particularly those of a regional nature;
- Concentrated diplomatic efforts to resolve disputes through the use and strengthening of multilateral institutions; and
- A desire to focus on regional problems and institution building.

Holmes discusses the emergence of middle powers following the Second World War and the influential role of middle powers in the early days of the United Nations (Holmes, 1979, 40-5). Middle powers, according to Holmes, took on the role of mediators or go-betweens in these international organizations in response to the needs of the international community (Holmes, 41). Carsten Holbraad, in his work *Middle Powers in International Politics* (1984), contends that middle powers exercise a strong influence in international organizations because middle powers utilize such organizations to strengthen their voices in the international system (Holbraad, 1984, 69). Bernard Wood, in *The Middle Powers and the General Interest* (1988), further suggests that, in international organizations,

> it is likely to be in the middle powers' interest to pursue at least a generalized strengthening of multilateral decision making as one approach to reducing the disproportionate control of the oligopolistic major powers.

DeWitt and Kirton contend that middle powers not only pursue frequent mediation and go-between roles within international organizations, but they also become involved in peacekeeping and other behaviors that act in order to maintain the status-quo in the international system (DeWitt and Kirton, 1983, 26). According to Michael Hawes (1984), peacekeeping and mediation roles go hand in hand for middle powers, and in the case of Canada these two roles have become so representative of Canada's foreign policy that they become 'calling cards for Canada's middle-powermanship' (Hawes, 1984, 6). Andrew Cooper et al. (1993) note that peacekeeping under the auspices of the United Nations is one of the important functions of middle powers (Cooper and et al., 1993, 20). South Korea over the past ten years became involved in numerous peacekeeping missions, particularly in Southeast Asia.

Middle powers have also been categorized as 'first followers.' While 'first followers' rarely, if ever, establish international regimes, they actively support them and the hegemon that created them. Therefore, first followers support and pattern their own foreign policies according to the hegemon's orientation. First followers, recognize that the norms and rules of the international system protect their interests. As such, first followers actively support the behaviors of the hegemon as long as it falls within the accepted norms and rules of the international system (Cooper et al., 20-1). Carsten Holbraad (121) notes that the notion of 'first follower' was first characterized during the Cold War era, wherein middle powers sought refuge with a hegemon against an opposing bloc. Despite the end of the Cold War, middle powers have not abandoned institutions or norms established originally by the hegemon. On the contrary, middle powers came to rely on embedded liberal institutions as necessary tools of diplomacy, especially due to a lack of bipolarity. However, the lack of bipolarity resulted in greater independence among the 'first followers' including South Korea, which sought to establish normalized relations with North Korea despite US consternation.

Middle powers also support international norms and institution building. As DeWitt and Kirton (1983) discuss, 'middle powers' recognize the importance of protecting international norms through persistent preservation, enrichment and further development (DeWitt and Kirton, 26). Middle powers, perceiving their enlightened self-interest in the rendering of durable and common values among states seek to protect and further these values through international conventions and treaties. For example, the Universal Declaration of Human Rights— an authoritative source for the norms agreed upon by the international community— draws references from middle powers and non-governmental organizations (NGO) indigenous to them. Gareth Evans (Evans, 1995), the former Australian Foreign Minister, underscores these points in a speech he made:

The international community cannot simply turn away from being involved in protecting human security in many of those situations which might previously have been regarded as wholly internal in character.

Many regard the generous the foreign aid policies of the Scandinavian countries, another group of 'middle powers,' as a model for other countries. Scandinavian countries, on the whole provide, on a per capita basis, significantly more foreign aid than the United States, Japan, the United Kingdom, Germany, or France. Middle powers view overseas development assistance (ODA) as one vehicle through which they can continue to maintain international norms. ODA allows middle powers to act as mediators by providing an economic bridge between developed countries and less developed ones (Pratt, 1990, 14). Olav Stokke (1989) also supports the internationalist orientation of middle powers in regard to aid policies. The aid policies emerge from a desire for moral responsiveness to global poverty and reflect domestic socio-political values (Stokke, 11).

Does South Korea Exhibit the Behavior of a Middle Power?

Scandinavian countries, Canada, and Australia are well established 'middle powers.' However, do relatively new 'middle powers,' especially Asian NICs, with a long tradition of political authoritarianism and insularity behave like their European counterparts? Preliminary evidence suggests that Asian 'middle powers,' especially Taiwan and South Korea, provide significant support for international development and peace. This section examines South Korea's newfound diplomatic endeavors and assesses the extent to which it fits 'middle power' theory.

South Korean system maintenance activities examined include involvement in UN peacekeeping missions and the growing role of Overseas Development Assistance (ODA) in that country's overall foreign policy orientation. South Korea's involvement in both of these areas changed dramatically beginning in 1991. In September of 1991 that South Korea became a full member of the United Nations and agreed to honor UN covenants and treaties, including the Universal Declaration of Human Rights. As a full member, South Korea then had the opportunity to participate in U.N. peacekeeping. The South Korean government decided in October of 1991, one month after its membership, to become involved in peacekeeping operations. However, over the years, significant internal debate over the appropriate role of South Korea in peacekeeping ensued.

The year 1991 also marked a turning point in South Korea's ODA programs with the establishment of the Korea International Cooperation Agency

(KOICA). While South Korea provided overseas assistance prior to 1991, the creation of KOICA centralized and focused international cooperation programs, grant aid and technical cooperation programs under the direction of the Foreign Ministry. South Korea's admission to the United Nations also set the stage for its multilateral aid and peacekeeping activities.

Since its acceptance into the United Nations as a member, South Korea has continued to be an active participant. Despite the financial setbacks and the recent economic crisis in East Asia, South Korea's desire for a broadening role in the UN both economically and diplomatically has not faltered. In the past three years South Korea's contributions to the United Nations have remained steady at approximately US$40,000,000 between 1997 and 1999 (Korean Foreign Ministry, 2001). In addition in 1998 South Korea began to self-identify as a middle power. This is especially important because it illustrates an embracing of the middle power role by the foreign policy establishment of South Korea. In a speech made to the Graduate School of International Studies at Korea University Foreign Minister Hong Soon-young (Ministry of Foreign Affairs) stated:

> Korea in the 21st century must stand as an Asian power and a middle power, firmly rooted in the changing dynamics of the region. It must also have a clear sense of what it can and cannot do as a middle power situated between the world's most powerful nations.

The recognition of the niche diplomacy of middle powers, along with the foreign policy emphasis on globalization, place South Korea in an ideal position to utilize a middle power type foreign policy.

According to Cooper, Higgott and Nossal (1993, 9), middle powers pursue multilateral solutions to international problems, embrace compromise positions in international disputes, and model their diplomacy on the principles of 'good international citizenship'. As an outgrowth of their international activism, middle powers frequently assume roles as mediators and become involved in UN peacekeeping operations (Stokke, 1989, 9). In fact, Bernard Wood (1988, 11) states that the creation of UN peacekeeping forces allowed middle powers to create and assume their mandate in the international system. Peacekeeping operations (PKOs) stabilize the international system by creating a transitory stage that prevents the exacerbation of conflict as the implementation of conflict resolution proceeds (Young, 527).

Additionally, South Korea with its well-trained and institutionalized military provides an ideal infrastructure for peacekeeping involvement. South Korea's initial decision to dispatch troops, as part of the Cambodian peacekeeping mission, occurred on July 15, 1992. In fact, the role of peacekeeping has become so interwoven into the foreign policy of Canada that Michael K. Hawes (1984, 6) stated: "Mediation and peacekeeping have become the calling cards of Canada's middlepowermanship". South Korea in many ways followed these traditional 'middle powers' principles in its peacekeeping invovlment. In fact, in some cases South Korea's contribution exceeds all other OECD nations. In support of South Korea's commitment to further involvement in peacekeeping, Sung-joo Han (1993, 230), the creator of South Korea's foreign policy vision of 'New Diplomacy' stated, "We will contribute to U.N. Peace Keeping Operations and international peace and security, thereby also securing our place in the international community". Following the Cambodian peacekeeping efforts, South Korea became involved subsequently in other missions abroad, including Somalia, Georgia, Angola, and East Timor.

Summary of South Korea's Contribution to United Nations' Operations

In December 1992, the United Nations asked South Korea for a financial contribution to the peacekeeping efforts in Somalia. (Yonhap, December 22, 1992). South Korea quickly responded to the United Nations' request. Kim Che-sop, Director-General of the Foreign Ministry's International Organizations Bureau, stated that South Korea would contribute "according to its capability" (Yonhap, December 30, 1992). The decision to send troops to Somalia required deliberations within the government. After over a year of discussion, South Korea dispatched troops. While the government pledged to the United Nations the use of 540 officers and infantry, 154 engineers and medical personnel and 36 military observers in July 1992, the actual contingent sent to Somalia took shape differently than originally promised. In April 1993, the South Korean government decided to send a 250 person Army Corps of Engineering Unit to Somalia rather than combat troops. Cost considerations and public opposition to sending troops abroad due to lingering memories of South Korea's role in the Vietnam war contributed to the scaled down contribution (Yonhap, 8 April 1993). Additionally, between the time of the original commitment and the date of South Korea's deployment of engineers, Somali attacks on UN peacekeepers became more widely publicized.

A contingent of 250 engineers from South Korea represented its first active participation in a UN peacekeeping effort. Given that at the height of the UN involvement, 28,000 peacekeepers operated in Somalia, South Korea's contingent of peacekeepers reflected the country's lukewarm commitment to the overall mission. Clearly, many South Koreans and politicians remained ambivalent about troop commitment abroad. South Korea participated in a number of peacekeeping missions since United Nations Operations in Somalia (UNOSOM) II, but in comparison to other countries, it committed only a small number of troops.

Following Somalia, South Korea's peacekeeping contributions increased dramatically in 1994 and 1995. In September 1994, South Korea joined the UN Mission for the Referendum in Western Sahara. South Korea sent 42 medical officers to assist in the UN efforts in monitoring the cease-fire in the area and to monitor the general election. The commitment of forty-two medical officers to Western Sahara's *Mission des Nations Unies pour le Referendum au Sahara Occidental* (MINURSO) represents the largest contribution made by any particular country to the mission.

After Western Sahara, peacekeeping troops were dispatched to Georgia. On August 24, 1993, the UN established the United Nations Observer Mission in Georgia (UNOMIG) to monitor the agreed upon cease-fire between the Government of Georgia and the Abkhaz authorities in Gudauta. The contingent's mission consisted of investigating reports of violations of the ceasefire and attempt to resolve such incidents with the parties involved in the violation. The peacekeeping mandate, expanded in July of 1994, came to include not only the implementation of the cease-fire agreement, but also the verification of weapons and troop withdrawal from the security zone and the monitoring of Georgian troop withdrawal from the Abkhazia region. In October of 1994, South Korea sent 6 military observers to assist in monitoring the ceasefire in Georgia (Kim, 1995). While South Korea's contribution to UNOMIG is quite small, it represented the average contribution of states involved in this mission. The overall small UN representation resulted from a joint operation with CIS (Commonwealth of Independent States) countries, which also sponsored a peacekeeping contingent in the area. UNOMIG served to assist and observe CIS peacekeepers.

South Korea sent troops and personnel to UN operations in India and Pakistan to partake in the United Nations Military Observer Group in India and Pakistan (UNMOGIP) beginning in November 1994 and became involved in UN Angola Verification Mission (UNAVEM III), established in March 1995. By this time, South Korean involvement became routinized with a pattern of cooperation involving the executive branch and the legislature fully institutionalized. During an interview, Jong-Moon Choi, Deputy Director of U.N. Division I of the Ministry of Foreign Affairs, stated that South Korea planned to become part of the UN Angola Verification Mission III (UNAVEM III). In the course of the interview, Mr. Choi explained that South Korea planned to send 200 engineers to Angola pending the Korean National Assembly vote on July 12, 1995 (Moon, 1995). The vote, according to Mr. Choi, was a technicality because the members of the National Assembly already consulted with other party members and agreed to send troops.

South Korea's recent peacekeeping involvement occurred in East Timor. In May of 1999, Portugal and Indonesia entrusted the UN with organizing a 'popular consultation' to determine if the people of East Timor accepted or rejected special autonomy for East Timor within the Republic of Indonesia. UNAMET (United Nations Mission in East Timor), therefore, was to oversee the transition period between the 'popular consultation' and the implementation of the decision of the East Timorese people. From October 1999 to the present, South Korea supported actively UN initiatives in East Timor. South Korea provided 419 members of the infantry battalion and 25 staff members of Force Command (Mission of the Republic of Korea to the United Nations, 2001). In addition to peacekeeping personnel, South Korea also provided US $250,000 in humanitarian assistance and US $400,000 to the United Nations Transitional Administration in East Timor (UNTAET) Trust Fund (Mission of the Republic of Korea to the United Nations, 2001). In June of 2000, the Korean government also planned to contribute US $600,000 for the training of East Timorese in close consultation with the United Nations. Apart from sending troops to a variety of peacekeeping missions, South Korea also supports the UN stand-by arrangement for peacekeepers. South Korea agreed to keep on staff peacekeeping forces and has been a very strong supporter of the controversial Rapidly Deployable Mission Headquarters (RDMHQ).

In sum, South Korea's peacekeeping efforts expanded dramatically since its commencement in 1992. As a middle power, South Korea's initiative in the East Timor and the Indo-Pakistan UN operations demonstrate a substantial commitment to international peace. South Korean contributions increased dramatically over the years and domestic politics and emergent popular opinion increasingly supports these commitments. Furthermore, South Korean political institutions reached a tacit consensus about the need for the country to play an active role in international affairs.

Overseas Development Assistance (ODA)

The creation and continuance of international aid programs can also act as a system stabilizing activity. According to Olav Stokke (1989, 276) foreign aid serves as a vital instrument for achieving peace and economic stability in the international system. Multilateral aid provides the middle power with an opportunity to cooperate with other states while bilateral assistance promotes its own commercial, strategic, and diplomatic interests. In the case of South Korea, the government not only consolidated its foreign aid program but also increased expenditures during the past ten years. This section examines South Korean ODA in greater detail and explores the characteristics of ODA in terms of recipient nations and compares its foreign aid policies with more established 'middle powers'.

While a variety of motivations regarding the provision of foreign aid exist, the middle powers studied by Stokke including Canada, Denmark, Norway,

Sweden, and the Netherlands all referred to a moral imperative as the main motive for their international aid programs (Stokke, 278). Furthermore, he concluded that 'middle powers' formulate national interest in general terms such as the pursuance of peace and international stability, sometimes associated with the concept humane internationalism. The core of humane internationalism is (Stokke, 10):

> an acceptance of the principle that citizens of the industrial nations have moral obligations towards peoples and events beyond their borders; it implies a sensitivity to cosmopolitan values, such as the obligation to refrain from the use of force in the pursuit of national interests and the respect for human rights.

South Korea echoes this moral imperative in its diplomatic initiatives. In a speech discussing South Korean foreign policy at the beginning of the new millennium Hong Soon-young, (Ministry of Foreign Affairs) stated:

> Morality is more and more the name of the game in diplomacy. For all players on the global stage, large or small, doing what is right in the eyes of others will be a key consideration in foreign policy decisions of the policy decisions of the 21st century.

Apart from the moral imperative that drives the aid programs of many middle powers, economic benefits accrue from such assistance. Margaret Catley-Carlson discusses the economic benefits of aid by stating that in the case of Canada (Catley-Carlson, 1988, 321):

> In the long run, international development will benefit us all. As one of the most export-dependent of the major industrial nations, and as the only one without sure access to a large-scale consumer market such the European Community or the United States, Canada has a very strong interest in promoting global economic growth.

'Middle powers' often lack a powerful military to impose order and structure of their liking on the international system. As such, the foreign aid they provide helps assure international stability without the need to use coercive tools of national security. For example, in the case of Canada's Overseas Developmental Assistance, moral imperatives, and national security mesh. Craford Pratt stated that (Pratt, 1994, 362-3):

> [There are] persuasive long-term Canadian interests in international stability and in the successful management of a wide range of issues that can be dealt with only on an international basis and are severely exacerbated by intensification of mass poverty in developing countries. The long-term interests powerfully reinforce the ethical arguments for major and generous development assistance.

Australia's overseas aid program report for 1995-1996 also highlights the role of developmental assistance for the furtherance of stability. The report states the importance of following Developmental Assistance Committee

(DAC) guidelines provided to all OECD members. One primary guideline for developmental assistance addresses the integration of political and economic stability through, responsible government, popular participation, concern for the environment, and the encouragement of market strategies for economic growth (Australia's Overseas Aid Program, 1995, 7). Foreign assistance reflects the outgrowth of a middle power's vested interest in systemic stability, economic self-interest, and a moral responsibility to less fortunate states.

South Korea's Overseas Developmental Assistance (ODA)

When discussing South Korea's motivation for its involvement in the area of ODA, Sooyong Kim and Wan-Soon Kim contend that the motives for ODA range from a pure humanitarian desire to reduce poverty to the commercial and political interests of suppliers (Kim and Kim, 1992, 19). Korea's main agent for ODA, the Korea International Cooperation Agency (KOICA), describes its aid philosophy as founded on humanitarian motivations (Korea International Cooperation Agency, 1994, 4):

> Korea shall provide aid based on broad principles of 'humanitarian considerations' and 'recognition of interdependence' striving to implement cooperation programs according to the nation's long-cherished spirit of 'mutual help' as well as in the spirit of Korea's own founding principle 'Hong-ik In-gan' meaning to strive for the well-being of humankind.

South Korea's growing role in ODA also resulted from its increased economic strength. In the words of Kim and Kim (21), "the Korean economy can now afford" to give aid. South Korea provided some developmental assistance before 1991, but these programs were initiated on a case-by-case basis and not coordinated between government ministries. The first attempt at ODA by South Korea, in 1963, consisted of receiving a group of trainees from developing countries as part of a US Agency for International Development (AID) program. South Korea sponsored a few other similar programs in 1965 and 1967, but in 1987 steps taken established South Korea's role as a donor country. In 1987, the Economic Development Cooperation Fund (EDCF) was created. This fund began with US$37.9 billion intended for bilateral loans to developing countries. South Korean bilateral assistance consists of three categories: developmental loans, grants, and technical cooperation (Kim and Kim, 29). EDCF disburses of loans and KOICA provides grants and technical assistance.

Economic Development Cooperation Fund (EDCF)

An EDCF loan can fall into one of the following two categories (Kim and Kim 41):

- Loans made directly to governments or corporations of developing countries or;
- Loans to Korean corporations for equity investment or ventures in developing countries.

There are five types of EDCF loans provided to developing countries (Export-Import Bank of Korea 2):

- *Development Project Loan*: funds required by the recipient government or corporations of developing countries to conduct specific projects under its economic development plan.
- *Equipment Loan*: funds required by the government or corporations to procure equipment and other materials needed for industrial development projects under national development plans in specific sectors or specific regions.
- *Two-Step Loan*: funds provided to the government or financial institutions so that they can make sub-loans to end-users in order to procure equipment and other materials needed for their industrial development projects.
- *Commodity Loan*: providing funds by the government or corporations to import the commodities bilaterally agreed upon as part of an economic stabilization program.
- *Project Preparation Loan*: funds required by the government or corporations for the preparation of development projects including feasibility studies or detailed designs.

While no restrictions or requirements exist regarding the goods and services from South Korean companies, the loans continue to benefit South Korean businesses almost exclusively because they are won denominated. Given that South Korea frequently experiences a balance-of-payment problem, dollar denominated foreign aid would prove too costly and come into conflict with the country's economic development strategy. Unlike many OECD nations, the South Korea government continues to regulate its banking and financial systems very strictly. Furthermore, a more cynical view suggests that large Korean *chaebols* engaged in construction, benefit from these loans which ultimately represent a tax on Korean citizens and transfer payments to the firms. Despite this drawback, the significant increase in ODA reflects a positive trend in South Korea's new diplomacy. In the year following the establishment of KOICA, all types of South Korean ODA increased substantially. Table 6.1 chronicles the increase in South Korea's EDCF loans from 1987 to 1996.

Table 6.1 South Korean ODA from 1987 to 2001 in US$ Millions

Type of ODA	1987	1990	1993	1995	1996	2001
Bilateral	1.42	12.25	60.12	71.46	123.31	N/A
Multilateral	22.08	48.91	51.44	44.53	35.58	N/A
EDDF Loans	n.a.	8.99	27.44	21.35	69.90	10.18
ODA/GNP	0.02	0.02	0.03	0.03	0.03	N/A
Total ODA	23.50	61.16	111.56	115.99	159.15	N/A

Source: Ministry of Finance and Economy and for 2001 data, *Korea Times*, May 8, 2001.

Note that in 1993, South Korea's total loans increased dramatically. As explained in the table, Poland received a large loan. In 1989, as part of South Korea's Northern Policy, President Roh Tae Woo visited Poland, promising that South Korea would provide US $50 million for development. The support promised by president Roh was not finalized until 1993 when US $42.4 million dollars went to Poland to assist in the development of Telecommunications. Apart from the jump in EDCF loans– explained by the Poland project– South Korea's EDCF loans continued a steady rise from 1992 to 1994. This steady increase in EDCF funds can be expected to continue in light of Sung-joo Han's comments in his speech to the Korean Council on Foreign Affairs, a speech that is still considered a guide for South Korea's MFA:

> It is now time for us to assume responsibilities commensurate with our standing in the international community. An increase in aid to the developing world and in contributions to relevant international organizations is the very first step we have to take toward this end. With this in mind, we are planning to invigorate such mechanisms as the Economic Development Cooperation Fund (EDCF) and Korea International Cooperation Agency (KOICA).

However, as a result of the Asian economic crisis, South Korea experienced harsh budgetary constraints and became a recipient of IMF loans. As a result, South Korea's foreign aid programs suffered. In 2001, for example, the *Korea Times* provided information about overseas loans totaling $10.18 million, a major decline from previous years. However, South Korea remains committed to foreign aid despite its economic problems. In a speech at the Third United Nations Conference on the Least Developed Countries in Brussels on May 14, 2001, Hwang Doo-yun, the Minister of Trade stated that while ODA as a percentage of GNP has declined in many countries, South Korea attempts to orient efforts toward "human capacity building, active participation in international trade, and mobilization of financial resources" (Hwang, 2001). In other words, the strategy involves leveraging limited funds with technical assistance and vocational training programs within Korea for foreign nationals.

Korea International Cooperation Agency (KOICA)

While EDCF concerns itself with bilateral loans, KOICA remains responsible for the provision of equipment, project aid, disaster relief aid, development studies, the acceptance of trainees, the dispatch of the Korean Youth Volunteers, and the dispatch of experts and medical doctors (Korea International Cooperation Agency, 1993, 8). KOICA provides bilateral grant aid which largely commercial and diplomatic ties between states (Kim and Kim, 30). Due to the diplomatic nature of grant aid, KOICA falls under the jurisdiction of the Ministry of Foreign Affairs (MFA). Therefore, grant applications involve a request to the MFA through a South Korean embassy abroad or a KOICA representative in one of their six overseas offices in Canada, Argentina, Thailand, Indonesia, China and Vietnam (KOICA, 1994, 17).

According to Table 6.1, South Korean grant aid steadily increased with a large amount of growth occurring during the first full year of KOICA's existence. Most observers expect a continued increase in South Korea's ODA over the years, with KOICA as one of the primary disbursement agencies. In an address to the World Summit for Social Development in Copenhagen March 1995, President Kim Young Sam supported South Korea's international bilateral grant programs by stating (Kim, 1995):

> ...we [South Korea] will also gradually increase the level of our support for the development of human resources of the developing countries. Since the 1980s, the Republic of Korea has also been operating a variety of manpower training programs for developing countries, including the dispatch of experts to such countries to provide technical help in the field. By expanding these endeavors, the ROK plans to provide technical training for more than 30,000 people from developing countries by the year 2010.

Multilateral Aid

South Korea's share of overall multilateral aid program ranks higher in comparison to other OECD Developmental Assistance Committee members (Kim and Kim 43). On the surface, this fact appears encouraging, but South Korea includes in its multilateral aid figures all subscription payments to multilateral institutions, thereby inflating its statistics. In addition, South Korea includes loans provided through its EXIM Bank on its ODA statistics. It appears that neither Canada nor Australia includes such items in their calculations of ODA. The inclusion of these loans inflates South Korea's ODA above its 'real' level.

Eventually South Korea will alter its reporting procedures to become more rationalized with other countries to secure its acceptance into the OECD. Table 6.1 illustrates that South Korean ODA never exceeded 0.05% of GNP. In contrast to other DAC members, South Korea's clearly lags in contributions as suggested in the table. EDCF officials contend that to become a member of the OECD, South Korea must give comparable amounts of international assistance (Ahn, 1995).

South Korea made consistent efforts to bring its level of ODA up to the level of other DAC countries. In 1990, the Economic Planning Board, subsequently eliminated and its functions taken over by the Ministry of Finance (MOF), announced the goal for increased foreign aid in the future (Chang, 1995). While this statement illustrates South Korea's movement toward increased levels of ODA, officials in both KOICA and EDCF assert that the goals set by the EPB remain unattainable and unrealistic (Ahn, 1995; Chang, 1995; Park, 1995).

Conclusion: Increased Globalization of South Korean Foreign Policy

While the recent economic crisis in East Asia affected negatively the ODA of several middle powers in the region, the international community expects South Korea's increased role in international affairs to continue. The recent warming of relations with North Korea and Kim Dae Jung's visit to Pyongyang likely presents new opportunities for South Korean diplomacy and foreign aid. An improving South Korean economy enhances the prospects for future increases in international assistance.

This study demonstrated the logic and reality of South Korean international assistance. The interviews conducted provided significant consensus regarding the value of becoming an increased regional and global player. Like other 'middle powers', South Korea emphasizes cooperation through multilateral institutions. South Korea's activism focuses not only on other Asian nations, such as Cambodia, Mongolia, North Korea, and Vietnam, but also global crisis locations, including the Balkans, Angola, and East Timor. South Korea's image will improve as its foreign aid program expands in the future. Furthermore, policy makers in the country clearly realize that foreign aid, reflects enlightened self-interest, rather than charity. It is this enlightened interest that pushes South Korea increasingly toward globalization. South Korea has embarked on a more complicated and challenging foreign policy since the end of the Cold War and its middle power type activities have been met with great success. It is both within South Korea's interest and the interest of the international community that South Korea continues its constructive and growing role in global and regional affairs despite economic dislocations caused by the Asian Economic Crisis.

Domestically, internationalism became institutionalized over the years. South Korean leaders, the bureaucracy, and legislature now realize the importance of global cooperation and participation. In addition, the 1997 election of Kim Dae Jung, the first president from an opposition party, will increase South Korea's clout in areas of human rights and democratization. South Korea, a model for political transition from authoritarianism to democracy, demonstrates the value of economic reform and political democracy to the world as its international image changed from an authoritarian pariah to a global team player.

References

Ahn, E. and Park Jong-kyu (1995), Export-Import Bank of Korea—Loan officers, personal interview, 21 June.

AUS Aid (1995), *Australia's Overseas Aid Program 1995-1996– Budget Related Paper No. 2*, Australian Government Publishing Service, Canberra.
Catley-Carlson, M. (1988), 'Aid: A Canadian Vocation', *Daedalus*. vol. 117, pp.319-333.
Choi, Jong-Moon (1995), Deputy Director of U.N. Division 1, Ministry of Foreign Affairs, personal interview, 12 July.
Cooper, A., Higgot, R., and Nossal, K.R. (1993), *Relocating Middle Powers*, University of British Columbia Press, Vancouver.
DeWitt, D. B. and Kirton, J.J. (1993), *Canada as a Principle Power: A Study in Foreign Policy and International Relations*, John Wiley and Sons, Toronto.
EDCF, *A Guide to the Economic Development Cooperation Fund*, Export-Import Bank of Korea, Seoul.
Evans, G. (1995), Speech at the La Trobe University Conference: 'Australia's Commitment to Global Multilateralism and its Implications for the Asia Pacific Region', 2 July.
'Exim Bank to Bolster Role as Export Credit Agency', *Korea Times*, May 8, 2001.
FBIS-EAS-93-066, *Yonhap*, 8 April, 1993.
FBIS-EAS-92-251, *Yonhap*, 30 December, 1992.
FBIS-EAS-92-247, *Yonhap*, 22 December, 1992.
FBIS-EAS-92-142, *Yonhap*, 23 July, 1992.
Han, Sung-joo (1993), 'New Korea's Diplomacy Toward the World and the Future', Speech at the Korean Council on Foreign Affairs, 31 May.
Hawes, M. (1984), *Principle Power, Middle Power or Satellite ?: Competing Perspectives in the Study of Canadian Foreign Policy*, University of Toronto Press, Toronto.
Holbraad, C. (1984), *Middle Powers in International Politics*, St. Martin's Press, New York.
Holmes, J. W. (1979), *The Shaping of Peace Vols. 1 and 2*, University of Toronto Press, Toronto.
Hwang Doo-yun (2001), Speech at the United Nations Conference on the Least Developed Countries in Brussels, Belgium , May 14, 2001.
Kim, Bong-joo (1995), Director of Economic Cooperation Division II, Ministry of Foreign Affairs, personal interview, 25 June.
Kim, Sooyong and Wan-Soon Kim (1992), *Korea's Development Assistance*, International Charter for Economic Growth, San Francisco.
Kim, Wook (1995), Director of the North American Division I, Ministry of Foreign Affairs, personal interview, 6 July.
Kim, Young Sam (1995), Address by President Kim Young Sam at the World Summit for Social Development, Copenhagen, 11 March.
KOICA (1993), *Constructing A Human Society in Which We Can Live Better Together*, KOICA, Seoul.
KOICA (1994), *Annual Report 1994*, KOICA, Seoul.
Ministry of Foreign Affairs (2001), *Korea's Contribution to International Organizations*, www.mofat.go.kr/web/in.nsf, 9 July.
Ministry of Foreign Affairs (2001), *Diplomacy in the 21st Century*, www.mofat.go.kr/speech.nsf, 9 July.
Ministry of Foreign Affairs (2001), *Foreign Policy Agenda of the Republic of Korea in the New Century*, www.mofat.go.kr/speech.nsf, 9 July.
Pratt, C. (1990), *Middle Power Inernationalism*, McGill-Queen's University Press, Ontario.
Stokke, O. (ed.) (1989), *Western Middle Powers and Global Poverty*, The Scandinavian Institute of African Studies, Stockholm.
Wood, B. (1988), *The Middle Powers and the General Interest*, The North-South Institute, Ottawa.

Chapter 7

East Timor Independence: The Changing Nature of International Pressure

Thomas Ambrosio

Introduction

Dewi Fortuna Anwar, a foreign policy advisor to President BJ Habibie remarked, "Why do we have to encounter so many international problems when we have already so many problems at home? Why do we need East Timor and why don't we just let them go?" (Deutsche Presse-Agentur, 1999). For almost two and a half decades after Jakarta's successful invasion of the former Portuguese colony, East Timor constituted a part of the Republic of Indonesia. During the summer of 1976, Indonesia annexed the region with the consent of an East Timorese 'provisional government' of its own creation. Despite possessing the right to self-determination under international law, East Timor received a muted international response to this act of aggression. East Timorese self-determination became a victim of a permissive international environment buttressed by the logic of the Cold War. Rather than opposing an ally, the United States and Australia acquiesced to Indonesia's control in order to secure and further their strategic goals in South East Asia. When the International Court of Justice– ruling on a suit brought by Portugal against Australia– stated that it had no ability to adjudicate on the lawfulness of Indonesia's 1975 invasion, Indonesia's territorial gains seemed secure well into the late 1980s and early 1990s.

However, with the unprecedented changes in the international system following the end of the Cold War, a dramatic shift occurred in Indonesia's international environment. Rather than providing tacit support to Jakarta's continued occupation of East Timor, its Cold War allies began to seriously question the territory's political status. As Indonesia's strategic value declined, human rights and economic issues became more prominent in Washington and Canberra's thinking. The Indonesian economic crisis led to the delegitimization of Indonesian President Suharto both at home and abroad. His resignation in May 1998 had dramatic implications for the East Timor question: Suharto's handpicked successor, BJ Habibie, announced in January 1999 that his country would allow the East Timorese to hold referendum which would determine its political future. At the end of August 1999, almost eighty percent of the East Timorese voted for independence, although the massive violence that engulfed East Timor committed by pro-Indonesian militias dampened any jubilation in the days following the referendum.

What factors led to East Timorese self-determination? Precisely, how and when did the United States and Australia change its orientation toward Indonesia? In answering these questions, this chapter explores the interplay between globalization, ethnic conflict, and the enforcement of norms in the international system. It shows how the shift from the bipolar system to what Robert Paster called the 'Liberal Epoch' (Paster, 1999, 341-9)– in which economic issues and humanitarian norms have largely supplanted geopolitics and strategic concerns as the primary motors of interstate relations– delegitimized Indonesia's hold on East Timor. Although Indonesia committed massive human rights abuses in East Timor, Jarkarta, too, the Cold War also victimized it. Several countries– such as Pakistan, Yugoslavia, and Indonesia– became insulated from foreign criticism despite their undemocratic internal policies and corrupt political structures because of their strategic value to the West during the struggle between communism and capitalism. Once the Cold War ended, their advantaged positions evaporated and these states became the objects of either international reproach (Pakistan and Indonesia) or irrelevance (Yugoslavia prior to the wars in Slovenia, Croatia, and Bosnia). In a highly globalized international system, these states became increasingly susceptible to international pressure to reform their political system or fundamentally change their policies. In Indonesia, concerns with the continuing crackdown in East Timor mixed with the Asian economic crisis of 1997-8 to prompt Australia and the United States to abandon Suharto in hopes of political change and economic reform. The independence of East Timor was a portentous outcome of this process. This chapter explores the evolution of US and Australian policies over the years and its impact on Indonesia's policy regarding East Timor. Complex linkages among Indonesian domestic politics and its foreign policy accounted for the country's behavior toward East Timor. This chapter also examines these linkages.

Decolonization, Invasion, and Annexation

For centuries, the South East Asian archipelago held strategic value for European and Western powers. During the sixteenth century, control over the region secured trade routes from the Far East to Europe. Portugal, the first of the European colonizers and the last to relinquish its colonies, began to establish forts throughout the lucrative Spice Islands. However, the Portuguese established control over what eventually became East Timor only in the mid-seventeenth century. Soon thereafter, the island of Timor became divided between Portugal and the Netherlands with the Dutch consolidating their control over nearly all the archipelago during the rest of the seventeenth and eighteenth centuries. Portuguese control over East Timor remained secure until Japan's occupation during the Second World War.

The East Timorese and Allied resistance to Japanese occupation is amongst the most heroic and tragic chapters of World War II. However, East Timorese assistance to the Allied cause did not result in independence. Instead, Lisbon successfully and brutally restored its rule in East Timor. Despite changing international norms regarding the legitimacy of colonialism, Portugal steadfastly refused to relinquish its overseas possessions. However, an April 1974 coup against the remnants of the fascist dictatorship in Portugal ushered in radical changes in the metropoles' relations with its colonies with the Portuguese 'Junta of National Salvation' announced that it would allow East Timor to determine its own political status. The East Timorese were given a choice between remaining with Portugal as an autonomous possession, independent statehood, and union with Indonesia.

Three political factions emerged in the colony, each supporting one of the options. The platform of the Timorese Democratic Union (UDT) sought a federation with Portugal. The Timorese Social Democratic Association, which later became FRETILIN (the Revolutionary Front for an Independent East Timor), was a radical leftist movement seeking East Timorese independence. And lastly, the Timorese Democratic People's Union (APODETI), largely a creation of the Jakarta regime, desired integration into Indonesia. FRETILIN was the most popular faction in the region, followed closely by the UDT. APODETI failed to ignite significant support because people perceived it as nothing more than Jakarta's puppet. Nevertheless, Indonesia made it clear that it would support nothing less than annexation. Armed conflict between UDT and FRETILIN strengthened Jakarta's position. Because of the fighting, the Portuguese colonial administration decided to withdraw from the island in August 1975. Soon thereafter, Indonesian forces began to launch raids across the border in preparation for a full invasion. FRETILIN, which found itself in *de facto* control of the territory after an unsuccessful UDT coup attempt, attempted to preempt further Indonesian interference by unilaterally declaring independence on 28 November 1975. Indonesian security forces immediately presented a document that called for the integration of East Timor with Indonesia to the leaders of APODETI, the UDT, and two minor factions (Krieger, 1977, 40). The parties signed the document under pressure and Jakarta used this as a pretext for its invasion a week later.

Indonesia's full-scale invasion of East Timor began early on 7 December 1975 with Indonesian troops committing widespread human rights violations. Soon thereafter, an Indonesian-created 'provisional government' was formed without the participation of FRETILIN. Despite criticism from the United Nations General Assembly, a 'popular representative assembly' requested Indonesia 'to accept, in the shortest possible time... the full integration of the people and territory of East Timor into the unitary state of the Republic of Indonesia without any referendum' on 31 May 1975. Two and one-half months later, President Suharto signed a 'bill of integration', formally annexing the territory.

Indonesia's military occupation of East Timor, without the consent of the residents, violated international law's provision pertaining to self-determination and provided only a thin veneer of legitimacy (International Platform of Jurists for East Timor, 1995). However, the international reaction to Indonesia's actions was solely rhetorical. After a contentious debate, the UN General Assembly passed Resolution 3485 on 12 December, 1975. This resolution "strongly deplore[d]" the military invasion and called upon Indonesia to withdraw from the territory and allow the East Timorese "to exercise their right to self-determination and independence". Less than two weeks later, the UN Security Council unanimously adopted Resolution 384 which, like the General Assembly's resolution, recognized 'the inalienable right of the people of East Timor to self-determination and independence' and called upon Indonesia to withdraw. The Security Council, however, refused to identify the invasion as a breach of the peace or an act of aggression and did not invoke its Chapter VII enforcement powers to punish Indonesia for its actions. Six months later, the Security Council issued another resolution (389 of 22 April 1976) that was equally hollow and passed with the abstentions of Japan and the United States.

The General Assembly's involvement continued a bit longer, but it too failed to take any punitive action against Indonesia. At the end of each year from 1975 to 1982, the General Assembly passed a perfunctory resolution on East Timor with fewer states voting for the resolution each year. In fact, none of the resolutions received a majority of the total number of possible votes and passed only because states abstained or were purposefully absent. (Kreiger, 129-33). Furthermore, the relative condemnation of Indonesia weakened each successive year to the point that by 1979, Resolution 34/40 called for neither a direct nor an indirect Indonesian withdrawal. After 1982, the General Assembly perennially deferred consideration of the 'Question of East Timor', thus giving its tacit consent to Indonesia's occupation.

None of the great powers countered Indonesia's brutal domination over East Timor. As one scholar concluded, "The United States... had no intention of supporting any further United Nations action on East Timor and had been urging other powers to come to terms with Indonesia's 'irreversible' action, while Britain, France, and to a lesser extent the Soviet Union adopted a passive attitude on the question" (Korman, 1996, 284). In fact, the two states best positioned to apply pressure against the Jakarta regime, the United States and Australia, quickly recognized Indonesia's de facto sovereignty over East Timor.

Indonesia's Cold War Strategic Value

Indonesia played a central role in US and Australian strategic thinking during the Cold War, especially after America's defeat in Vietnam. The implied logic of America's containment policy challenged the spread of communist influence throughout the world. Often, this meant that the United States aligned itself with states whose leaders did not possess a commitment to democracy or human rights. In short, America often willingly discounted human rights violations whenever geopolitical gains vis-à-vis the Soviets materialized. Indonesia's invasion of East Timor fell well within this *realpolitik* paradigm.

After Suharto emerged victorious, in the coup and counter-coup that toppled the pro-leftist Sukarno regime in 1965-6, Indonesia began to shift toward a pro-Western, anti-Communist alignment. The United States responded with pledges of support and cooperation. Furthermore, the US government reasoned that excessive pressure against the Suharto regime regarding the Timor issue would create a counterproductive anti-Western backlash that would destabilize the fragile regime (Declassified Documents Reference Service (DDRS), Fiche # 1980-85B). In 1975, with the fall of Saigon, securing Indonesia firmly in the Western camp became imperative.

In a memorandum from Secretary of State Henry Kissinger to President Gerald Ford just prior to Suharto's visit to the White House, Kissinger outlined American security interests in Indonesia. He stated, "Since the late 1960's, our policy has been to give solid support to the Suharto Government's efforts to rehabilitate and develop Indonesia's economy, since we have looked on Indonesia as potentially the most stabilizing element in Southeast Asia" (DDRS Fiche #1994-239). Hanoi's victory had important implications for Indonesia's relationship with Washington: Indochina's fall has further eroded Jakarta's confidence in U. S. intentions toward Asia. Jakarta in the two years preceding Vietnam's fall had already grown anxious over declining US support for Indochina, as well as over what it saw as reduced support for Indonesia itself" (DDRS Fiche #1994-239). Furthermore, according to US policy makers, Jakarta saw a renewed threat from communist forces– "The Suharto Government fears that infiltration and subversion in Southeast Asia will now intensify and that North Vietnam will try to thwart regional cooperation among Southeast Asian nations as well as to compete with Indonesia for regional leadership" (DDRS Fiche # 1994-239). All three of these factors would play a role in affecting US policy toward East Timor. America's national interest became interwoven with Indonesia's political stability and resistance to a perceived communist threat from the insurgents. US policy sought to reassure Jakarta of strong US commitment toward resisting communism.

While preparing for President Ford's visit to Indonesia, political order in East Timor collapsed and the National Security Council (NSC) produced a 'briefing book' on the situation in Indonesia and East Timor (DDRS Fiche # 1994-233). It identified the first two purposes of the president's visit as a desire to "demonstrate the significance and importance we attach to our relations with Indonesia and to 'reassure our friends in Southeast Asia that we remain fully committed to supporting them". The question of East Timor was explicitly addressed and the briefing book reported that the State Department urged Ford to tell Suharto that the US "would view incorporation of this territory into Indonesia as a 'reasonable solution". However, the NSC advised Ford to "avoid any such direct endorsement of Indonesian actions on Timor, and limit [himself] to an expression of support for self-determination and a peaceful resolution of the situation". Later, the National Security Advisor Brent Scowcroft was advised to tell the president to 'remain noncommittal both publicly and in private discussions with Suharto' on the East Timor issue (DDRS Fiche # 1994-233). However, the original NSC briefing book cited Indonesian fears that 'Timor might become a base for Communist insurgents' and urged Ford to tell Suharto that the US 'fully [understood] Indonesia's concern over developments in Portuguese Timor' (DDRS Fiche # 1994-239). Consequently, the United States ceased to be neutral on the topic of East Timor.

Immediately preceding Ford's visit to Indonesia, Scowcroft received a supplemental briefing paper on East Timor for use by the president (DDRS Fiche # 199-233). Several sections remain sanitized, but a number of points are clear. First, the US would not take a strong stand against any possible Indonesian actions: "Since none of our interests are involved, expressions of concern and support for a peaceful solution are as far as we should go. Beyond this, we should avoid any statement which could possibly be interpreted as expressing support for any side's position...'. Scowcroft's overall suggestion was that the president "both publicly and privately remain noncommittal on this issue". More importantly, the memorandum advised Ford not to explicitly reject Indonesia's forcible annexation of the region, but rather to make coy statements about the need for the parties themselves to resolve the problem. This advice belies the fact that American policymakers knew that at least some prominent military officials surrounding Suharto were advising him to invade, although the details on this matter remain sanitized (DDRS Fiche # 1995-183).

According to the memo: "Our judgment is that no dramatic step up in Indonesian intervention will take place at least until President Ford has departed Indonesia and that Suharto remains sensitive to the problems of possibly embarrassing the United States". The advice suggested Ford should state that "[America's] concern is that there not be unnecessary bloodshed and that the situation not adversely affect our friendly relations with the countries involved". These documents indicate clearly that the official US position during the summit precluded making Indonesian policies toward East Timor a detriment to US-Indonesian ties.

The Ford administration, with its noncommittal stance on the possible Indonesian invasion of East Timor, did not necessarily give a 'green light' to Jakarta, but certainly did not give a 'red light' either. When Jakarta launched its offensive just twelve hours after Ford left Indonesia, it seemed clear that Washington issued tacit consent. Subsequently, the United States' acceptance of Jakarta's acts of aggression and human rights abuses sealed America's complicity. The logic of America's strategic interests in Indonesia even overcame the Carter administration's supposed emphasis on the promotion of human rights worldwide. On 19 July 1977, the State Department's Deputy Legal Advisor recognized 'the validity of the sovereign authority of Indonesia in East Timor' (Korman, 1996, 286). In a 1978 Article, Zbigniew Brzezinski, Carter's National Security Advisor, identified Indonesia as one of the key Third World states that the US needed to improve relations (Kohen and Taylor, 1979, 95). Subsequent policy under the Reagan and Bush administrations likewise tended to look the other way as Indonesia continued its repressive policies in East Timor.

Similar to the US, the logic of Cold War alliances also drove Australian policy toward Indonesia. Geographic proximity and historical connections with the East Timorese people, who aided Australia in halting Japanese expansion in the South Pacific during the Second World War, drove Australia's policy toward Indonesia. However, given Indonesia's large population and Australia's desire to develop stronger relations with Southeast Asian nations, Canberra's merely accepted the Indonesian *fait accompli* in East Timor.

Since the early 1970s, with the end of the conservative era in Australian government, Canberra's strategic focus shifted away from exclusive ties to Europe and toward closer links with its Southeast Asian neighbors (Kohen and Taylor, 103). Australia's relationship with Indonesia assumed primary importance because "The Indonesian archipelago forms an umbrella over the Australian continent, and a hostile regime in Jakarta could cause Canberra immediate, practical problems" (Ibid, 103). Also, Indonesia's geography makes it a necessary bridge between Australia and the other states of South East Asia. The possibility of a pro-Communist East Timor posed a much more direct national security threat for Australia than for the United States. As one observer put it, East Timor could become a "South East Asian Cuba" (Djelantik, undated). At the very best, East Timor's independence could have created a 'balkanization' of the region, thus legitimizing the establishment of micro-states which could in turn become ripe for manipulation and infiltration by communist supporters.

The Australian government's position on the future of East Timor started to coalesce during 1974 (Akashi, 1995). A July 1974 visit to Canberra by Jose Ramos-Horta, a leading figure in the pro-independence movement, met a cool reception from Foreign Ministry officials who did not want the government "to become prematurely identified in Indonesian eyes with any particular Timorese faction" (Akashi 1995, 6). Foreign Minister Don Willesee refused to meet with him. Two months later, Prime Minister Gough Whitlam met with Suharto and gave the Indonesian leader what amounted to Australia's blessing for the annexation of East Timor (Akashi, 7):

> ...Whitlam said that he favoured the integration of East Timor into Indonesia following an internationally acceptable act of self-determination. He also told Suharto that the independence of East Timor would be economically unviable and a threat to the stability of the region, and that incorporation into Indonesian [sic] was the best option.

Canberra needed an act of Indonesian incorporation that avoided the overt use of force and contained a veneer of legitimacy. When reports of Whitlam's acquiescence became public, he came under sharp attack through the press and from both sides in the Federal Parliament. Nevertheless, he refused to deviate from his pro-Indonesian policies. In April 1975, Whitlam again met with Suharto and reiterated his support for the integration of East Timor into Indonesia, though he stressed that Canberra would disapprove of the use of force. However, once Indonesia began to launch border incursions into East Timor in preparation for its invasion, Australia's responded with only rhetorical condemnation, but refused to change its policy. This policy continued even after the October killing of five Australian press corps members in the border town of Balibo. In mid-November, the Governor-General of Australia replaced Whitlam with a caretaker government and called for new elections to be held on 13 December. The defeat of Whitlam's Labour government by the Liberal-Country Party held open the possibility for a change in Australia's East Timor policy.

Between the removal of Whitlam and the victory of the Liberal-Country Party, Indonesia invaded East Timor. The caretaker government, headed by Malcolm Fraser, voted for the relatively weak General Assembly resolution passed immediately after the invasion that condemned Indonesia. However, the new government, also led by Fraser, largely followed the policies of its predecessor. When Australia's delegation spoke before the UN Security Council on 16 December he noted his country's desire for East Timorese self-determination, but refused to condemn Jakarta's actions (Krieger 1977, 77-8). This change, in Australian rhetoric a little over a week after the invasion, betokened a shift by the Fraser government back to the policy of its predecessor. The US State Department document of March 1976 noted (DDRS, Fiche# 1992-99):

> When the Fraser Government came to office, it was somewhat embarrassed to find that there were no visible alternatives to Whitlam's Timor policies, which Fraser and Foreign Minister Peacock had criticized while in opposition. There followed a period of seeming vacillation on Timor by the new Government, in which Fraser and Peacock refused to recognize Fretelin's [sic] unilateral declaration of independence in Timor, but at the United Nations called for Indonesian withdrawal. Having established a public posture for the record, however, the Fraser Government now supports the Security Council resolution of December 1975, accepts Indonesian control of Timor as a fait accompli, and has taken pains to mend its fences with Indonesia.

By early 1976, the Australian government accepted the inevitability of East Timor's incorporation into Indonesia, and Fraser's visit in the fall of 1976 solidified this policy shift. When the UN General Assembly voted on the East Timor question in October 1976, Australia abstained. This de facto recognition became official policy on 20 January 1978 with a statement by Foreign Minister Andrew Peacock (Krieger, 333):

> This is a reality with which we must come to terms... Accordingly, the Government has decided that although it remains critical of the means by which integration was brought about it would be unrealistic to continue to refuse to recognize de facto that East Timor is part of Indonesia.

A year later, in 1983, the new Prime Minister Bob Hawke reaffirmed the *de jure* recognition of Indonesia's control over East Timor. In 1989, Australia and Indonesia signed the 'Timor Gap Treaty' that established a maritime delimitation between the two countries and allowed for natural resource exploitation.

Both the US and Australia accepted the Indonesian *fait accompli* in East Timor on the basis of the logic of the Cold War. Unlike in the United States, where East Timor never occupied high level of salience in the public consciousness, a major lacunae between official Australian government policy and the public's pro-East Timorese feelings existed (Jackson, 2000). Nevertheless, the importance of Indonesia as a security partner in South East Asia suppressed concerns of self-determination and human rights. With the end of the Cold War, however, Indonesia's place in the strategic vision of Washington and Canberra dropped considerably.

Post-Cold War US and Australian Strategic Thinking

With the collapse of the global bipolar struggle between the United States and the Soviet Union, Indonesia's geopolitical importance decreased significantly. Bill Clinton's ascension to the presidency in 1993, coincided with the beginning of the post-Cold War international system, and thus allowed the new administration to revamp America's policies toward its historic allies. Meanwhile, Australia and Indonesia increased their strategic cooperation with Indonesian stability seen as crucial for long-term Australian stability.

Shifting US Policy

In the seven years prior to Clinton's election, economic ties between the US and Indonesia increased dramatically with US exports to Indonesia tripled from $795 million to $2.8 billion (Niksch, 1996). At the same time, however, US-Indonesian relations took a dramatic downturn. In 1992, the US Congress banned all aid to Indonesia for training and new weapons under the Department of Defense's International Military Education and Training program because of Indonesia's human rights abuses in East Timor (US House of Representatives [HR 5368 Sec. 599H], 1993). In particular, the videotaped massacre of unarmed civilians during a politically charged funeral procession helped to galvanize anti-Indonesian members of Congress (Federal News Service, 6 March, 1992).

Upon taking power, the Clinton administration indicated an interest in taking a tougher stance against Indonesia over the East Timor question (Wallace, 1993). Unlike the previous two administrations, Clinton refused to block a resolution of the UN Human Rights Commission expressing 'deep concern' over rights violations in East Timor (Toronto Star, 4 April, 1993). Furthermore, Clinton raised the issue directly with Suharto at several meetings (Niksch). However, the Clinton administration did not go as far as some preferred. It refused to de-recognize Indonesian sovereignty over East Timor or impose sanctions against Jakarta. While it scuttled the proposed sale of US-built F-5 fighters from Jordan to Indonesia, the administration also opposed legislation that would suspend other US arms sales to Indonesia (Niksch). Some in the American press began to question Clinton's commitment to human rights (McGrory, 1994). The administration responded by arguing that increased trade and political ties between the United States and Indonesia would improve the latter's human rights policies in the long run (Bluestein and Lippman, 1994).

While the Clinton administration modified its initial stance of greater human rights policy emphasis in East Timor, the shift away from the Cold War strategy became readily apparent. The administration placed human rights onto the agenda of US-Indonesia relations. Although tempered by the need to reach bilateral trade agreements, Clinton raised the issue of human rights while in Jakarta and the administration's top human rights official explicitly stated that Indonesia's human rights record factored into future US-Indonesian relations (Jacob, 1995; Sciolino, 1994). Secretary of State Warren Christopher stated (Baltimore Sun, 1994): "The relationship between the United States and Indonesia can never reach its highest levels if the people of the United States don't [sic] have confidence that there is an effort here to respect the rights of all [its] citizens".

By the end of 1996, the Clinton administration's relatively soft policy toward Indonesia disintegrated as a result of several factors. Amid charges of illegal campaign contributions to Clinton's reelection campaign from Indonesia, a heightened military campaign against the East Timorese, and the award of the Nobel Peace Prize to two East Timorese rights activists, constructive engagement came under increased media and Congressional scrutiny (Babcok and Marcus, 1996; Serrano, 1996; Sanger, 1996). Increasingly, administration officials and members of the US Congress began questioning the United States' close relationship with Jakarta. By the time the Asian economic crisis hit the archipelago, the legitimacy of a pro-Indonesian policy had effectively collapsed.

Tenacious Australian-Indonesian Relations

Given the greater importance of Indonesia in Australian strategic thinking, human rights issues factored less in maintaining close than those between Jakarta and Washington. A close personal relationship between President Suharto and Prime Minister Paul Keating during the early-1990s led to secret negotiations on a security agreement between their two countries. The 'Agreement on Maintaining Security' (AMS), signed in mid-December 1995 and hailed as critical components of Australian foreign and defense policies, formed the cornerstone of Indonesian-Australian relations (Brown et. al, 1995-96). While the agreement did not establish a defensive alliance, it helped foster Indonesia as Australia's most important security partner in the region. In 1996 John Howard, Keating's successor, affirmed his support for the AMS. In a 1997 strategic review of Australian foreign policy, entitled *Australia's Strategic Policy*, the Howard government stated that "Indonesia is our most strategic relationship in Southeast Asia" (Department of Defence, 1997). The report also outlines areas of cooperation between the two states and the potential impact of East Timor on their relationship:

- Moreover, Indonesia is likely to have similar strategic perceptions on regional security. The AMS would suggest that Indonesia now sees its security interests and ours more closely

aligned and is prepared to work with Australia in pursuing common objectives. This provides an important opportunity to strengthen further our relationship.
- While the management of the defence relationship is somewhat complicated by the focus within Australia on [the Indonesian Armed Forces'] role in internal security, especially in East Timor, we need to resist efforts to make this strategically important relationship hostage to individual incidents– and close cooperation on a range of issues provides us with broad influence, including on human rights.
- While Australia's Indonesia policy was coming under increasing fire from the Australian public, the government's relationship with Jakarta appeared secure at the time of the Asian Economic Crisis.

Regardless of the human rights abuses, both the United States and Australia maintained close relations with Indonesia. In particular, Australia, due to its geographical proximity to Indonesia, could not alter its policies as readily. The United States, however, increasingly reevaluated its links to Indonesia in the aftermath of the Cold War. However, close economic ties between the US and Indonesia precluded any punitive action. Indonesia's relationship with both countries and its management of East Timor experienced dramatic change as a result of the Asian Economic Crisis.

The Asian Economic Crisis and the Problem of Suharto

The Asian Economic Crisis began in mid-1997 and devastated Indonesia: real GDP fell by 20% in eighteen months; its currency, the *rupiah*, at one point lost over 85% of its value against the dollar; unemployment soared; and ethnic violence erupted throughout the country. Of the states afflicted by the Asian Economic Crisis, it struck Indonesia the hardest. In the World Bank's 1998 annual painted a particularly grim picture of Indonesia's economic disaster by stating that "Indonesia is in deep crisis. A country that achieved decades of rapid growth, stability, and poverty reduction, is now near economic collapse. ... No country in recent history, let alone one the size of Indonesia, has ever suffered such a dramatic reversal of fortune" (Hill, 1999, 1). Within a year of the Indonesian economy's dramatic downturn, President Suharto resigned after some three decades of nearly unquestioned power. Besides shifting the political balance in the country, the Asian Economic Crisis proved an important catalyst for Jakarta's decision to relinquish control over East Timor by weakening the ruling elites economically based legitimacy.

Beginning in the last two months of 1997, Indonesia's economic and political situation deteriorated sharply. A number of Indonesian banks closed in early November and many of the needed economic reforms never materialized because they jeopardized the Suharto family interests. Furthermore, President Suharto fell worryingly ill in early December, thus raising the specter of political turmoil to the already alarming economic situation. Very quickly, Indonesia's currency and stock market plummeted and the government lost control over the money supply, thus fueling inflation. In just a few months, the entire Indonesian middle class saw its newfound wealth erased and unemployment increased dramatically as the construction and property development sectors disintegrated (McLeod, 1999).

Soon after the crisis spread to the archipelago, the International Monetary Fund (IMF) went to work with Jakarta in an effort to stem the collapse of the Indonesian economy. In October 1997, the IMF and the Indonesian government reached an agreement on a new round of loans. The 'conditionality agreement' with the IMF set tough requirements for aid that the Suharto regime immediately began to rescind in order to protect family business interests. For example, Tommy Suharto, the son of the president, had his clove monopoly protected despite IMF demands for the demonopolization of Indonesian businesses (Jakarta Post, 1997). The amount of the IMF package remained unclear, as were the specific expenditure items (McCleod, 221). More importantly, the Suharto regime began to publicly question the IMF's 'belt-tightening' requirements.

All of this led to a worsening of Indonesia's economic position in January 1998. The New Year began ominously with "an implausible budget, widening rifts with the IMF (in spite of a high-profile signing ceremony in the middle of the month), and a clear indication of [BJ] Habibie's imminent ascendancy to the vice presidency" (Hill, 1999, 5-7). Habibie, a long-time family friend of Suharto, would eventually become president himself when Suharto stepped down in mid-1998. However, outside observers viewed him as a problem because of his emphasis on high-tech, publicly subsidized, and wholly wasteful industries during his term as State Minister of Research and Technology. Habibie's nomination to the vice presidency indicated Suharto's rejection of reforms required by the IMF (McDonald, 1998). Consequently, at one point in January, the rupiah dropped to Rp17,000 per dollar– one-seventh of its pre-crisis level.

A second IMF agreement softened the belt-tightening requirements but demanded greater microeconomic reforms. Unfortunately, the Indonesian government attempted to continue to 'muddle through' the crisis and failed to put forth a coherent and effective response. By March 1998, Suharto openly feuded with the IMF by insisting on an 'alternative' plan of 'IMF-plus' for his country, which would have entailed the creation of a currency control board that would peg the rupiah to the dollar (Shiner, 1998). Around the same time, Suharto's unveiled his new cabinet, "widely seen as a snub to the International Monetary Fund," since it included his eldest daughter Tutut and one of his leading cronies, Bob Hasan (Asian Wall Street Weekly, 1998). In effect,

Suharto told the international community no significant reforms would be undertaken. Consequently, international confidence in the regime, already at an all-time low, simply collapsed. Simultaneously, the government's harassment of political opponents and widening student protests against the regime pointed to a fundamental problem in Indonesia's system of governance. Many observers concluded that "the problem was not the Indonesian economy *per se* but more had to do with the Indonesian political leadership. Until and unless this problem was addressed there was no hope whatsoever of improving the national economy" (Singh, 2000, 80-1). As Suharto's domestic support began to collapse, his international support evaporated.

The US took an active interest in the Indonesian economic crisis. In mid-February, President Clinton spoke with his Indonesian counterpart about the economic situation several times to express US support for reforms (New York Times, February 22, 1998). After Jakarta rebuffed his first envoy, Clinton dispatched former Vice-President and former ambassador to Japan Walter Mondale to Indonesia with a series of messages for Suharto. The United States was extremely concerned with the Indonesian economic crisis; the U.S. wanted Suharto to strictly follow the IMF's reform package; and it wished to see greater democratization in Indonesia (New York Times, 25 February, 1998; Washington Post, 24 February). Significant debate within the Clinton administration about how strongly the U.S. should try to pressure Suharto ensued (New York Times, 27 February, 1998). While some with the administration strongly opposed Suharto, the State Department countered that no credible alternative to the current president exists (Los Angelos Times, 1 March, 1998). However, just hours after Mondale met with Suharto, administration officials testified before Congress and stated that the U.S. would refuse dispersal of IMF loans to Indonesia without 'appropriate progress' on dealing with "monopolies, subsidies, monetary policies, and [its] approach to the financial system" (Federal News Service, 3 March, 1998). This indicated a more confrontational stance against Suharto in order to pressure him into accepting reforms.

Canberra, too, considered the Indonesian economic crisis a priority in early 1998 with Australia ranking tenth as a market for Indonesian exports and sixth as a source of imports. Furthermore, Australians invested heavily in Indonesia with a total direct investment of some of A$2.5 billion (Djelantik). In January 1998, the upbeat Australian Prime Minister John Howard thought Indonesia could recover quickly and pledged US$1 billion ($1.52 billion) to the IMF's stand-by loan package (Australian Associated Press [AAP Newsfeed], 15 January, 1998). In a meeting with Suharto, however, Australian Foreign Minister Alexander Downer made it clear that Canberra supported the full and speedy implementation of the IMF-required reforms (Agence France Presse, 26

January, 1998). Howard expressed disappointed by what many perceived as Suharto's footdragging on reforms, although, at the same time, he argued for greater IMF 'flexibility' (AAP Newsfeed, 1 March, 1998).

Both the US and Australia began to take a tougher line with the Suharto regime in March 1998. As seen in the previous section, a shift in U.S. and Australian strategic thinking, precipitated by changes in the international system, made Indonesia less relevant for Washington and Canberra. Suharto's tenure in office was no longer necessary from a strategic standpoint and, in fact, his refusal to reform Indonesia's economy could lead to instability in the region and precipitate a complete economic catastrophe. As one scholar put it, "Indonesia was entering dangerous and uncharted waters. If the president was unwilling to adhere to his policy commitments, the economy was heading for the rocks, for no other political players could delay, alter, or countermand his decisions" (Pempel, 1999, 158). By the end of the spring, a growing sense in the United States and Australia that Suharto must depart crystallized. On 20 May, amidst growing student protests, US Secretary of State Madeline Albright called publicly for Suharto to agree to a timetable to step down from office (Lippman, 1998). The next day, some thirty-two years after seizing power, Suharto resigned. International pressure coupled with his refusal to implement reforms intensified the domestic factors that led to his ouster (Emmerson, 2000, 295-343).

International Pressure and East Timorese Independence

Since capturing East Timor, Indonesia's official policy stated that the East Timorese joined Indonesia of their free will (Krieger, 275-8). Although both Washington and Canberra accepted this during the Cold War, the Clinton administration gradually distanced itself from this position. While Australia backed Suharto and Indonesia's policy toward East Timor longer than the United States, Suharto's resignation created an opportunity for Australia to reevaluate its own policy toward the region. Similarly, Suharto's replacement, BJ Habibie, perceived an opportunity to make a sharp break from the past and to establish his 'bonafides' as a person that could inspire international confidence and foreign investment, both of which proved lacking at the time of his inauguration (The Canberra Times, 28 May, 1998). Habibie's inaugural address stated that his country would alter its policy toward East Timor (Agence France Presse, 21 May, 1998).

From inception, the Habibie government's policies on East Timor came under close international scrutiny and pressure. International observers saw Habibie's policies toward East Timor as a litmus test of his commitment to rejecting the negative policies of his predecessor and to embracing both democratic and human rights reforms. Initially, some rumors emerged that his administration would seek a 'reevaluation' of Jakarta's policies toward the area (Lakshmanan, 1998). However, in an interview with CNN, Habibie reiterated Indonesia's long-term policy (Shiner, 1998):

> East Timor is an integrated part of the Republic of Indonesia. ...We have done more in the last 20 years than the former colonial masters have done in the last 400 years. There's no need for a referendum in Indonesia. They will enjoy, as the others in Indonesia, the same values of life and quality of life.

Soon thereafter, however, Habibie began to soften his hard-line position and opened the possibility that Indonesia would accept some sort of 'special status' for the region with very limited autonomy (Spillius, 1998 and Aglionby, 1998). While East Timorese leaders rejected Habibie's position, clearly room for negotiation existed (Daily Telegraph, 10 June, 1998). Around the same time, Habibie ordered the release of over a dozen East Timorese political prisoners (Financial Times, 11 June 1998) and expanded his 'special status' proposal to include the withdrawal of thousands of Indonesian troops from East Timor (New York Times, 21 June 1998). Habibie also met with Bishop Carlos Belo– one of the two East Timorese leaders awarded the Nobel Peace Prize in 1996. After this initial flurry of activity, however, it looked unclear at the end of 1998 whether Habibie would take the steps necessary to bring a full resolution to the East Timorese situation in line with the East Timorese people's right to self-determination. In particular, many perceived Habibie's offer of symbolic autonomy the limit of his reformist policies (Jakarta Post, 28 December, 1998; 2 December, 1998).

A hardening of the US position on East Timor and a change in Australian policy toward the territory coincided with Habibie's desire to increase his international legitimacy in general, and the US and Australia in particular. Both countries perceived a limited window of opportunity in which to pressure Habibie to fundamentally alter Jakarta's policy on East Timor. US officials reported to Congress about an increase in American pressure on Indonesia in relation to human rights abuses in East Timor (Federal Document Clearing House, 24 July, 1998). The Clinton administration saw Indonesia as 'a priority' and urged "both sides to seize this opportunity to open a dialogue and initiate confidence building measures" (Federal Document Clearing House 4 June, 1998). The administration's basis of this dialogue would consist of a series of UN-sponsored talks aimed at settling East Timor's political status. Both the U.S. House of Representatives and Senate took action on the issue during 1998, passing a concurrent resolution demanding a referendum for East Timor (US Senate SR 237; US House Res 258). Thus, the Americans supported the 'problematizing' of East Timor's political status in which other options, presumably including independence, became a distinct possibility.

Even more dramatic than the policy changes in Washington, Canberra's radical shift would no longer acquiesce to Indonesia's claims of legitimate rule over East Timor. In December 1998, Australian Prime Minister John Howard wrote to Habibie urging him to grant East Timor autonomy and ultimately self-determination (Albinski, 2000). A month later, Australian Foreign Minister Alexander Downer announced that a full review of Canberra's policy toward East Timor and summarized the new policy as follows: "the long term prospects for reconciliation in East Timor would be best served by the holding of an act of self-determination at some future time, following a substantial period of autonomy"(Australian Ministry of Foreign Affairs, 12 January, 1999). This statement, although important because it permitted the possibility of eventual East Timorese independence, also denoted that "this adjustment to Australian policy does not alter the Government's position which continues to recognise Indonesian sovereignty over East Timor." Furthermore, the statement raised a number of questions. How much autonomy would be sufficient? How long is a 'substantial period'? Does the phrase 'some future time' refer to a point in the short, medium, or long-term in the future? Australian Foreign Minister Alexander Downer placed Canberra's expected timeframe at "10 years time or whatever the period might be" (Agence France Presse, 12 January, 1999). Despite the substantial timeframe, East Timorese leaders welcomed the policy shift (Radio Renascenca [Lisbon], 12 January, 1999; BBC Monitoring Asia-Pacific, 12 January ,1999; and Agence France Presse, 12 January, 1999).

Suharto's resignation motivated Canberra's new East Timor policy. Australia took advantage of Habibie's proposal for limited autonomy, which he did to bolster his image in the West, and proposed a more substantial, if ill-defined autonomy. More generally, the fall of Suharto provided an opportunity to change a rather unpopular policy amongst the Australian public (Thayer, 1999).

Jakarta for its part expressed its concern and deep regret. Although Indonesian officials argued that the Australian policy shift would "have an adverse effect on the search for a just, comprehensive and internationally acceptable solution on the issue" (Thayer, 1999). This merely represented an attempt to curb the increasing pressure from the international community over its occupation of East Timor. It became clear to Indonesian officials that international pressure would be unyielding. As one analyst put it: "The collapse of [Indonesia's] economy and the overthrow of the Suharto regime has made the [Indonesian] Government more susceptible to foreign pressure, and the pressure inevitably includes the need to settle the East Timor conflict" (The Press [Christchurch, NZ], 20 January, 1999). When combined with the estimated high cost of maintaining its hold over the rebellious region, the collapsing economy, and the Habibie government's shaky hold over the country, international pressure served as a 'tipping' factor which made continued control over East Timor harmful to Indonesian national interests.

On 27 January, Indonesian Foreign Minister Ali Alatas announced that Indonesia would allow a referendum in East Timor to determine the region's political future. After more than two decades of Indonesian rule and senseless brutality at the hands of Jakarta, East Timor was finally given the opportunity to achieve its independent. In the aftermath of this dramatic decision Indonesian Finance Minister Ginandjar Kartasasmita explained the reasons for the government's decision quite succinctly: "we [the Indonesian government] want to turn a new leaf, it is part of the reforms of the Habibie administration" (FBIS-WEU-99-030).

Conclusions

On 9 May, 1999, Indonesia and Portugal signed an agreement that formed the basis of the United Nations Assistance Mission East Timor (UNAMET) to conduct a referendum in East Timor. Although delayed twice and occurring under the threat of violence, UNAMET held the referendum on 30 August 1999 in which more than three-quarters of the East Timorese rejected Jakarta's offer of 'special autonomy'– which meant in effect that they supported independence. The subsequent rampage by pro-Indonesian militia groups, backed by the Indonesian military, left many East Timorese dead and entire urban centers destroyed. In response, the United Nations Security Council approved the formation of the International Force East Timor (INTERFET) which was charged with restoring order in the former colony. In early October, the Indonesian People's Consultative Assembly formally accepted the result of the East Timorese referendum. As the assembly's speaker Amien Rais bluntly put it: "Timtim [East Timor] is now no longer a part of Indonesia. It's finished" (Deutsche Presse, 6 October, 1999).

In the early 1990s, Indonesia fully secured control over East Timor and the international community generally accepted the status of the enclave. However, at the end of the decade, Indonesian officials felt pressure from abroad to permit the region's independence. The decision to allow for a self-determination referendum in East Timor departed radically from Indonesian state policy toward its sprawling archipelago. The potential for the further weakening of Indonesia, precedented by East Timor's departure, continues to threaten to pull the country apart in such places as Aceh, Borneo, the Molucca Islands, Sulawesi, and West Papua. Nevertheless, President BJ Habibie felt compelled to relinquish control over East Timor as the new president who sought to portray himself as a reformer in an environment of mounting international pressure. The confluence of changing norms within the international system, economic crisis, and heightened economic interdependence accounted for this dramatic turn of events.

Both the US and Australia accepted Jakarta's invasion and brutal subjugation of East Timor as part of a Faustian bargain to block communism's spread during the Cold War. With the end of that ideological struggle, however, human rights and economic issues took precedence over geopolitics and strategic value. In the United States, the newly-elected Clinton administration raised the East Timor issue as a potential impediment to US-Indonesian relations. Although it often did not live up to its rhetoric, the Clinton presidency began a policy shift that increasingly delegitimized continued Indonesian occupation of East Timor. Australia's East Timor policy lagged behind America's for good reason: the strategic value Indonesia possessed for Washington was far greater for Canberra given the latter's immediate proximity. Nevertheless, the Asian Economic Crisis that began to sweep throughout Asia in 1997 altered radically the relations between Indonesia and its two democratic allies.

Indonesia was quite possibly the hardest hit by the Asian Economic Crisis. Both the US and Australia had an important stake in convincing President Suharto to undertake economic reforms. In addition to the high level of trade and investment that both states had in Indonesia, neither the US nor Australia wanted to see the economic crisis spread to the political realm and potentially cause the country to collapse. Soon after the International Monetary Fund presented its loan package and conditionally agreement, Suharto himself emerged as the primary impediment to reform. Although domestic forces were likely decisive in driving the long-time dictator from office, increasing international pressure made Suharto's continued rule untenable. Consequently Suharto's handpicked successor, BJ Habibie, became the country's president.

Habibie, himself a problematic figure for promoting international confidence in Indonesia's new regime, attempted to improve his international image to alleviate the ongoing economic crisis. It became acutely important to undertake policies which would instill the perception that Habibie's policies represented a sharp break from the past. Despite some initial vacillation on the East Timor issue, allowing increased autonomy for the region and a UN-sponsored referendum on eventual independence became part of this plan. The decision to utilize East Timor in this political makeover reflected continued changes in US and Australian policies as both countries perceived a window of opportunity to push Indonesia into relinquishing East Timor. Jakarta's announcement of late January 1999 that it would finally allow the East

Timorese to exercise their right to self-determination nearly two and a half decades after Portugal departed from the colony was one positive consequence of the Asian Economic Crisis.

References

Aditjondro, G.J. et al. (1995), *International Law and the Question of East Timor*, Catholic Institute for International Relations, London.

Agence France Presse, 'Australia Tells Indonesia it must Press Ahead with Reforms', 26 January, 1998.

Agence France Presse, 'The Full Speech of Indonesian President Habibie', 21 May, 1998.

Agence France Presse, 'Australia Policy Shift on East Timor Receives Mixed Response', 12 January, 1999.

Agence France Presse, reproduced as 'Minister: Indonesia Wants to End 'Costly' E Timor Problem', in *Foreign Broadcast Information Service*, FBIS-WEU-99-030, 30 January, 1999.

Aglionby, J. (1998), 'Habibie Sees His Troubles Multiply', *Guardian* (London), 11 June, p. 17.

Akashi, Y. (1995), 'The East Timor Question in Australia-Indonesia Relations, 1974-78: An Australian Perspective', Centre for Australian Studies Working Papers, Nanzan University.

Albinski, H.S. (2000), 'Issues in Australian Foreign Policy: East Timor', *The Australian Journal of Politics and History* v.46, no.2. [Accessed through *Infotrac*.]

Asian Wall Street Journal Weekly, 'President's Cabinet Choices Seen an Apparent IMF Snub', 23 March 1998, A4.

Australian Associated Press Newsfeed [AAP Newsfeed], 'Howard Says No Immediate Concern from Indonesia', 15 January, 1998.

Australian Associated Press Newsfeed [AAP Newsfeed], 'Fed: Suharto must Make IMF Reforms, IMF must Be Flexible: PM', 1 March, 1998.

Australian Ministry of Foreign Affairs, Alexander Downer, 'Australian Government Historic Policy Shift On East Timor', 12 January 1999, <http://www.dfat.gov.au/media/releases/foreign/1999/fa002_99.html>

Babcock, Charles R. and Marcus, Ruth. 'Indonesian Gift Points Up What Some Call a Loophole', *Washington Post*, 16 October, 1996, A6.

Baltimore Sun, 'Clinton Gently Pushes Indonesia on Rights', 17 November ,1994, A1.

Blustein, P. and Lippman, T.W. (1994), 'Clinton Says Trade Boosts Rights Issue', *Washington Post*, 15 November, A1.

Blustein, P. (1998), 'Clinton Chooses Mondale as Envoy to Indonesia', *Washington Post*, 24 February, D3.

Brown, G., Frost, F. and Sherlock, S. (1995-96), 'The Australian-Indonesian Security Agreement-Issues and Implications', Department of the Parliamentary Library (Australia), Research Paper 25, <http://www.aph.gov.au/library/pubs/rp/1995-96/96rp25.htm>

Canberra Times, 'Signs Habibie could Break with the Past', 28 May, 1998, A9.

Declassified Documents Reference System [DDRS], CDROM Id: 1980010100257, 'American Embassy Djakarta', Annual Report on Relations with Communist Countries, 26 December 1966 (Fiche#: 1980-85B).

Declassified Documents Reference System [DDRS], CDROM Id: 1992050101285, Department of State, 'Australia and Portuguese Timor', 1 March 1976 (Fiche#: 1992-99).
Declassified Documents Reference System [DDRS], CDROM Id: 1994090102862, Kenneth M. Quinn, 'Memorandum for Brent Scowcroft: Presidential Talking Points on Portuguese Timor', 4 December 1975 (Fiche#: 1994-233).
Declassified Documents Reference System [DDRS], CDROM Id: 1994090102861. Thomas J. Barnes, 'Memorandum for Brent Scowcroft: Forwarding of State Briefing Books on Indonesia to the President', 25 November 1975 (Fiche#: 1994-233).
Declassified Documents Reference System [DDRS], CDROM Id: 1994090102943, Henry A. Kissinger, 'Meeting with Indonesian President Suharto', 5 July 1975 (Fiche#: 1994-239).
Declassified Documents Reference System [DDRS], CDROM Id: 199507010288, American Embassy, Jakarta, 'Briefing Memo: Last Portuguese Timor Developments', 4 December, 1975 (Fiche#: 1995-183).
Department of Defense (1997), *Australia's Strategic Policy*, Commonwealth of Australia.
Deutsche Presse-Agentur, 'Indonesian Government Favours Independence for East Timor', 28 January, 1999.
Deutsche Presse-Agentur, 'Indonesian Assembly Agrees to Endorse East Timor Vote', 6 October, 1999.
Djelantik, Sukawarsini. 'Indonesia, Australia And East Timor Diplomacy', <http//www.smug.adelaide.edu.au/ppiasa/nuansa/suke/> [On file with author.]
Emmerson, Donald K., (1999), 'Exit and Aftermath: The Crisis of 1997-1998', in D.K. Emmerson, (ed.), *Indonesia Beyond Suharto: Polity, Economy, Society, Transition*, M.E. Sharpe, Armonk, pp. 295-343.
Federal Document Clearing House, 'Testimony July 24, 1998, John Shattuck Assistant Secretary of Democracy, Human Rights and Labor Bureau, Department of State, US House International Relations: International Operations And Human Rights: Human Rights in Indonesia', 24 July, 1998.
Federal Document Clearing House, 'Testimony June 04, 1998 Aurelia E. Brazeal, Deputy Assistant Secretary For East Asia and The Pacific Department of State, US House International Relations: Asia and Pacific U.S. Policy Options Toward Indonesia', 4 June, 1998.
Federal News Service, 'Hearing of the East Asian Affairs Subcommittee of the Senate Foreign Relations Committee', 6 March, 1992.
Federal News Service, 'Hearing of The Foreign Operations Subcommittee of The Senate Appropriations Committee', 3 March, 1998.
Financial Times (London), 'Indonesian Leader Releases 15 Political Prisoners from East Timor', 11 June, 1998, 1.
Flynn, K., (1998), 'All Eyes on New Indonesian Cabinet as Suharto Begins Seventh Term', *Agence France Presse*, 12 March.
Hill, H. (1999), *The Indonesian Economy in Crisis*, St. Martin's Press, New York.
Jackson, M. (2000), 'Something Must Be Done? Genocidal Chaos and the Decision to Intervene: World Responses to Mass Murder', Paper presented at A Century of Killing: Genocide and Ethnic Cleansing in the 20th Century, University of South Dakota.
Jacob, P. (1995), 'Human Rights a part of Agenda in Ties with U.S., Indonesia Told', *The Straits Times* (Singapore), 21 April, 19.
Jakarta Post, 'What About Monopoly on Clove Trading?', 2 December, 1997, 1.
Jakarta Post, 'Self-Determination Must Not Threaten Nation's Unity: Habibie', 2 December, 1998.
Jakarta Post, 'Hope for Habibie-Belo Meeting Wanes Rapidly', 28 December, 1998.

Kohen, A. and Taylor, J. (1979), *An Act of Genocide: Indonesia's Invasion of East Timor*, Tapol, United Kingdom.
Korman, K. (1996), *The Right of Conquest: The Acquisition of Territory by Force in International Law and Practice*, Clarendon Press, Oxford.
Krieger, H. (ed.), (1977), *East Timor and the International Community: Basic Documents*, Cambridge, Cambridge University Press, United Kingdom.
Lakshmanan, I.A.R. (1998), 'Indonesia's New Leader Pledges Array of Changes', *Boston Globe*, 26 May, A1.
Lim, L.Y.C., (1999), 'The Challenges for Government Policy and Business Practice', Paper presented at the Asia Society's Conference entitled The Asian Economic Crisis, February. <https://wwwc.cc.columbia.edu/sec/dlc/ciao/conf/ass07/ass07_a.html>
Lippman, T. W. (1998), 'Albright Encourages Suharto to Leave Office', *Washington Post*, 21 May, A34.
Mann, J. (1998), 'U.S. Backs Suharto Despite Calls for Reform', *Los Angeles Times*, 1 March, A1.
McDonald, H. (1998), 'As 'Dr Strangelove' Rises, the Rupiah Falls even Further', *Sydney Morning Herald*, reproduced by *Australasian Business Intelligence*, 22 January, pp.1 and 8.
McGrory, M. (1994), 'Human Rights Retreat', *Washington Post*, 7 July.
McLeod, R.H. (1999), 'Indonesia's Crisis and Future Prospects', in K.D. Jackson, (ed.), *Asian Contagion: The Causes and Consequences of Financial Crisis*, Westview Press, Colorado.
New York Times, 'Clinton and Suharto Talk', 22 February, 1998, sec.1, p.3.
New York Times, 'Mondale to Visit Jakarta to Press Suharto on IMF Reform Plan', 25 February, 1998, A6.
New York Times, 'Indonesia Leader Offers Proposal on East Timor', 21 June, 1998, sec.1, p.7.
Niksch, L. (1996), 'US-Indonesian Relations', (Congressional Research Service, number 94-223F, 1996).
Paster, R.A. (ed.), (1999), *A Century's Journey*, Basic Books, New York.
Pempel, T.J. (1999), *The Politics of The Asian Economic Crisis*, (ed.), T.J. Pempel, Cornell University Press, NY.
The Press (Christchurch, NZ), 'Indonesia Sees Sense', 20 January, 2000, p. 10.
Sanger, D.E. (1996), 'Administration Moves to Defend Indonesia Policy After Criticism', *New York Times*, 17 October, A1.
Sanger, D.E. (1998), 'Indonesian Faceoff: Drawing Blood Without Bombs', *New York Times*, 8 March, sec.4, pg.1.
Sanger, D.E. (1998), 'U.S. Faces Hard Choice as Suharto Balks at Economic Reform', *New York Times*, 27 February, A3.
Sciolino, E. (1994), 'Clinton Is Stern With Indonesia On Rights but Gleeful on Trade', *New York Times*, 17 November, A1.
Serrano, R.A. (1996), 'Gingrich Seeks Probe of Donation', *Los Angeles Times*, 14 October, A23.
Shiner, C. (1998), 'Suharto Touts Alternative Reforms', *Washington Post*, 2 March, A13.
Shiner, C. (1998), 'Indonesian Leader Says He Hopes to Accomplish 'Mission Impossible'', *Washington Post*, 3 June, A24.
Singh, B. (2000), *Succession Politics in Indonesia*, St. Martin's Press, New York.
Spillius, A. (1998), 'East Timor Rejects Habibie Peace Offer', *Daily Telegraph*, 10 June, p. 17.
Taylor, J. (1999), 'Australia Policy Shift on East Timor Welcomed by Campaigners', 12 January, *Agence France Presse*.

Thayer, C.A. (1999), 'Australia-Indonesia Relations: The Case of East Timor', Paper presented at Australia and East Asian Security into the 21st Century, Taipei, Taiwan, 9 October.

Toronto Star, 'U.N. Resolution Vote May Signal Shift in American Policy Toward Indonesia', 4 April, 1993, F3.

Wallace, C.P. (1993), 'U.S. Concern Over East Timor May Signal Asian Policy Change', *Los Angeles Times*, 2 April, A5.

Chapter 8

Japan's Regional Environmental Foreign Aid: Responding to Global and Regional Realities*

David M. Potter

Introduction

As Japan's economic development increased from the 1950s and into the 1980s and sustained and substantial trade surpluses developed, significant pressure mounted on Japan to increase its global commitment. '*Gaiatsu*', or foreign pressure, from the United States in the 1980s further exacerbated this increased demand for Japan to share it's newly acquired wealth. Furthermore, Japan's image in the Pacific region remained tarnished from its World War II aggression and its post-War economic expansion heightened concern over Japan's growing military and economic power. Japanese foreign policy makers believed that foreign aid could alleviate its negative World War II image, soothe relations with the United States, and assist the country in penetrating the Asian markets further. All of these external forces became integrated with domestic politics as the Japanese became increasingly concerned about the need for a globalized and internationalized Japan.

This chapter examines Japan's environmental aid activism in the 1990s. In the 1970s, Japan emerged as a key foreign aid donor, especially to Asian countries. Despite its global reach, Asia remains a key component of Japan's aid policy; conversely, Japan became the largest bilateral aid donor to every country in East, Southeast and South Asia. The Japanese government's newfound interest in aid policy for environmental conservation took advantage of the opening of an international policy window in the mid-1980s. While OECD nations and developed nations expected Japan to increase is official development assistance (ODA) as its economy grew, numerous and serious impediments arose, especially an inadequate institutional support for increasing Japan's ODA. This chapter examines Japanese environmental aid policy at the end of the century and explores how an initially reactive foreign aid policy has

---

* The author thanks Sudo Sueo and Robert Compton for their helpful comments on earlier drafts. Responsibility for the text, of course remains with the author.

developed. It argues that three factors continue to limit a proactive environmental foreign aid style in Japan: the lack of institutional adjustment within the aid program; a corresponding lack of effective voices articulating a unified and concerted approach to environmental issues; and continued ambivalence about environmental protection by aid recipients.

Policy Environment

Any discussion of what happened to aid policy in the last decade must take into account two factors in the overall policy environment, namely the Heisei recession of the 1990s and the ongoing climate of administrative reform. Both have had various impacts on environmental aid policy. The Heisei recession provoked a reassessment of the overall aims and priorities of aid policy in light of a continuing a structural fiscal debt problem. This re-examination could result in a diminution of environmental protection as other policy issues displace it on the issue agenda or to a recommitment to environmental aid as discussions of priorities affirm its importance. Second, the limited administrative reform achieved under the Hashimoto cabinet (1995-8) may strengthen bureaucratic policy making and implementation capacity, by creating new nodes of policy innovation and leadership. Conversely, restricted budgetary resources and bureaucratic jurisdictional rivalry may create an environment of uncertainty and directionless aid policy based on inter-bureaucratic compromises.

As expected, the sum of political, economic, and administrative changes in the 1990s created a mixed bag for environmental aid policy. Scholars agree generally that policy innovation eluded the Japanese bureaucracy for much of the postwar era, but these events of the last decade made drastic changes and creative leadership next to impossible. The truncated political realignment, necessitated by the LDP's loss in the 1993 House of Representatives' election fragmented the party system in the Diet and made coalition politics inevitable. Beginning in 1994, the LDP resumed power, either in a coalition or as a sole cabinet party, but the policy leadership it exercised until 1993 evaporated. Other opposition parties championed environmental protection, but the politics of coalition government accorded them little room to create and sustain new policy. For example, the cabinet of Prime Minister Hosokawa Morihiro, crafted by a non-LDP coalition in the wake of the 1993 elections, included Hironaka Wakako as Director-General of the Environment Agency. Hironaka, a member of the Komeito, was well-known for her advocacy of environmental issues. Yet the coalition lasted less than a year and subsequent Environent Agency directors lacked the portfolio and recognition Hironaka brought to the post.

At the political agenda level, political reform overshadowed environmental policy in the Diet by the electoral stalemate, the political jockeying for administrative reforms, and prolonged recession. The recession, if anything, refocused political attention on economic growth as a top policy goal. Government fiscal policy consistently relied on Keynesian stimulus packages mostly domestic public works despite the lack of positive results. Political leadership in aid policy in the late 1990s was limited to a series of annual cutbacks in the aid budget. While environmental protection remained a part of the aid agenda, it increasingly competed with economic issues of the economy, both domestically and internationally. Policy makers perceived environmental protection and economic growth as mutually exclusive.

While environmental concerns have been a part of Japan's politics since the 1960's, there is a decided lack of voices at the national level urging a significant reconsideration and definition of environmental aid. Public opinion polls on foreign aid and Japan's international contributions tend to reflect the contradictions of environmental awareness. A nationwide survey on Japan's contribution to the UN, conducted in October, 2000, found that 45.7% of respondents favored environmental issues as an appropriate contribution, well ahead of human rights and social issues (Cabinet Office, 2000). The survey allowed for multiple responses, however, so it is unclear whether this environmental awareness constitutes solid support for environmental protection. Indeed, some aspects of this policy area appear decidedly unpopular. In a poll conducted two months later, only 12% of respondents thought the reduction of the flora and fauna reduction from economic development constituted an important issue requiring future resolution. This issue ranked the second lowest among the issues selected as requiring resolution. Most domestic environmental issues ranked significantly higher than international environmental issues (Kahoku Shimpo, 2001).

Despite marked improvement in Japan's domestic environment in the 1970s and 1980s, the truncated political realignment of the 1990s failed to create a domestic constituency for enhanced environmental foreign aid. In her recent survey of Japan's international environmental policy, Anny Wong (2001) found that the bureaucracy has assumed the lead role in defining environmental foreign policy. No other set of domestic actors– politicians, the business community, the media, academia, think tanks, or NGOs– possess either the interest or capability to significantly alter the bureaucratic perspective on this issue. Lam Peng-Er (1999) found that contrary to the experience of Western Europe and North America, the Japanese case demonstrated that replacement of materialist values with post materialist values never took place. Rather the two overlap. As a result, post materialist sensibilities supporting broader concern about the environment coexist with continuing concerns about traditional issues of economic growth and stability especially in the era of the Heisei recession. Economic growth and stability comprised the broad national consensus in the postwar political economy and public policies favored industrial development as a national priority. While environmental activism in Japan increased dramatically following a number of well publicized 'pollution cases' in the 1960s and early 1970s, policy makers continue to organize priorities according to material orientations. Unlike in Western Europe, which experienced the emergence of numerous 'green and ecological parties', Japanese political parties continued to emphasize the personalistic and materialistic orientations and values. Not surprising, none of the political parties that emerged since 1993 made the environment a policy priority.

As expected, the dearth of political parties focusing on environmental issues also correlates with the limited impact of environmental interest groups on public attitudes. Lise Skov (1996) demonstrates, for example, that the ecology boom of the early 1990s established an 'Earth Day' in Japan, but little else. The environmentalism became a faddish commodity to wear and consume, but not one based on any sophisticated or enduring attachment to ecologism. Moreover, the domestic and localized nature of these interest groups precludes significant impact on citizen attitudes about regional and global environmental issues. Further complicating the issue, environmental concerns tend to have lower salience than economic issues among the general public in most industrial democracies. Public awareness and concern tends to fluctuate in relation to other concerns, especially economic ones (Vogel and Kessler, 1998). The prolonged recession of the 1990's tended to concentrate disproportionate public attention on domestic economic issues.

Administrative reform affected the foreign aid program directly in two ways. The first is through consolidation and the second through ministerial reshuffling. Fierce budgetary competition and jurisdictional rivalry characterized the postwar Japanese bureaucracies. Beginning with the Hashimoto cabinet, the government has sought to reform and stream-line the Japanese bureaucracy and thereby increase the power of elected officials over bureaucrats. The old decentralized aid policy making structure, known as the 'four ministries and agencies' system (*yon shouchou taisei*), combined with an equally decentralized implementation process, contributed to bureaucratic entrenchment and recalcitrance.

Consolidation most directly affected the primary implementation agencies. In October 1998 the Overseas Economic Cooperation Fund, the primary foreign loan aid-implementing agency, was merged with the Export-Import Bank of Japan into the new Japan Bank for International Cooperation (JBIC). The two halves of the new bank continue to carry out their former functions, but the new agency represents a victory for the MITI perspective in foreign aid, as it ratifies the long-standing ambiguity between foreign aid and other forms of public finance to support the internationalization of Japanese companies. Under the ministerial reforms effected in January, 2001, oversight power regarding the functions of the former Overseas Economic Cooperation Fund (OECF), originally possessed by the Economic Planning Agency (EPA), transferred to the Ministry of Foreign Affairs (MFA). As a result of these reorganizations, both lead aid-implementing functions of the Japan International Cooperation Agency (JICA) and OECF came under the supervision of a single ministry for the first time since the inauguration of Japan's formal aid program in the 1960s. A proposal floated by the Koizumi cabinet's Office on Reform of Special Legal Entities in June, 2001, would further the consolidation by merging formally JICA and the Japan Bank for International Cooperation (JBIC).

Bureaucratic reshuffling has also affected aid policy-making. In January 2001, the Economic Planning Agency (EPA) combined with several other agencies to become the new Cabinet Planning Agency, in the process losing its jurisdiction over loan aid policy to MFA. The Ministry of International Trade and Industry (MITI) was renamed the Ministry of Economy and Industry and, but international economic cooperation remains in its portfolio. The Ministry of Finance (MF) suffered the greatest change, separating its functions into three agencies. The Finance Ministry's (*Zaimu-shou*) International Division retains jurisdiction over multilateral aid. Despite these changes, foreign aid policy formulation remains convoluted with all three ministries crafting policy.

A potential improvement consisted of upgrading the Environment Agency to ministerial status in January 2001. As the environment moved up on the aid agenda in the late 1980s and early 1990s, the Environment Agency expanded its role in aid policy making, acting as a voice of support for the new policy. To that extent, its new cabinet status should enhance that voice. Its Global Environment Division is given jurisdiction, *inter alia*, over overseas environmental cooperation. The ministry's portion of the aid budget, however, likely will remain small: the Environment Agency controlled less than 10% of the ODA budget in the late 1990s. The ministry's exclusion from the *yon shouchou taisei*, or its successor, decreases its ability to directly affect aid policy.

Administrative reform does little, if anything, however, to streamline the aid implementation process. More than a dozen agencies still receive some portion of the ODA budget each year. While the aid budget makes up a small percentage of the total government budget, it remains crucial for some agencies. JICA and the OECF depend on it as their raison d'etre; the Ministry of Agriculture, Forestry, and Fisheries views an expanded aid role as a necessary correlate to its declining domestic relevance and budgetary resources constraints. The best that has been achieved to date is the creation of the ODA Agencies Contact Council (*ODA Kankei Shouchou Renraku Kyougikai*) in March, 2000 designed to facilitate communications among implementing agencies.

Decentralization continues to foster divergent understandings of the nature and purpose of foreign aid. Most scholars agree that the main division in the aid program lies between the MFA and MITI. Each perceives aid in terms of its broader mission, and each continues the long-standing practice of issuing its own annual foreign aid 'white paper'. Furthermore, the contrasting policy orientations found in each agency remain in effect. MITI understands foreign aid as a portion of broader economic interactions (trade and DFI) intended to support Japanese industry abroad. Its policy of reintroducing tied aid in the form of yen loans in Japan's aid response to the 1997 Asian financial crisis, demonstrates the continuation of a mercantilist bent in that ministry's orientation. MFA, in contrast, sees the aid as closely related to Japan's international political position. It views aid as a tool of foreign policy with which to seek support from critical recipient countries and to demonstrate Japan global leadership in international affairs. A comparison of the 1992 ODA Charter and MITI's 1997 White Paper on Economic Cooperation illustrates this contrasting policy orientation. The former, produced under MFA auspices includes support for democratization, support for demilitarization, and support of the environment as fundamental principles to the aid program. MITI's 1997 White Paper, on the other hand, calls for greater privatization of economic cooperation with Asia, demonstrating a clear intent on reducing governmental aid flows in favor of expanded private sector trade and investment.

Lastly, administrative reform has done little or nothing to strengthen aid administration capacity. Despite continual official statements about the need to improve aid effectiveness and administrative capacity, the entire thrust of bureaucratic change in the 1990s has been to reduce the size of the national civil service, both in terms of number of agencies and personnel. This can hardly benefit an aid bureaucracy that is already small by international donor standards. There is a general consensus among scholars of Japan's foreign aid that a larger staff, particularly those with technical expertise, would go a long way toward the government's stated objective of increasing aid effectiveness. As we shall see below, technical transfer and project monitoring are important elements of the new environmental aid, and both require staff competencies not usually attributed to Japan's aid bureaucracy.

Overview of Environmental ODA

Environmental protection remains a policy commitment of the aid program. During the 1990s, evolving Japanese aid policies reflected a change that correlated with developments in other OECD nations and multilateral organizations including the World Bank and the IMF. The government began a concerted shift toward including environmental considerations in its foreign aid policy. Thus, the Japanese government's evolving policies came to mirror established OECD and multinational donor agencies' standards. Equally important, environmental protection cooperation provides a mechanism to demonstrate Japanese policy leadership in facing global issues (Asuka-Zhang, 2000).

The 1990s began with a series of policy statements, the first by Prime Minister Kaifu at the Arche Summit in 1989, to increase ODA for environmental purposes. At the 1992 Earth Summit in Rio de Janeiro, the Japanese government pledged $700 million in environmental aid over five years, a pledge which it fulfilled a year early in 1996. New policy initiatives also complemented funding increases during the decade. In 1992, the MFA published its ODA Charter, in which environmental protection, along with human rights, limitations on recipient government defense spending, and democratization, became priority areas for assistance. The same year MITI established its Green Aid Program to assist with industrial pollution control efforts in developing countries. Also since 1993, the Japanese and United States governments have collaborated on the Common Agenda as part of the bilateral New Economic Partnership. Environmental cooperation, along with global population, AIDS, international drug issues, and children's welfare, forms the core of that cooperation. Joint projects included coral reef protection, the establishment of a joint committee on environmental cooperation with Eastern Europe, and aid for a forest management-training center in the Philippines. Then in 1997, the MFA established the 'Initiative for Sustainable Development (ISD) toward the 21st Century'. Throughout the 1990s environmental protection and conservation remained stated policy objectives within the aid bureaucracy.

The Japanese government also improved environmental impact assessment procedures and requirements for aid projects. Between 1989 and 1992 both the OECF and JICA established guidelines to better insure environment-friendly implementation of aid projects (Potter, 1994). In 1993, the OECF established the Environment and Social Development Division, and upgraded it to the Environment and Social Development Office in 1997. In 1995, it also revised its project guidelines with emphasis on improving their effectiveness. The revised guidelines require recipient governments to undertake environmental impact assessments "for all projects with substantial environmental impacts" (OECF, 1998, 44), beginning in 1997. Environmental conditions have also been attached to the consultancy phase of project development (MITI, 1998), thereby helping to ensure that environmental considerations inform the project decision-making process from formulation to implementation. The assessment process remains flawed, however, because environmental considerations are usually not binding on contractors and follow-up assessment is rare (Dauvergne, 2000; Asuka-Zhang, 2000).

New lending rules now make it easier for aid recipients to apply for low interest and extended repayment schemes for environmental projects. Since 1997, loans for projects to combat global warming now carry a 0.75% interest rate with 40-year repayment periods, which are the lowest concession rate terms the Japanese government offers.

Despite the numerous positive developments involving environmental aid, the absolute volume of aid declined in the 1990s. Japan continues to channel a portion of its aid through multilateral organizations but the decline in ODA budgets, in tandem with the fiscal difficulties in the government as a whole, impacted negatively this kind of funding. In 1995, for example, multilateral aid comprised just over 28% of the total aid budget (Waga Kuni, 1996) from 1998 to 2000, multilateral contributions comprised just under 20% of the total (MFA, 2000). Japan remains the largest subscriber to the Asian Development Bank, an organisation in which Japan also exercises significant leadership. It remains a major contributor to the World Bank and the various UN development agencies. Consequently, Japan found it convenient to channel environmental aid funds through such agencies. It is the largest supporter of the International Timber Trade Organization (ITTO), discussed below, and the Tropical Forest Action Plan the ITTO administers. Japan also supports conservation and development efforts through the Global Environment Fund (GEF), Food and Agriculture Organization (FAO), United Nations Environment Program (UNEP), and the Consultative Group on International Agricultural Research (CGIAR). It co-financed conservation projects with the World Bank and the Asian Development Bank (ADB), and has used portions of its Japan Special Fund to support environmental projects in tandem with the ADB, World Bank, Interamerican Development Bank, and the African Development Bank.

These aid inititatives have been matched by a continued commitment to environmental issues in overall foreign policy. In 1992, Keidanren– Japan's largest business federation– inaugurated its Nature Conservation Fund to support environmental efforts in developing countries. By 2000 it had funded nearly 300 projects (Keidanren, 2000). Japan hosted the Third Session of the Conference of the Parties to the United Nations Framework Convention on Climate Change (COP3) in 1997. That meeting adopted the so-called Kyoto Protocol, which commits the parties to reducing greenhouse gases depending on their levels of economic development. The protocol laid the groundwork for the difficult negotiations at COP 6 in the Netherlands in November, 2000. Members of the Japanese delegation that played prominent leadership roles included Yoriko Kawaguchi, a former MITI official and managing director of Suntory, Ltd., who subsequently became Minister for the Environment. She chaired the panel on greenhouse gas emissions and forest absorption.

Table 8.1 presents official figures for environmental aid in the 1990s. Environmental ODA comprised roughly 15% to 25% of total aid in the 1990s, with the proportion increasing over time. The Foreign Ministry's 2000 annual report on ODA states that aid for environmental protection comprised one-third of the total aid budget in 1999. However, as Table 8.2 demonstrates, no environmental protection sector existed for most of the last decade. Official statistics still apportion aid amongst the traditional sectors found in Japan's aid program since the 1970s. This finding is consistent with Hook and Zhang's (1998) contention that ODA implementation in the 1990's, official pronouncements to the contrary notwithstanding, changed little from over the years. Where, then, is the aid for the environment?

Table 8.1 Japan's Environmental ODA, 1990-1999

Year	Amount (hundred million yen)	% of Total ODA
1990	1,654	12.4
1991	1,127	7.2
1992	2,803	16.9
1993	2,280	12.8
1994	1,941	14.1
1995	2,760	19.9
1996	4,632	27.0
1997	2,447	14.5
1998	4,138	25.7
1999	5,357	33.5

Source: *Waga Kuni no Seifu Kaihatsu Enjo* [Our Country's Development Assistance], vol. 1, (1996), Gaimusho Keizai Kyoryoku-kyoku, [MFA Economic Cooperation Division], Kokusai Kyoryoku Suishin Kyokai, Tokyo, p. 109; *Waga Kuni no Seifu Kaihatsu* Enjo vol. 1, (2000), Gaimusho Keizai Kyoryoku-kyoku, Kokusai Kyoryoku Suishin Kyokai, Tokyo, p. 108.

Table 8.2 Japan's Bilateral ODA by Sector, Selected Years

Sector	1993 (%)	1995 (%)	1998 (%)
Social Infrastructure	22.64	26.6	20.2
Economic Infrastructure	36.67	44.47	39.0
Productive Sectors	12.08	11.67	12.4
Commodity/Program Loans	3.67	2.17	11.6
Environmental Protection	0.0	0.0	1.0
Other	28.61	17.2	24.6

Source: *Waga Kuni no Seifu Kaihatsu Enjo*, vol. 1, (1994), Gaimusho Keizai Kyoryoku-kyoku, Kokusai Kyoryoku Suishin Kyokai, Tokyo, p. 123; *Waga Kuni no Seifu Kaihatsu Enjo*, vol. 1, (1996), Gaimusho Keizai Kyoryoku-kyoku, Kokusai Kyoryoku Suishin Kyokai, Tokyo, p. 109; *Waga Kuni no Seifu Kaihatsu Enjo* vol. 1, (1999), Gaimusho Keizai Kyoryoku-kyoku, Kokusai Kyoryoku Suishin Kyokai, Tokyo, p. 164.

Part of the aid program's environmental improvement in the last decade involved refraining from projects that clearly harm the environment. In the 1970's, JICA and the OECF supported private sector operation of the Philippine Sintering Corporation a Kawasaki subsidiary and the PASAR Copper Smelting Plant (also in the Philippines). Domestic and international environmental groups criticized widely this case as an example of Japan exporting industrial pollution overseas (Tsuru, 1999). Japanese aid also exacerbated the deforestation of tropical timber in Southeast Asia to meet domestic demand for wood and wood products (Dauvergne, 1997).

In reaction to strong criticism from NGOs and indigenous groups, the government suspended a number of high-profile projects including the Sardar Sardovar Dam in India in 1990 (part of the World Bank Narmada Dam complex); and a loan for the Calaca II coal-fired power plant in Luzon in 1992. It also demurred on a Philippine National Oil Corporation plan for a geothermal power plant in Mindanao in 1991 (Potter, 1994). The latter 1990's witnessed no such dramatic developments, suggesting that major advances in 'environmental aid' was achieved by eliminating environmentally detrimental projects from initial consideration.

A great deal of Japan's environmental aid consists of infrastructure and social development projects under a different rubric (Potter, 1994). The OECF lists as environmental aid the following: development projects for irrigation, water supply improvement, flood control, and waste disposal in addition to afforestation, pollution control, and other problems. If anything this tendency increased in the course of the last decade. In 1997, in addition to announcing the Kyoto Initiative, the government decided to expand fields eligible for environmental loan terms to also include urban mass transit systems that alleviate traffic congestion, hydroelectric projects, natural gas generating facilities, and rehabilitation of facilities to enhance energy and resource conservation (OECF, 1998). While good reason exists to consider such measures as contributing to protection of the environment, the ambiguity between traditional sectoral definitions and the new policy remain.

The ambiguous definition of environmental aid derives from two causes. First, despite statements about improving aid quality, volume remains the dominant measure of ODA. Japan emerged as the largest bilateral donor in 1989, and maintained that position since 1992. Its 1999 outlays, over $15 billion, was one and a half times larger than the United States, the second-largest OECD donor. As top donor, expectations suggest that Japan will continue to make significant contributions to the alleviation of environmental problems in developing countries (OECD, 1994).

Yet, environmental aid as a percentage of overall aid volume lagged behind total aid, averaging 15% of total ODA between 1990 and 1996. Fluctuating levels of such aid characterized the first half of the 1990s, with percentages ranging from a low of 7.2% in 1991 to a high of 27% in 1996. MFA (1999) claims that in 1998, 24% of total ODA went to environmental protection. The higher average of around one-quarter of ODA coincides with the expanded sectoral definition of environmental aid that went into effect at the time of the Kyoto Initiative in 1997.

Second, Japan defines environmental assistance in terms compatible with its traditional emphasis on loan aid for capital projects. Since 1992, the Japanese government equates environmental aid in terms of sustainable development, a term that appears repeatedly in official documents. Yet the ambiguity of the term creates confusion. The closest common definition that the international community arrived at derives from the Bruntland Commission in 1987. It defines development as that which "meets the needs of the present without compromising the ability of future generations to meet their own needs". Shigeto Tsuru (1999) notes that the document 'Agenda 21', issued at the Rio Summit, fails to define the term precisely, and further observes the tension between the goals of economic growth, sustainable development, and free trade put forth in that document. In practice, sustainable development can be variously defined to cover a series of issues.

The ambiguity pertaining to environmental aid and sustainable development is manifest in Japan's aid program. The vagueness of the term 'sustainable development' allows aid policy makers to fund a variety of projects that best meet the aid program's overall profile. Moreover, it accommodates the bifurcation in aid policy exemplified by the different approaches to which MFA and MITI subscribe. In keeping with its primary mission as the lead foreign policy agency, MFA's definition tends to reflect current international issues. Its 1996 statement on economic cooperation in the environmental sector defined such aid in terms of specific aid sectors, including improvement of the residential environment, water supply and sewage systems, waste disposal facilities; air and water pollution control measures; forestry conservation; disaster prevention; and natural environment conservation (MFA, 1997). All of these comprise sectors Japan funded previously. Its 1997 Initiative for Sustainable Development toward the 21st Century (ISD) added human security– expressed as the absence of environmental destruction that poses a threat to human existence– to the criterion enveloping sustainable development. The ISD reconfigured the definition-by-sector approach to include five priority sectors: air and water pollution; global warming (the centerpiece of the Kyoto COP3 summit); preservation of the natural environment; water problems; and development of environmental awareness (MFA, 1999). The ISD retains, however, the long-standing tendency of MFA to reduce its definition of environmental aid to a sectoral list.

MITI's rival Green Aid Plan, inaugurated in 1992, follows that agency's main mandate of industrial promotion. The Green Aid Plan provides Japanese expertise on pollution control to developing countries through technical assistance (largely through engineering associations closely affiliated with the ministry) intended to help recipients develop their own capacity to solve energy and environmental problems. The Green Aid Plan specifically excludes support for restoration from pollution damage (arguably another area of Japanese expertise), forest conservation, and desertification (MITI, 1999, 135-41). Its 1997 assessment of environmental issues in East Asia, the product of a ministry-sponsored research group composed solely of ministry officials and corporate representatives, focused on issues of industry, industrial pollution, and developing government environmental regulations. The report frankly stated that ODA should stimulate further private efforts at environmental conservation in East Asian countries. It further argued that, at current levels, aid could not be expected to alleviate significantly the environmental problems the region faces. The emphasis once again focuses on the industrial aspects of the problem. While overlap between the two ministries' approaches exists, (e.g. support for acid rain reduction) the two main agencies in the bilateral aid program operate their respective programs largely independent of one another. In neither case, moreover, do we find a comprehensive vision for environmental cooperation.

The International Tropical Timber Organization (ITTO) and Japan's role in it further highlights the ambiguities inherent in its approach to assistance for the environment. The ITTO, established in 1980 and headquartered in Yokohama beginning in 1986 provides Japanese policy makers with a unique opportunity to shape environmental policy dealing with deforestation. Japan plays a leading role in the organization: its financial contribution represented 34% of the organization's total budget in 1994 (Feinerman and Fujikura, 1998), and it remains the largest donor to the present. The organization's purpose, to develop tropical forests for timber production while at the same time preserving forest resources, reflects a conservationist rather than environmentalist orientation. In this sense, it both exploits and preserves tropical forests. Japan's position on tropical timber reflects its own history of managed forestry, consisting of timber exploitation and reforestation (Feinerman and Fujikura, 1998; Totman, 1998), and its conservationist orientation derives from being the world's largest tropical timber consumer. Japanese companies, some current contributors to the ITTO's voluntary fund and Japanese domestic timber management policies played a significant but indirect role in overexploitation of tropical forests in Southeast Asia (Dauvergne, 1997).

Only recently the ITTO shifted its orientation away from conservation and toward tropical timber protection. Its primary efforts have been directed at plantation reforestation. In 1994 the signatory states to the new ITTA agreed to trade tropical timber only from sustainably managed forests by 2000 (Feinerman and Fujikura, 1998, 277).

Feinerman and Fujikura criticize the ITTO and Japanese policy on tropical forestry as being overly reliant on the market. They note that "even as of 1997, Japan has no policy to limit the use of tropical timber despite the scale of domestic consumption, current and predicted" (277). Continual reliance on market mechanisms to determine tropical timber trade, combined with efforts at reforestation appears inadequate. Peter Dauvergne (1997) argues that Japanese ODA for forest conservation, bilateral and through the ITTO, does not offset past or current corporate practice. "Little evidence exists to concrete changes to

Japanese trade practices or to the attitudes of corporate leaders", (180-1) who fail to link corporate practice with deforestation. "Japanese government reforms have focused on reshaping the least potent element– ODA– and even these have made only marginal improvements" (181).

Support for NGOs

During the 1990s, NGOs increased their presence in environmental aid programs. Unlike traditional environmental citizen movements that become mired in confronting bureaucracies and operate in a highly localized manner, NGOs seek cooperation and possess an international focus. Both the MFA and the Ministry of Posts and Telecommunications (MPT) provide funding for NGOs. The MFA established its NGO Project Subsidy Scheme in 1989, providing funds for small-scale projects that cannot be effectively assisted by official agencies and which meet humanitarian criteria of contributing to local people's livelihoods and welfare. NGOs are eligible to receive subsidies of 1 to 10 million yen to cover up to one-half of total project non-operating costs and plan their projects independent of direct government involvement. To assist NGOs, the MFA established a Small-Scale Grant Aid Program disbursed by Japanese embassies to NGOs in developing countries. In 1990, the MPT established a separate International Volunteer Savings Scheme. Using its jurisdiction over the vast Japanese postal savings system, the MPT instituted a program by which subscribers could donate 20% of the interest on their savings for the promotion of international cooperation. Organizations may apply for assistance to fund travel, living expenses and wages of personnel needed to complete development projects overseas. In its first year of operation, the scheme disbursed 913 billion yen, about ten times as much as the MFA's NGO Project Subsidy Scheme (A Guide to Japan's Aid, 1992, 97-9).

Tables 8.4 and 8.5 show data by category of expenditure from the two major NGO support schemes. As the data shows, NGOs do not appear likely to augment the official environmental aid program in any meaningful way.

Environmental aid projects account for approximately 10% of each subsidy program in any given year. MFA's NGO support scheme remains a tiny portion of the overall aid budget, between two and four percent annually. In 1999 the ratio of NGO subsidies to the overall aid budget was 1 to 42, and the lowest among the top five OECD donor countries and the fourth lowest in the Development Assistance Committee (DAC) of the OECD (MFA, 1999). Both the MFA and MPT subsidy programs have been adversely affected by the general fiscal climate of the late 1990s, so it is doubtful that significant new government resources will be available in the near future.

Table 8.3 MFA Support for NGOs by Category (%), Selected Years

Category	1995	1996	1998
Medicine /Health	39.4	29.2	32.6
Agriculture	6.2	4.7	11.0
Technical Training	17.7	17.8	10.6
Women in Development	6.2	3.4	7.9
Environment	11.4	8.3	9.1
Regional Industry	7.3	9.2	3.7
Other	11.8	27.4	25.1

Source: Gaimusho [MFA], *Waga Kuni no Seifu Kaihatsu Enjo* [Our Country's Development Assistance], Tokyo: Keizai Kyoryoku Suishinkai, (1999), 196.

Table 8.4 MPT Support for NGOs by Sector (%), Selected Years

Sector/Year	1995	1996	1998	2000
Medicine /Health	33.2	31.3	33.2	35.4
Agriculture	12.7	13.6	12.7	15.5
Technical Training	8.7	10.1	8.7	7.1
Environment	33.2	22.2	23.8	23.6
Education	10.1	11.1	11.3	7.4
General Welfare	7.2	9.4	8.1	11.0
Food	1.8	1.9	1.8	0.0
Technical Training	8.7	10.1	1.8	0.0

Source: Ministry of Posts and Telecommunications [MPT]. URL http://www.zaimu.mpt.go.jp/tokei/indexe.html. Searched January 26, 2001: Yuseisho [MPT], *Kokusai Boranteia Chokin* [Almanac of International Volunteers], (2000), Okurasho Shuppankyoku, Tokyo.

The primary impact of NGOs continues to be limited mostly to specific projects. Agenda setting, in which civic groups attempt to alter official policy, currently appears to be beyond Japanese NGO capabilities (Potter, 1998). The MFA continues to view them as new to the field of development and thus institutionally weak. Alan Rix (1993) argues that the aid bureaucracy sees NGOs in instrumental terms, as conduits for promoting official views of foreign aid. He concludes that official agencies do not regard NGOs as partners in development. Recent interactions suggest that modal contacts involve application for subsidies by NGOs. While a few NGOs recently participated in the planning stages of specific projects, formal interactions appear to be of the 'Kondankai' type in which private organizations attend meetings arranged by bureaucrats. In short, the institutional links between voluntary and public development agencies remains shallow and defined largely by the bureaucracy.

Environmental ODA to Asia

Japan's ODA targeted the Asian region throughout the postwar period. Asian countries not only receive a disproportionate share of Japanese bilateral aid, typically 70% in any given year, it also became the locus of new Japanese aid initiatives. Recent examples include the Asian Monetary Fund (AMF) and the Miyazawa Initiative, both put forward in the wake of the 1997 Asian financial crisis. The abortive AMF, in particular, represented Japan's attempt to demonstrate active leadership in dealing with an Asian economic problem (Sudo, 2000, 108-9). If anything, the aid debates engendered by budgetary contractions in Japan since 1998 refocused ODA policy makers' attention on the region. In 1998, Japan's aid budget contracted by nearly one-third, disproportionately affecting Asian countries since they receive 90% of yen loans (OECF, 1999).

MITI's Green Aid Plan has focused solely on the region, with projects establishing environmental research centers in Thailand and China beginning in 1992, followed by Indonesia, the Philippines, Malaysia, India, and Vietnam over succeeding years. Japan has also tried out new measures in the region. In 1997, MFA began to work on the East Asian Acid Rain Monitoring Network under the auspices of its Initiative for Sustainable Development (ISD). That year it also established the Japan-China Model City Plan with the Chinese cities of Dalian, Chongqing, and Guiyang designed to encourage greater conservation efforts consistent with Japanese experience in those municipalities (Asuka-Zhang, 2000; Taya, 2000). It supports plantation afforestation efforts in Southeast Asia, a continuation of aid efforts which started in the 1980's (see Potter, 1994). For the most part, environmental aid to Asia followed the contours of the overall aid program– largely bilateral and project-based. These countries' experience reflects the promise and the limitations of Japan's environmental aid approach.

The emphasis on aid to Asia has its logic. Not only does the region represent a sphere of Japanese foreign policy priority, regional rapid economic growth increased the salience of environmental issues. MITI (1999) notes that rapid industrialization in the region resulted in rapid and severe acceleration of environmental problems. Past commercial relations between Japan and Asian countries dictate that regional environmental problems will involve Japan. Peter Dauvergne (1997) traced the links between Japanese companies and successive deforestation in the Philippines, Indonesia, and now Malaysia, and recent attempts to limit that damage. Moreover, as Asian countries have industrialized, they also have become a source of transnational pollution that affected Japan. China represents a potential threat to Japan's own environment. China's rapid industrialization, based on inefficient technologies created very high levels of sulfur emissions from industrial and other sources. A recent study comparing

China to the OECD countries showed 1996 levels of sulfur emissions produced by that country to be second only to the United States (which has a much larger economy) and well above levels produced by the other developed countries (Washizu and et. al, 2000, 138.) Those emissions contribute to a growing problem of acid rain that falls on the Korean peninsula and Japan. Thus, providing China with technology to address sulfur emissions represent enlightened Japanese self-interest. In 2001, amidst a serious review of bilateral aid to China that was sure to result in reduced allocations, the Japanese government announced its continued commitment to environmental aid to China for that reason (Asahi, June 4, 2001).

The interaction between host countries and the aid provider determine the extent to which the policies succeed. While aid policy formulation initially takes place in Tokyo, its success or failure also involves the host countries' ability to use the aid and benefit from it. Yet, scholars consistently overlook recipient government preferences as an aspect of the foreign aid program funding (Potter, 1996). Those preferences are crucial to assessing Japan's ability to meet its commitments. Indifference in recipient governments will limit environmental aid effectiveness. Developing countries, moreover, do not perceive the merits of environmental protection in the same way as developed countries do. The 1992 Rio Summit and subsequent international fora demonstrated the tradeoff between rapid economic growth and environmental preservation, choice developing countries are reluctant to make. Furthermore, powerful patron-client relationships in key Asian countries support unsustainable exploitation of natural resources as a necessary condition of regime maintenance (Dauvergne, 1997). A 1991 survey by the Economic Planning Agency found developing country officials evenly split between those who supported greater levels of environmental protection and those who felt that environmental protection efforts should be carried out "if they do not damage economic growth". Moreover, a significant minority considered economic growth to be a main priority (EPA, 1991, 87.)

Such sentiments are of particular importance to Japan because it relies on recipient government's requests for project funding. With the partial exception of China (Asuka-Zhang, 2000), Japan will consider financing aid projects only when the host nation's agency provides an official request for funding. The request principle represents basic aid philosophy, constituting a unique feature of Japan's aid programs (Sudo, forthcoming). In any case, the overall priorities of recipient governments figure in the calculations for funding in terms of which projects ultimately receive funding and the extent of appropriated monies.

In Asian cases that Japan provides foreign aid, environmental requests represent a small minority of cases. Instead, the recipient priorities reflect the salience of economic and technological issues confronting the recipients. A 1990 survey of Southeast Asian political and economic leaders revealed a strong preference for Japan's greatest contribution to continue in the area of economic and technological development. Additionally, environmental protection efforts ranked low on their list of priorities in that survey (Kansai Doyukai Kokusai Mondai Iinkai, 1990, 95). During a state visit to Japan to attend a World Bank-sponsored donors' meeting in June 2001, Cambodian Prime Minister Hun Sen outlined six priority areas for which his government wanted Japanese ODA; none was for environmental conservation. The 1997 financial crisis in the region reinforced that predisposition toward economic and technological aid.

Asian governments possess a relatively new awareness about environmental aid. While most governments in the region now have environmental conservation agencies, their attention to such issues dates mostly from the late 1980s and early 1990s. New initiatives and bureaucratic arrangements take time to solidify, and new agencies often face hostility from existing agencies threatened by the new agencies' mandates. Years of governmental preoccupation with economic development and the lack of foreign aid, until recently, for environmental abatement and protection, have made it difficult for environment agencies throughout Asia to muster the financial resources or the political capital necessary to enact major environmental reforms. An earlier study (Potter, 1994) cited cases from Thailand and Indonesia and concluded that the environment agencies in those countries suffered in their attempts to sway policy from inadequate technical expertise and mandates limited largely to data collection and policy advice. Typically, in 1993 the Indonesian government established an organization to protect tropical timber, composed of companies that had been granted timber licenses. Given Indonesia's forestry record under the New Order (see Dauvergne, 1997), this conservation policy amounted to setting the fox to guard the henhouse. Only modest improvements took place over the past decade.

In its 1997 assessment of the Asian environment, a MITI advisory panel listed lack of funding and inadequate technical expertise as continuing limitations on government efforts to implement environmental measures. In a recent study of Chinese compliance with international environmental treaties, Michael Oksenberg and Economy (1998) found that a lack of funding, inadequate technical training, and insufficient and overlapping jurisdictions all hampered efforts at environmental conservation. Finally, earlier research (Potter, 1996) suggests that new agencies and mandates in developing country governments confront a steep learning curve as they attempt to negotiate Japan's aid system for the first time. Significant delays in concluding aid agreements and subversion of agency goals occur as they attempt to accommodate donor comparative advantages and preferences.

As a result of the preoccupation with economic development and the bureaucratic maneuvering required by the aid recipient, interest in Japan's environmental aid among Asian nations remain sub-optimal. A 1997 MITI study admitted as much, noting that "it has been difficult to get requests from developing countries, and especially in the pollution control and global environment fields, requested have extremely limited" (33). MITI targets precisely these areas under the Green Aid Plan. Yet, between 1992 and 1995 pollution control comprised only 13% of total bilateral environmental ODA; meanwhile, sewer and water projects accounted for two-thirds of such aid (34). In sum, the redefinition of traditional infrastructure sectors as environmental aid looks less like sleight of hand and more like an attempt to find common ground with key recipients.

Recipient ambivalence about environmental preservation indirectly impacts ODA. Most Asian countries are long time recipients of Japanese aid, with bilateral programs dating from the 1960's and 1970's in many cases. Incrementalism results in Japanese aid commitments in the 1990's for the same and similar projects it previously supported. Some of this subsequent aid supports efforts to reform the technology of power plants, a significant improvement for local environmental conditions. However, the demarcation between developmental and environmental aid remains unclear and much of it remains allocated towards projects that reflect minor environmental orientations.

Recipient capabilities pose another problem. In principle, the OECF now requires environmental impact assessments on all loan projects, which are conducted by recipient governments prior to the commitment of funds. Given the lack of technical skills and funding available for such work in developing country governments, however, the Japanese government found it expedient to provide assistance for EIAs (Environmental Impact Assessment) (OECF, 1998). Given the low levels of manpower in the aid field, however, real limits exist in terms of how much aid personnel can do in this area. Moreover, recipient government commitments to the maintenance of environmental aid projects, once the donor terminates its support remains an uncertain proposition in some countries (Taya, 2000).

As noted above, current definitions of what constitutes environmental aid remain elusive and ambiguous. Current discussions between Vietnam and Japan highlight the ambiguity of environmental aid definitions. In 1998, Japan and Vietnam formalized a long list of development projects to be considered for ODA funding between 1999 and 2001 (Potter, 1996). Proposed 'environmental projects' included:

- Installation of equipment to existing thermal power plants to mitigate environmental impacts;
- Sea dike construction and drainage improvement to alleviate coastal flooding in the Mekong Delta and Ho Chi Minh City;
- Improvement of solid waste disposal in Hanoi and Ho Chi Minh City; and

- Construction of a satellite imaging system to improve monitoring of natural resources and the environment.

Interestingly, projects to construct wind power plants and rehabilitation of an operating thermal power plant "for improving generation efficiency and environmental impact" were included under a separate 'power' category (MFA, 1998). In practice, it appears that in the Vietnamese and other Southeast Asian recipient cases, environmental projects are considered as such based only on interest and repayment conditions for environmental projects outlined above.

Two environmental projects, one in China and another in Nepal, illustrate the successes and difficulties of Japan's technical assistance capabilities. The Chinese project involved the provision of environmental expertise and the construction of a training center in Shanghai in the early 1990s. In her review of the project, Taya Chikako (2000) argues that the provision of experts and the funding of facilities succeeded only partially. Experts, who used pollution control experience from Osaka, formed the core of technical experts assigned to this project. Two obstacles hindered utilization of the received assistance. First, the original intention– to use the center to train environmental experts throughout East Asia– failed to materialize because many Asian engineers and scientists perceived the field of environmental engineering as limited in career opportunities. Second, she notes that the highly centralized nature of Chinese administration acts as a serious brake on the lateral transfer of information and expertise between agencies even within China. As a result, the value of Japanese technical assistance provided employment for Japanese scientists but failed to benefit the recipient county.

In contrast to the Chinese case, the Nepali example succeeded because the Japanese worked with local volunteers and used appropriate technology to address problems as perceived by local residents. Taya acknowledges the success of a technical assistance project that sought to improve the use of natural resources by local people in Nepal. The distinguishing characteristic of the project, the use of resident Japan Overseas Cooperation Volunteers (JOCV) volunteers who generated conservation proposals, provided greater potential for programmatic success. Furthermore, she notes that the continuance of the project, post-aid, increased with local participation and their high regard for it. This model, similar to the one used by the US Peace Corp and other volunteer agencies succeed at the local level rather than national level. Its impact on aid budget and technical resources remains limited, thereby making them less likely to receive the support of the Japanese aid community and the host country governments.

A final issue involves aid tying. MITI enthusiastically promoted the transfer of pollution abatement technology from Japan to Asia on the grounds that Japan has a great deal of experience in the development of such equipment.

Indeed, a significant portion of regional pollution abatement projects includes installation of abatement equipment in power plants and other large-scale facilities supported by earlier yen loans. Such assistance raises the appearance of inflexibility and impropriety as the loans become contingent on service provision by Japanese contractors. Despite widespread international criticism of aid tying in the 1970's and 1980's, Japan in 1997 revived the practice for loans that carry the special environmental loan interest rates. In 1998 MITI further announced the resumption of tied loans under the Miyazawa Plan, which provided aid to alleviate the 1997 Asian financial crisis. Chris Johnstone (1998) argues that the resumption of aid tying will once again link environmental aid to Japanese commercial interests.

Conversely, Shouchuan Asuka-Zhang (2000) contends that the overall diminution in the awarding of project contracts to Japanese companies in the last decade limits the amount of Japanese pollution technology export. Asuka-Zhang notes that environmental aid and aid in general declined according to OECF data from 1995 to 1998. Data from OECF annual reports for prime contracts awarded for large-scale environmental aid projects (the OECF baseline is one hundred million yen, and it does not provide public data for contracts smaller than that) in Asia, Japanese companies do not figure prominently. Mostly European companies and occasionally Chinese firms successfully bid on environmental projects in Southeast Asia. Despite the smaller share of environmental expertise by Japanese firms, several Japanese consultancies, including Pacific Consultants and Nippon Koei (both have decades of experience in the region), still receive significant awards for the development of project outlines and guidelines.

Despite shrinking ODA figures and the declining market share of Japanese firms in environmental consulting, Japan still possesses a strong opportunity for becoming a major environmental actor in the Asia region. Japan possesses the necessary funds and technical expertise for providing leadership and other Asian countries are gradually increasing their concern over issues of environment and conservation. However, greater export of Japanese technology via the aid program will surely raise objections in Asian capitals about a return to a mercantilist aid strategy. Policy makers in Japan must devise the appropriate mechanism and policy guidelines for administering aid. The Nepali case noted above seems promising in this regard.

Conclusion

How does Japan's environmental foreign aid policy measure up at century's end? While Japan remains mired in a decade long recession, an increasing commitment to environmental aid exists. Despite a decade of fiscal and bureaucratic retrenchment the share of environmental aid as a percentage of ODA increased in the past decade. Furthermore, Japanese bureaucrats possess a wealth of experience from the 1990s, which should guide the formulation and implementation of Japan's environmental aid program. As top bilateral aid donor, Japan will remain a significant source of environmental assistance for the foreseeable future, even in terms of grants and technical assistance, which together comprise one quarter of the aid budget. Given donor fatigue and absolutely smaller technical assistance and grant programs in other donor countries, Japan's environmental grants and technical assistance will constitute a significant contribution simply because of the size of Japan's aid program relative to other donors. This coupled with Japan's tradition of concentrating aid on the Asian region bodes well for Asian nations that seek to tap into these resources. To date, Japan is the leading bilateral donor in every country. Whether Asian countries are interested in such aid remains a problem.

As for environmental aid effectiveness, a murkier picture emerges. Given shrinking budgets and very modest increases in aid staff over the 1990's, Japan's aid program cannot significantly enhance its oversight and follow-up functions. The Overseas Economic Cooperation Fund's (OECF) policy of requiring recipient governments to carry out environmental impact assessments on proposed projects externalizes a function it cannot implement in-house. The loose definition of what constitutes an environmental aid project also complicates the issue because foreign aid will increasingly need to satisfy multiple expectations.

Finally, Japanese policy leadership remains weak, despite the fact that top donor status carries with it the expectation of policy initiative. As noted elsewhere (Potter, 1994) Japan's environmental aid policy, like its environmental foreign policy in general, emerged in reaction to the opening of a transnational policy window in the 1980's. Globalization and regionalism prompted the development of Japanese environmental aid policies on a reactive, rather than proactive basis. In this sense, Japanese foreign policy reflects a reactive tendency and innovation remains elusive. The use of terms like 'Initiative for Sustainable Development' not only conform to widely used terminology but also masks a lack of internal consensus regarding the formulation, implementation, and evaluation of Japanese environmental aid. While administrative reform partially reduced the decentralized nature of aid policy making, bureaucratic inertia in Japan remains the dominant modus operandi. To date, the aid bureaucracies remain unable to craft an innovative role in international environmental protection.

In sum, while Japan's concern about its aid policy reflects the current thinking in Europe and the United States, its actions primarily adverse effects Japan's investment and aid on the environment in recipient countries. While avenues exist for developing countries to avail themselves of Japanese environmental aid, they must navigate a complicated and contradictory Japanese bureaucracy. While greater incentives for recipients exist, Japan's foreign aid must improve significantly before it can be classified 'green'. Incrementalism and bureaucratic balancing, both within Japan and between the recipient country and Japan, remain the order of the day.

References

Asuka-Zhang, S. (2000), 'Greening and Decarbonizing: Japan's Development Assistance', *East Asia*, vol. 18, pp. 75-95.

Dauvergne, P. (1997), *Shadows in the Forest: Japan and the Politics of Timber in Southeast Asia*, MIT Press, Cambridge.

Dauvergne, P. (2000), 'The Rise of an Environmental Superpower? Evaluating Japanese Environmental Aid to Southeast Asia', in J. Maswood, (ed.), *Japan and East Asian Regionalism*, Routledge, London, pp. 53-67.

Feinerman, J. and Fujikura, K. (1998), 'Japan: Consensus-Based Compliance', in E. B. Weiss and H. K. Jacobson, (eds.), *Engaging Countries: Strengthening Compliance with International Environmental Accords*, MIT Press, Cambridge, pp. 253-90.

Gaimusho Keizai Kyoryokukyoku (2000), *Waga Kuni no Seifu Kaihatsu Enjo* [Japan's Official Development Assistance], Keizai Kyoryoku Suishinkai [Association for the Promotion of Economic Cooperation], Tokyo.

Gaimusho Keizai Kyoryokukyoku (1999), *Waga Kuni no Seifu Kaihatsu Enjo*, Keizai Kyoryoku Suishinkai, Tokyo.

Gaimusho Keizai Kyoryokukyoku (1996), *Waga Kuni no Seifu Kaihatsu Enjo*, Keizai Kyoryoku Suishinkai, Tokyo.

Gaimusho Keizai Kyoryokukyoku (1994), *Waga Kuni no Seifu Kaihatsu Enjo*, Keizai Kyoryoku Suishinkai, Tokyo.

Hook, S. and Zhang, G. (1998), 'Japan's Aid Policy Since the Cold War: Rhetoric and Reality', *Asian Survey*, Vol. 38, pp. 1051-66.

Kahoku Shimpo [Tohoku Region Newspaper], January 1, 2001. p.1.

Kansai Doyukai Kokusai Mondai Iinkai (1990), 'Keizai Kyoryoku wa Nozomu ga Kankyo Hokai wa Gomen', [Economic Development is Desirable but Not With Environmental Degradation], *Kokusai Kaihatsu Janaru* [International Development Journal] (April) 95.

Lam, P. (1999), *Green Politics in Japan*, Routledge, London.

Ministry of Foreign Affairs of Japan (1997), *Japanese Economic Cooperation in the Environmental Sector*, http://www.mofa.go.jp/policy/global/environment/pamph/199706/ evn_sect.html., Searched December20, 2000.

Ministry of Foreign Affairs of Japan (1998), *Long List of Future Candidate Projects for Vietnam (FY 1999, FY2001)*. http://www.mofa.go.jp/policy/oda/longlist/ list.html., Searched January 26, 2001.

Oksenburg, M. and Economy, E. (1998), 'China: Implementation Under Economic Growth and Market Reform', in E.B. Weiss and H.K. Jacobson, (eds.), *Engaging Countries: Strengthening Compliance with International Environmental Accords*, MIT Press, Cambridge, pp. 353-94.

Organisation for Economic Cooperation and Development (1994), *OECD Environmental Performance Reviews: Japan*, Organisation for Economic Cooperation and Development, Paris.

Overseas Economic Cooperation Fund (1999), *Annual Report*, Overseas Economic Cooperation Fund, Tokyo.

Overseas Economic Cooperation Fund (1998), *Annual Report*, Overseas Economic Cooperation Fund, Tokyo.
Potter, D. (1999), NGOs and Japan's Role in Post-Cold War Asia, in W. Head and E. Clausen, (ed.s.)., *Weaving a New Tapestry: Asia in the Post-Cold War World*, Praeger, Westport, pp. 189-209.
Potter, D. (1996), *Japan's Foreign Aid to Thailand and the Philippines*, St. Martin's Press, New York.
Potter, D. (1994), 'Assessing Japan's Environmental Aid Policy', *Pacific Affairs*, vol. 67, pp. 200-15.
Skov, L. (1995), 'Environmentalism Seen Through Japanese Women's Magazines', in L. Skov and B. Moeran, (ed.s.), *Women, Media, and Consumption in Japan*, Curzon Press., Surrey, pp. 170-96.
Sudo, S. (forthcoming), *The International Relations of Japan and Southeast Asia*, Routledge, London.
Sudo S., (2000), 'Toward a Japan-U.S.-ASEAN Nexus', in M. Nishihara, (ed.), *The Japan-US Alliance*, Tokyo: Japan Center for International Education, Tokyo, pp. 103-20.
Taya, C. (2000), *ODA to Ningen no Anzen Hosho* [ODA and Human Security], Yuhikaku, Tokyo.
Totman, C. (1998), *The Green Archipelago: Forestry in Preindustrial Japan*, Ohio University Press, Athens.
Tsuru, S. (1999), *The Political Economy of the Environment*, Athlone Press, London.
Tsushosangyosho Keizai Kyoryoku Kyoku [MITI Economic Cooperation Bureau] (1999), *Keizai Kyoroku no Genjo to Mondaiten* [Conditions and Problems of Economic Cooperation], Tsushosangyo Chosakai Shuppanbu, Tokyo.
Tsushosangyosho Tsusho Seisaku Kyoku (1997), *Ajia no Kankyo no Genjo to Kadai* [Conditions and Issues of Asia's Environment], Tsuhosangyo Chosakai Shuppanbu, Tokyo.
Vogel, D. and Kessler,T. (1998), 'How Compliance Happens and Doesn't Happen Domestically', in E. Weiss and H. Jacobson, (eds.), *Engaging Countries: Strengthening Compliance with International Environmental Accords*, Cambridge: MIT Press, Cambridge, pp. 19-37.
Washizu, A. and et. al, (2000), 'Chugoku ni Okeru SOx Hishutsu no Jitsujo Bunseki', [The Study of the Current Status of Chinese SOx Emissions], in T. Kojima, (ed.), *Chugoku no Kankyo Mondai* [China's Environmental Problems], Keio Gijuku Daigaku Shuppankai, Tokyo, pp. 131-80.
Wong, A. (2001), *The Roots of Japan's International Environmental Policies*, Garland, New York.
Yuseisho [MPT] (2000), *Kokusai Boranteia Chokin* [International Volunteer Savings Fund], 2000 Nen Hen [Annual Edition], Okurasho Shuppankyoku, Tokyo.

Chapter 9

Prospects for a Regional Human Rights Mechanism in East Asia

Hidetoshi Hashimoto

Introduction

Over the last thirty years, and especially during the post-Cold War era of the 1990s, non-governmental organizations' (NGOs) and inter-governmental organizations' (IGOs) role in international politics increased dramatically. It appeared that increased transnational issues of the environment, AIDS, trade, and human rights' advocacy would create a era of international politics, based on IGOs, NGOs, corporations, and regional mechanisms and regimes. At the same time, the power of the state experienced relative decline in contrast to the years following World War II. Despite these changes, some regions of the world, especially Europe experienced greater integration and transnational activities through the European Union. Other regions, in particular East Asia, many states derived its legitimacy through the promotion of economic nationalism, regional cooperation remained fairly weak and civil society existed in an embryonic stage. However, democratization and globalization finally impacted East Asia in the 1980s, with increasingly 'free and fair' elections being held in South Korea, Taiwan, the Philippines, and Thailand. The 1990s experienced a plethora of NGOs in East Asia as civil society throughout the region strengthened.

In 1995, 200 East Asian non-governmental organizations (NGOs) banded together to draft the 'Asian Human Rights Charter: Our Common Humanity'. A remarkable exercise in regional cooperation, the charter's promulgation in 1998 in Kwangju South Korea raises the question of whether a parallel governmental initiative might someday evolve. Regional inter-governmental human rights organizations (RIGHROs) share similar characteristics with regimes and regional inter-governmental organizations (RIGOs) evident for some time in Europe, the Americas and Africa. The foundation for these regional human rights regimes include treaties such as the European Convention for the Protection of Human Rights and Fundamental Freedoms (1950) and its eight supplements; the Inter-American Convention on Human Rights (1969) as adopted through the Organization of American States (OAS);

and the African Convention on Human and Peoples' Rights (1981) adopted through the Organization of African Unity (OAU). Regimes reflect a regional orientation toward human rights issues enforced by emerging supranational organizations, states, and NGOs. To date, however, these types of mechanisms promoting regional cooperation and problem solving remain elusive in the East Asian region.

This chapter investigates the prospects of establishing a regional human rights mechanism in East Asia, focusing on the contributions of nongovernmental organizations (NGOs) to its development. In addition to exploring the progress and obstacles in creating a regional human rights mechanism in Asia, this chapter reports the results of a survey and a series of interviews conducted to assess the attitude of NGOs toward the creation of an East Asian RIGHRO. Realizing the limitations of states in the creation of a RIGHRO, based on past relations among Asian states and the strong levels of attachment to the concept of 'national sovereignty', this chapter also explores the extent and methods by which NGOs can assist in its creation. Historically, NGOs played little known but critically important roles in the development of intergovernmental human rights organizations. Evidence from the survey and interviews suggests strong support among NGO staff for creating an East Asian RIHGO. Furthermore, interviews and survey question responses reveal a number of specific obstacles that hindered the development of an East Asian RIGHRO.

Evaluating Effectiveness of Regional Human Rights Mechanisms

Historically, regional human rights mechanisms proved more effective and useful for promoting and protecting human rights than established multinational human rights mechanisms available through the United Nations. While UN affiliated entities, including the Human Rights Committee and the Committee Against Torture serve a vital purpose, their effectiveness overlooks regional particularities involving the needs, priorities, and conditions of the countries within particular regions. Thus, the United Nations encourages the establishment of regional human rights regimes, justified as essential elements in any successful international human rights system in a diverse, conflict-ridden world.

Conceptual frameworks such as functionalism (Ashworth and Long, 1999; Thompson, 1979; Wallerstein, 1979; and Haas, 1964), regional integration (Mattli, 1999; Kim, 1998; Mansfield and Milner, 1997; Cantori and Spiegel, 1970; Deutsch et al., 1969; and Nye, 1968), interdependence (Keohane and Nye, 2000; and McKibbin, 1994), and global civil society (Pomeranz and Topik, 2001; Bull and Watson, 1985; and Mitrany, 1966) best explain the emergence of RIGOs. Scholars recognize increasingly the interdependent nature of international relations based on global cooperation (e.g., networking, collaboration, coalitions, and alliances) with diminishing impact of national cultures, economies and borders. Functionalists call this web of interdependence 'functional integration'. Functional activities include a wide range of spheres involving social, cultural, economic and humanitarian concerns.

Since the end of World War II, functional integration among the countries in East Asia increased steadily as bilateral and regional trade relations flourished. The increasing flows of capital, goods, services, investments, communications, tourists and cultural exchanges permit reference to East Asia as a complex regional political and economic entity. Many expect the complexity to increase over the next few decades at a pace much faster than many other regions of the world.

According to functionalist theory, the web of mutually dependent linkages may lead to political, social, economic and cultural institutional arrangements and connections. Despite the tense relations between North and South Korea recent prospects for cooperation increased with President Kim Dae-Jung's visit to Pyongyang. In the case of the People's Republic of China (PRC) and Taiwan, political and military relations remain unsettled, but trade links between the two have become well entrenched with PR China becoming the major destination of Taiwanese capital. In East Asia, geographical proximity, common cultural tradition and heritage, and technological advancement in communications and transportation provide the impetus for functional collaboration, which increases awareness that "we share a common destiny" (Kim, 1998). Regional integration may gradually transfer power from the sovereign state to new regional structures and arrangements or strengthen existing ones, including Asian Pacific Economic Cooperation (APEC), Association of South East Asian Nations (ASEAN), and the Asian Development Bank (ADB). From these older institutions arrangements, an Asian Union (AU) or East Asian Forum (EAF) could emerge.

Functional integration takes place not only in commerce and cultural exchange arenas but in the field of human rights as well (Christenson, 1997; Olivera and Tandon, 1994). NGOs, including those oriented towards human rights exhibit the behavior of transnational 'sovereign-free-actors', by establishing strategic linkages across national borders (Rosenau, 1990). NGOs communicate, collaborate and build relationships across national boundaries through extensive transnational consultation, meetings, and exchange of information. NGOs transcend the territoriality of the state and operate across borders as they deal with complex and sensitive issues (Gordenker and Weiss, 1996). Human rights NGOs facilitate democratization and seek to build a human rights regime and culture. The web of linkages created represent regional integration in East Asia.

NGO Leaderships' Values and Beliefs Regarding RIGHRO

Evidence from interviews and surveys of leaders from NGOs indigenous to Japan, South Korea, Taiwan, Hong Kong and Mongolia and international NGOs which focus their activities in East Asia suggest that NGOs play an important role in crafting a RIGHRO in East Asia. The leadership of the NGO reveals support for, indifference to, or opposition to, regional integration for the formation of East Asian human rights institutions. Their diverse views tells us much about the range of their views and the substance of their concerns and remaining challenges regarding the formation for a RIGHRO. Twenty-four NGOs responded to the mailed questionnaire, and thirteen in-depth interviews both, by mail and in person, of international experts constitute the source of the data analyzed in the following sections.

For this study questionnaires were sent to 128 human rights NGOs and 45 individuals in South Korea, Japan, Taiwan, Hong Kong, Mongolia, The Philippines and Indonesia. The NGOs that responded numbered twenty-four (24), accounting for an 18.8% mail return. They identified themselves and their primary focus according to the following categories as depicted in Table 9.1.

While the selection of NGOs do not reflect a stratified sample, by any means, they are fairly representative of the types of organizations involved in human rights activities throughout Asia. These organizations reflect the diversity NGOs foci, including country, region or global orientations. This broad selection allows an examination of the goals, mission, and strategies of NGOs resident in Asia.

Table 9.2 provides background information on the interviewees' expertise and country of origin. The experts selected represent half dozen nationalities, five different occupational types and present residence in five countries. The primary backgrounds as depicted in the table include law, education, and NGO administration. All interviewees selected possess experience with human rights issues in general and specifically as it applies to East and South East Asia.

NGOs and Regional Institution Building?

From the point of view of those promoting RIGO development, the most effective human rights implementation systems consist of regional mechanisms (Leary, 1990, 13). Experts agree that regional arrangements take into account similar cultural, legal, and intellectual traditions. At the same time, the lack of enforcement frequently stymies the effectiveness of these

Table 9.1 NGOs Surveyed

Organization Name	Origin Country	Operational Foci
Taiwan Association for Human Rights	Taiwan	Taiwan
Asian Center for the Progress of Peoples	Hong Kong	East and S. East Asia
Asia Monitor Resource Center	Hong Kong	East and S. East Asia
Christian Conference of Asia	Hong Kong	East and S. East Asia
Asian Human Rights Commission	Hong Kong	East and S. East Asia
Information Center for Human Rights and Democratic Movement	Hong Kong	Hong Kong
Jesuit Social Center	Japan	East and S. East Asia
The Investigation Team on the Truth About Forced Korean Laborers in Japan	Japan	Japan
The Association for Solidarity with Foreign Migrant Workers	Japan	Japan
Women's Democratic Club	Japan	Japan
Japan Federation of Bar Association	Japan	Japan
All Japan Federation of Buraku Liberation Movement	Japan	East and S. E. Asia
Asia-Pacific Human Rights Information Center	Japan	Asia and global
The Committee of World Conference on Religion and Peace	Japan	South Korea
People's Solidarity for Participatory Democracy	South Korea	South Korea
Human Rights Committee for the Korea Youth Progress Party	South Korea	South Korea
The Lawyers for a Democratic Society	South Korea	South Korea
The International Human Rights of Korea	South Korea	South East Asia
Working Group for an ASEAN Human Rights Mechanism	The Philippines	Mongolia
The Mongolian Human Rights Committee	Mongolia	Mongolia
Mongolia Committee	Mongolia	China
Human Rights in China	United States	East and S. E. Asia
Human Rights Watch Asia	United States	US and Global
Amnesty International/ USA	United States	Global

Notes: NGOs broken down by type: International organization (INGO)= 6; Regional organization (RO)=7; National organization (NO) =10; and Local community organization (LC)=1.

organizations. RIGOs possessing legally binding authority perform better than those lacking a regional support mechanism. For example, the regional court in Strasbourg decides cases authoritatively with full jurisdiction. However, no UN court exists with a comparable court mechanism covering the full range of human rights and UN Conventions lack enforcement mechanisms and procedures. While UN established international human rights standards exist, the protection mechanisms remain elusive and institutionalized weakly. As a result, increased activity exists to establish the International Criminal Court (ICC), which primarily deals with genocide, crimes against humanity, war crimes, and the crime of aggression (Lee, et. al, 1999).

Table 9.2 Characteristics of Leaders Interviewed

Occupation	Nationality	Position*	Residence
Professor	Korean	No	South Korea
Professor	Indonesian	No	Indonesia
Attorney	Taiwanese	No	Taiwan
Professor	American	No	Japan
Professor	Japanese	No	Japan
Professor	Korean	No	Japan
Professor	Korean	No	Japan
Director	US	Yes	United States
Director	US	Yes	United States
Vice Chair	Chinese	Yes	United States
Director	US	Yes	United States
Director	Unknown (not US)	Yes	United States
Professor	Chinese	Yes	United States

Notes: *Position refers to whether the person held a position with an IGO or NGO.

Ideally, as in the European case, RIGOs supplement and do not compete with the UN mechanisms and procedures but provide the benefits of decentralized authority. Decentralization of authority often creates greater legitimacy at the local levels. For example, an NGO conference in Bangkok in 1993 complained about the need to send human rights reports to distant Geneva and New York instead of to a more convenient regional venue. As with all regions of the world, the problems in Asia have regional characteristics and embedded networks (e.g., trafficking of women, drug trade, and child prostitution). Regional problems require regional coordination because the sources of the problem, in addition to the solutions, exist within the region. In the area of human rights, for example, a RIGHRO could address human rights in the context of regional economic development. For example, while many assume the universality of basic human rights, human rights issues dealing with migrant labor flows from less to more prosperous Asian countries should be addressed within the conditions of the region (i.e., level of economic development). In 1993, the Bangkok NGO Workshop of Human Rights in Asia concluded that remedial procedures for human rights violations are too important to consign to the Palais des Nations in Geneva, Switzerland. Because the global human rights protection mechanisms developed in the context of Western values and standard of living, it fails to address unique Asian development issues. A RIGHRO can adjust to regional realities.

Numerous respondents to the survey were insistent that RIGOs should not function at lower standards of 'internationally recognized human rights principles' and that they should not bypass international law. Therefore, if a country fails to an international treaty, the RIGO should deny entry into the system. For example, many NGOs express concern that ASEAN would create a human rights mechanism that lowers international standards. The non-signatory status of many ASEAN nations– to international human rights treaties– indicates a lack of willingness to enforce international standards and to even lower them. In such circumstances, lower human rights standards become reified by the newly established RIGHRO with member countries subverting higher international standards.

NGO Operational Connections to Regional Institutions

NGOs, often operate on small budgets, are accustomed to working in an environment of scarce resources and adapt by cooperating and collaborating with one another. For example, the director of a major NGO based in Washington, D.C., stated that it determines its priorities (e.g. trafficking of women, extra-judicial killings) and then sets its agenda, (e.g., in Burma, Thailand, Philippines, and Japan). By focusing on specific priorities, NGOs can leverage their funds by working with other NGOs and with regional institutions. In return, RIGOs rely on IGOs for information and implementation through partnerships. This particular NGO conducts research, advocacy and other projects jointly with partners. It shares and combines its resources with other NGOs. As the director summarized, it engages in the cross-fertilization of ideas because:

> From our point of view, our effectiveness and our ability to be successful depends upon our ability to work closely with NGOs as colleagues. NGOs have limited resources, play different roles and complimentary roles. This is an ad hoc division of labor in many cases. NGOs have different tactics and priorities. Generally there is recognition among the NGO communities that we have to work together. Voices are limited in terms of how much influence we can have. Working together we can have a better chance of being effective.

As issues dealt with by NGOs become increasingly transnational and sovereignty bound states fail to address global issues effectively, NGOs fill an important vacuum. However, NGO experience varying levels of funding, expertise, and effectiveness. The survey responses agree that NGOs need to cooperate on a global scale as a matter of 'movement solidarity'. According to the NGOs surveyed, 6 INGO, 9 NOs, and 7 ROs– for a total 92% of the all surveyed organizations– stated that a major operational strategy consists of cooperation or collaboration. In addition, six of seven organizational leaders asked this question mentioned that NGOs need to collaborate or cooperate with each other to achieve their organizational goals.

NGO surveys indicated that their cooperative work includes personnel exchanges, dissemination of reports, providing information exchanges, holding meetings, joint seminars, educational training sessions and workshops, implementing projects, supporting groups in other countries, doing research projects jointly, providing financial support and technical assistance, distributing publications, organizing regional networking and engaging in regular consultation. These forms of cooperation assist in facilitating regional integration by propagating notions of universal human rights by mediating skillfully between regional culture and 'internationally recognized standards and principles' of human rights. For example, some Asian governments excuse the low status accorded to woman based on 'Asian values'. However, collaboration and cooperation at the 1993 Bangkok NGO Workshop resulted in common ground that stipulated "cultural practices that seek to set aside or derogate from universally accepted human rights, including women's rights, must not be tolerated".

Linkages Among RIGOs and NGOS

Empirical evidence suggests clearly that NGOs tend to cooperate with each other as they seek to influence governmental actions and corporate behavior. The cooperative climate presents an ideal environment for crafting a RIHRO in East Asia. The surveys and interviews provide evidence that support for a RIHRO. Among those surveyed for this study, a spokesperson for one particular NGO stated that they must participate in the process of establishing a regional human rights mechanism. The spokesperson's reasoning suggested that collective action, on the part of the NGOs, creates an environment with multiple linkages between governments and NGOs. Being involved in the creation and maintenance of a RIGHRO can check the power of these governments and enhance the existing cooperation among NGOs. Furthermore, those interviewed all realized that coordination and cooperation among NGOs would ultimately determine the contours of any new RIGO and its effectiveness across national boundaries.

NGOs provide the catalyst for RIGOs effectiveness because they can operate more effectively in a globalized environment in contrast to sovereign states. Several regional mechanisms which lacked NGO participation languished until the infusion of their ideas and actions took place. As the director of a Latin American organization stated, that the African system existed only on a paper until NGOs facilitated the monitoring, reporting, and petitioning functions. By preparing complaints and presenting cases to the Commission, they became an integral part of its operation and its success.

In addition to facilitating integration and cooperation with RIGOs and among countries, NGOs frequently provide a crucial role in creating and maintaining an organization's transparency. Surveyed NGOs state that countries often tend to avoid transparency and instead seek to obfuscate information. NGOs perform a 'watchdog' function and some release reports revealing data and facts, thereby increasing transparency. The conferences and workshops organized provide the venue to disseminate information. Furthermore, as part of many NGOs victims assistance programs, NGOs provide family members with information, advocate certain positions, and intervene in litigation by filing briefs and serving as *amicus curiae*.

In sum, the survey elicited highly general justifications for NGO support as well as very specific expectations. Generally, most NGOs view RIGOs favorably. Leaders of NGO provided the following reasons:

- RIGOs provide a forum to exchange information between governments and NGOs;
- RIGO provide opportunities for collaboration between NGOs and government agencies;
- RIGO provides a forum through which NGOs can pressure governments to avoid ignoring non-state interests; and
- RIGO mechanisms could be used to protect human rights monitors and promote a civil society.

At a highly specific level, some respondents justified NGO participation in RIGO development; e.g., pressuring China on its human rights policy and influencing the Japanese government's development policy to take into account greater and more stringent human rights standards.

Significant advantages exist for NGO within RIGOs. The Asian branch director of a global human rights organization went as far as suggesting that even RIGOs organized and controlled by governments still provide tremendous opportunities for NGOs. Through a concerted effort at exposing the deficiencies of governmental information, incremental progress and alteration of the RIGO could take place according to this director. However, most believe that any RIGO successes amplifies when NGOs participate in its creation by defining appropriate roles for them. For example, NGOs can work with governments to protect human rights monitors, promote a civil society, or distribute aid. In this way, NGOs and the potential RIGHRO would more likely share a mutually beneficial common objective through a division of labor.

Socioeconomic Factors in East Asia Facilitating Regional Integration

Despite the numerous positive socioeconomic developments in East Asia, especially economic growth in Japan, PR China, Taiwan, South Korea and democratization in Taiwan, South Korea, and Mongolia, the region lags behind other Asian sub-regions in regional cooperation. The Association of South East Asian Nations (ASEAN), the South Asian Association for Regional Co-operation (SAARC) and South Pacific regions launched previously human rights initiatives in their respective region. A powerful PR China and Japan, with its checkered history regarding regionalism, coupled with a reclusive North Korea create an environment that remains detrimental for cooperation on a plethora of regional issues, including human rights. However, due to the integral nature of PR China and North Korea to the region, significant RIGO initiatives must include these countries. This section attempts to examine some of the positive trends and developments in light of some of these fundamental difficulties discussed above.

Past research on integration alludes to several factors that enhance or detract from ongoing integration. Major factors frequently mentioned include cultural, economic, social, demographic, political, legal, and international. While none of these factors alone guarantee the establishment of RIGO institutions, but each can facilitate integration.

Table 9.3 below shows the seven factors outlined above and how they pertain to East Asian nations.

As noted above, all the East Asian countries except Mongolia, experienced the strong influence of authoritarian Confucianism. While some scholars suggest that Confucianism hinders democracy and the protection of human rights, others suggest that some aspects of Confucianism actually assist in the development of democratic polities that respect human rights (Friedman 1999). One Chinese NGO official interviewed went as far as suggesting that there is nothing inherently anti-human rights about Confucianism. Confucianism teaches benevolence, the development of a strong work ethic, emphasis on education, respect for the elderly and other sources of social justice that form the basis of human rights. Despite these shared cultural values, however, many NGO leaders and academics surveyed noted major differences in local language and culture. These cultural differences coupled with Asian mistrust of Japan, as a result of World War II policies of aggression, establish the bases for antagonistic ethnic consciousness.

Barrington Moore (1966) posited that a strong middle class allows democracies to thrive. Over the past three decades, many East Asian countries experienced dramatic economic growth and improved distribution of wealth so necessary for democratic consolidation (Curtis, 1997). In particular, two new

Table 9.3 Salient Socioeconomic Factors and RIGO Formation

Country	Cultural Background	Socio-Economic	Social and Political	Legal Influence
Japan	Confucian, Buddhist, and Shinto	Mature economy	Democracy	Confucian and Western
PR China	Confucian and Buddhist	Growing economy relatively small middle class	One party rule with increased local autonomy	Marxist and traditional
Taiwan	Confucian	Established middle class	Democracy since 1987	Confucian and Japanese
South Korea	Confucian	Established middle class	Democracy since 1987	Confucian and Japanese
North Korea	Confucian and Marxist	Mass poverty	One party rule	Marxist and Soviet
Mongolia	Buddhist and Marxism	Rural; middle class non-existent	Struggling democracy	Marxist, Soviet, and Chinese

democracies, South Korea and Taiwan witnessed economic transformations followed by dramatic political changes. As a result, political culture and expectations from the state changed over time and citizens increasingly participate in grass-roots political activities, especially those oriented toward the environment, human rights, and other social justice causes. Therefore, if North Korea, PR China, and Mongolia experience sustained growth and political liberalization on behalf of their respective governments, the likelihood of the emergence of a strong civil society increases. At present, however, the relative disparities in economic performance and levels among East Asian nations hinder integration. As the EU experience suggests, harmonization of similar industrialized economies provide the maximum benefit for sustained economic growth.

Another positive factor for establishing a RIGHRO in East Asia is a growing civil society in the region. For the last decade, the number of NGOs working in various fields in South Korea, Japan, Taiwan and Mongolia increased dramatically. The growth of NGO in South Korea, Taiwan, and Mongolia is encouraging. However, civil society in East Asia, in contrast to many other regions lags considerably.

Underlying the growth of civil society and NGO activity in East Asia is the significant gererational shift taking place in all the countries in East Asia. This generational shift results in the replacement of a more traditional and less educated population with a younger, more liberal and better-educated cohort. Unlike their parents who attained political consciousness in an environment of scarcity and authoritarian control, the younger generation developed their political values under greater political liberalization and economic affluence. Numerous scholars, including Ronald Inglehart (1990), noted that post-materialist values promote greater citizen involvement in community organizations.

Increasing affluence and the development and deepening of civil society throughout much of East Asia would be futile without democratization. In East Asia, both North Korea and PR China refuses to embrace democracy. While PR China embraced elements of a market economy, North Korea currently faces economic collapse of its Stalinist economy. The experience of South Korea suggests that as economic growth becomes consistent, citizens demand increasingly their political rights. Once democratic transition takes place, the foundation for democratic consolidation exists. In a politically liberal environment, where the government makes explicit its commitment to democratic procedures, NGOs and civil society flourish. Thus, increasing economic development and political liberalization creates cautious optimism among many Chinese dissidents and students abroad.

Two other factors contribute indirectly to the establishment of RIGOs. Similarities in the legal system make it possible to create binding mechanisms for the enforcement of decisions made by supranational organizations. In the case of the European Union, thus far, the European Court of Justice developed a judicial system based up continental legal philosophy. In East Asia, some commonality exists in terms of the origin of the Korean, Taiwanese, Chinese, and Japanese legal systems. However, the communist legacy and a strong orientation toward guarding state sovereignty hamper the development of RIGOs. In light of these factors, one final catalyst deserves attention. International pressure and norms promote human rights, economic harmonization, and internal democratic processes. Pressure from the United States, Western Europe and international organizations and international NGOs provided additional leverage necessary to effect democracy in South Korea and Taiwan. Currently, significant international pressures make the maintenance of authoritarianism in PR China taxing for Chinese authorities. Even China perceives a need to mollify human rights critics. In 1991, for example, China began publishing its White Paper on Human Rights in 1991, hosted the Beijing Women's Human Rights Conference. It also accepted a visit of the UN Commissioner for Human Rights and opened contacts with Amnesty International. These instances indicate that the universality of human rights cannot be ignored without negative consequences.

Over the past decade, a growing sense of human rights and regional cooperation among NGOs developed. In 1995, a forum attended by Asian

NGOs drafted 'Asian Human Rights Charter: Our Common Humanity' was promulgated' as a declaration in Kwangju, South Korea in 1998 on the occasion of the 50th anniversary of the Universal Declaration of Human Rights (Asian Human Rights Commission, 1995). Thousands of activists from various Asian countries and more than 200 NGOs participated in the three-year period of drafting process. As the sub-title of the Charter "our common humanity" indicates, the Charter represents 'moral interdependence' and 'consensus building'. The Charter is evidence of the internationalization of human rights and acknowledges the increasingly important and intersecting forces of globalization on human rights issues.

The Charter possesses universalistic characteristics of human rights. It rejects any claim of the primacy of 'Asian values' and other appeals to cultural relativism and it strongly affirms universality and the indivisibility of human rights by stating "we believe that rights are universal, every person being entitled to them by virtue of being a human being". The Charter encompasses rights sometimes referred to as 'first generation' (civil and political) and of second generation (economic, social and cultural rights) as well as of progressive newer third generation (rights to peace, democracy and development).

The Charter also calls for the establishment of an enforcement mechanism, stating "there should be an inter-state convention on human rights, formulated in regional forums with the collaboration of national and regional NGOs". The Convention must address the realities of Asia. At the same time it must be fully consistent with international norms and standards. An independent commission or a court must be established to enforce the Convention. Access to the commission or the court must be open to NGOs and other organizations.

As expected, NGOs spearheaded the effort to create the Charter but governmental support for the creation remains weak. While NGOs appear to be taking the lead in the establishment of a East Asian RIGHRO, many governments in the region provide varying degrees of resistance while others support the establishment of a RIGHRO.

Objections and Progress Towards Establishing a RIGHRO in East Asia

Frequently, East Asian governments raise many arguments objecting to the elevation of human rights protection to a regional level. These arguments, both culture and national sovereignty related, illustrate the tenacity of the difficulties involved in coming to a regional consensus on this issue. Despite these drawbacks, significant progress involving increased numbers of signatories to international human rights covenants in the region demonstrate progress made to date. This section analyses the difficulties in creating a RIGHRO and progress made to date.

The most prominent objection to universal human rights consists of those based on the 'Asian values' argument discussed by many scholars (Chan, 1999; Roseman, 1998; Bary, 1998). As exemplified by speeches and writing by Mohamed bin Mahathir of Malaysia, Lee Kuan Yew and Kishore Mahbubani of Singapore, this argument suggest the cultural incompatibility of universal and western notions of human rights to East Asia. This perspective insists on traditional respect for authority over imported notions of democracy to justify particular policies that advocate the pursuit of rapid economic growth (Davis, 1998; Johnson, 1987). Leaders contend that rapid economic growth and 'catching up to the west' require concerted effort without high levels of dissent and it becomes necessary to sacrifice civil and political rights in order to achieve economic development.

While some authoritarian regimes successfully promoted economic growth, the record of these regimes cannot justify the suppression of human rights. Most African and Latin American governments that repressed human rights failed to promote economic growth, instead suffered from gross economic decline. Even in East Asia, some authoritarian regimes failed to promote and suffered from poor governance. The list of these countries includes South Korea, Thailand, the Philippines, North Korea, Cambodia, Laos, and Vietnam. In North Korea, for example, instead of promoting economic development or a higher quality of life for its citizens, the authoritarian regime engulfed the entire country in famine through mismanagement. As Amartya Sen noted, "no substantial famine has ever occurred in any country with a democratic form of government and a relatively free press", because democratic society exposes administrative mismanagement and mitigates conditions of famine and speeds up governmental and international response (Sen, 1999, 92).

Given the tendency for economic development to unleash a whole host of social problems including unsustainable urbanization, the decline of traditional authority, and new expectations for governments, political leaders tend to refrain from encouraging the development of civil society. With many Asian states trying to consolidate their authority, they tend to consider human rights as belonging "essentially within the domestic jurisdiction of sovereign state". Human rights implicate questions of national sovereignty, and some governments resent Western interference in the internal affairs of another country. For example, China– like Yugoslavia and Chile– insists that human rights belong to the domestic jurisdiction of an independent sovereign state. Therefore, human rights are country specific, contingent upon what the government offers. Governments' aversion to external accountability shows unwillingness for subjugation to a higher authority such as a regional human rights court. Although virtually all IGOs and many governments endorse the theory of inalienable human rights, when it comes to enforcement and implementation, strong opposition exists.

Because of China's growing political and economic importance, its support for a RIGHRO will determine whether such a mechanism will develop and become effective in the region. Unfortunately the political reality for China currently suggests a strong attachment to nationalist integrity that it perceives would be undermined with the initiation of such a mechanism. Because of the sovereignty issue, Asian countries prefer to deal with human rights issues internally. States remain wary about any RIGO that would expose a state to complaints filed by other states, individuals, and NGOs for human rights violations. However, due to international pressures, the need to prevent continued criticism from Western nations, and even internal criticism, increased receptivity to creating a basic set of human right standards exists. China for example, would derive considerable good will and improved international image if it sought to lead in the creation of a RIGHRO.

Setting up a RIGHRO involves a complicated and complex set of relationships among different countries and NGOs. Unlike in Western Europe, where close cooperation and a lessening of antagonistic national rivalry took place in the context of a 'democratic peace', East Asia experienced increased national rivalry as a result of the Cold War. The increasingly similar cultural background, history, existing political and economic framework of Europe differs significantly from the antagonistic and anomic development of East Asian political systems. Throughout modern European the fundamental social and moral question consisted of reaching the appropriate balance between order and freedom. The Magna Carta, the English Bill of Rights, and the French Declaration of Man and of the Citizens all illustrate this fundamental theme. Historically, in East Asia, the fundamental political question consisted of order and disorder. As such, the liberal philosophy taken for granted in Europe does not exist in East Asia. Confucianism emphasizes order and good governance while Western philosophy evolved around the principles of the Enlightenment.

Empirical examination of Asian governments' commitment to international treaties and conventions provide some positive prospects for the furthering of human rights in the region. Simultaneously, many Asian countries failed to accept international treaties and covenants. Even Japan, with the most established democracy and developed economy in East Asia, experiences serious human rights issues relating to World War II and its domestic treatment of Korean residents. Japan's persistent refusal to make adequate compensation to war victims (e.g., comfort women and forced conscripts) and attend war atrocities such as the Nanjing Massacre prevents countries in the region from building the necessary cooperative framework. Thus, the two countries that could provide leadership in crafting a RIGHRO remain stymied due to historical and present day realities.

The failure of ratification of many UN human rights treaties suggests that signing a treaty does not guarantee ratification. As such, failure to ratify casts doubts about the willingness of states to adhere to evolving international laws and norms. Furthermore, agreements or consensus at the regional level remains elusive. The table below provides evidence, through December 2000, regarding the extent to which Asian states have signed international treaties dealing with human rights. As the Table 9.4 suggests, PR China remains the main country in East Asia that systematically refuses to sign international treaties and covenants. Taiwan, excluded from the global family of nations, due to its dispute with PR China remains excluded from these treaties and covenants. North Korea, the last remaining Stalinist regime also refuses to sign many treaties and covenants. Overall, the record provides an optimistic view regarding future East Asian cooperation but does not capture the extent of nationalism and government based recalcitrance in establishing a RIGHRO.

Table 9.4 Signing and Ratifying International Human Rights Instruments

Country	CESCR	CCPR	OPT	OPT2	CERD	CEDAW	CAT	CRC
N. Korea	Yes	Yes	No	No	No	No	No	Yes
S. Korea	Yes	Yes	Yes	No	Yes	Yes	Yes	Yes
Japan	Yes	Yes	No	No	Yes	Yes	Yes	Yes
Taiwan	No	No	No	No	No	No	No	No
PR China	Yes*	Yes*	No	No	Yes	Yes	Yes	Yes
Mongolia	Yes	Yes	Yes	Yes*	Yes	Yes	Yes*	Yes

Notes: Yes– indicates signed and ratified; Yes*– indicates signed but not ratified; and No– indicates non-signatory and non-ratification.

Explanation of instruments: (CESCR) The International Covenant on Economic, Social and Cultural Rights; (CCPR) The International Covenant on Civil and Political Rights; (OPT) The Optional Protocol to the International Covenant on Civil and Political Rights; (OPT2) The Second Optional Protocol to the International Covenant on Civil and Political Rights; (CERD) The International Covenant on the Elimination of All Forms of Racial Discrimination; (CEDAW) The Convention on the Elimination of All Forms of Discrimination against Women; (CAT) The Convention against Torture and Other Cruel, Inhuman or Degrading Treatment or Punishment; and (CRC) The Convention on the Rights of the Child.

Conclusion

As economic growth and integration unfold in East Asia into the 21st century, governments and NGOs increasingly must address issues of human rights. Pressure is increasing both domestically in many countries and internationally to establish a comprehensive RIGHRO. The NGO leaders and scholars who work tirelessly to advance human rights and scholars who advocate increased protection of human rights will increasingly challenge the governments in the region. In the past, most governments objected to increasing protection of human rights on grounds that economic growth and the protection of national sovereignty take precedence. While the 'Asian values' argument attempts to rationalize government's record and policies on human rights based on religion, Confucianism both supports and refutes the Western notions of human rights.

NGOs in Europe and North America play a vital role in crafting and maintaining RIGHROs. In particular, they provide a check on state abuse of power and an independent non-governmental monitoring of international and regional treaties and conventions. As democracy becomes increasingly the form of government in the region and as political liberalization takes firmer hold, many expect a plethora of NGO to play a crucial role in the development of RIGHROs. NGOs, whether international, regional or national, tend to cooperate and collaborate with each other as illustrated by the Asian Human Rights Charter.

Several recommendations provided will facilitate the formation of a supranational human rights body in East Asia with independent investigation, adjudication, and enforcement power. First, both human rights-promoting governments and NGOs in their political activities need to persuade the non-signatories and non-ratifiers to sign and ratify existing international human rights treaties.

Second, in order to promote establish amicable relations among the countries in the region so as to foster regional integration, Japan needs to play an appropriate role. The Japanese government needs to commence war reparations and improve its domestic human rights orientation. Japanese development assistance needs to become more sensitive to human rights concerns and become less focused on Japanese commercial interests abroad.

Third, NGOs facilitate democratization by demanding accountability and transparency. Given their non-territorial character, they can assist in opening up North Korea and China in unique ways that eludes states. Increasing the quality and quantity of NGO in PR China and North Korea will create the appropriate climate in those countries so that they will become more in tune with the democracies in the region.

Fourth, the governments in the region must cooperate to establish the process, initiated by such countries as the Philippines and Indonesia, to establish national human rights commissions with advisory, educative, investigative as well as promotion and protection functions. This is consistent with the "Framework for Regional Technical Cooperation in the Asia-Pacific" adopted by the Teheran workshop in 1998, which urged governments to develop "national institutions for the promotion and protection of human rights".

Lastly, governments in the region should strengthen human rights education at all levels to create national, regional and global human rights cultures. This is consistent with the 'Framework for Regional Technical Cooperation in the Asia-Pacific', adopted by the Teheran workshop in 1998, which urged governments "to develop human rights education". The link between human rights education and RIGHRO promotes transnational solutions to regional problems. As citizens become aware of the transnational nature of these problems, support for RIGHRO will increase. Thus, an East Asian RIGHRO could become a valuable tool for all parties concerned.

References

Asian Human Rights Commission (1995), *Asian Human Rights Charter*, Asian Legal Resource Center: Unit 4, Hong Kong.
Ashworth, L.M. and Long, D. (eds.), (1999), *New Perspectives on International Functionalism (International Political* Economy), Palgrave, New York.
Bary, T. de (1998), *Asian Values and Human Rights: A Confucian Communitarian Perspective*, Harvard University Press, Cambridge.
Bora, B. and Findlay, C. (1998), *Regional Integration and the Asia*, Oxford University Press, Oxford.
Bull, H. and Watson, A., (eds.), (1985), *The Expansion of International Society*, Oxford University Press, Oxford.
Cantori, L. and Spiegel S. (1970), *The International Politics of Region: A Comparative Approach*, Prentice-Hall, Englewood Cliffs.
Chan, J. (1999), 'A Confucian Perspective on Human Rights for Contemporary China', in J. Bauer and D. Bell, (eds.), *The East Asian Challenge for Human Rights*, Cambridge University Press, New York.
Chang, I. (1997), *The Rape of Nanking: Forgotten Holocaust of World War II*, Basic Books, New York.
Christenson, G. (1997), 'World Civil Society and the International Rule of Law', *Human Rights Quarterly*, vol. 19, pp. 724-37.
Curtis, G. L. (1997), 'For Democratic Development: The East Asian Prospect', *Journal of Democracy*, vol. 8, pp. 139-45.
Davis, M. C. (1998), 'The Price of Rights: Constitutionalism and East Asian Economic Development', *Human Rights Quarterly*, vol. 20, 303-37.
Deutsch, K. and et al. (1969), *Political Community and the North Atlantic Area: International Organization in theLight of Historical Experience*, Greenwood Press, New York.

Friedman, E. (1999), 'Asia as a Fount of Universal Human Rights', in P. Van Ness, (ed.), *Debating Human Rights*, Routledge, London.

Gordenker, L. and Weiss, T. (eds.), (1996), *NGOs, the UN and Global Governance*, Lynne Rienner, Boulder.

Haas, E. (1964), *Beyond the Nation-State: Functionalism and International Organizations*, Stanford University Press, Stanford.

Inglehart, R. (1990), *Culture Shift in Advanced Industrial Societies*, Princeton University Press, Princeton.

Johnson, C. (1987), 'Political Institutions and Economic Performance: The Government-Business Relationship in Japan, South Korea, and Taiwan', in F.C. Deyo, (ed.), *The Political Economy of New Asian Industrialism*, Cornell University Press, Ithaca.

Keohane, R.O. and Nye, J.S. (2000), *Power and Interdependence*, Addison-Wesley, New York.

Kim, Chae-Han (1998), *Domestic Politics, Trade Negotiation and Regional Integration: the US, Japan and Korea*, Sowha Publishing Company, Korea.

Leary, V. A. (1990), 'The Asian Region and the International Human Rights Movement', in C. Welch, Jr. and V.A. Leary, (eds.), *Asian Perspectives on Human Rights*, Westview Press, Boulder.

Lee, R.S. (ed.), (1999), *The International Criminal Court: The Making of the Rome Statute Issues, Negotiations Results*, Kluwer Law International, The Hague.

Mansfield, E.D. and Milner, H.V. (1997), *The Political Economy of Regionalism: New Directions in World Politics*, Columbia University Press, New York.

Mattli, W. (1999), *The Logic of Regional Integration: Europe and Beyond*, Cambridge University Press, Cambridge.

McKibbin, W.J. with Sachs, J.D. (1994), *Global Linkages: Macroeconomic Interdependence and Cooperation in the World Economy*, Brookings, Washington, D.C.

Mitrany, D. (1966), *Working Peace System*, Quadrangle Books, Chicago.

Moore, B. (1966), *Social Origins of Dictatorship and Democracy*, Beacon Press, Boston.

Nye, J. (1968), *International Regionalism: Readings*, Little, Brown and Company, Boston.

Oliveira, M.D. de and Tandon, R. (1994), 'An Emerging Global Civil Society', in World Assembly, (ed.), *Citizens Strengthening Global Civil Society*, World Alliance for Citizen Participation, Washington, D.C.

Pomeranz, K. and Topik, S. (2001), *The World That Trade Created: Society, Culture, and the World Economy, 1400-the Present*, M.E. Sharpe, Armonk.

Roseman, H. (1998), 'Human Rights: A Bill of Worries', in W.T. de Bary and T. Weiming, (eds.), *Confucianism and Human Rights*, Cambridge University Press, New York.

Rosenau, J. (1990), *Turbulence in World Politics*, Princeton University Press, Princeton.

Sen, A. (1999), 'Human Rights and Economic Achievements', in J.R. Bauer and D.A. Bell, (eds.), *The East Asian Challenge for Human Rights*, Cambridge University Press, Cambridge, p. 92.

Thompson, K.W. (1979), *References Ethics, Functionalism, and Power in International Politics: The Crisis in Values*, Louisiana State University Press, Baton Rouge.

Wallerstein, I. (1979), *The Capitalist World Economy*, Cambridge University Press, Cambridge.

Chapter 10

Demilitarizing Okinawa: Globalization and Comparative Social Movements*

Vincent Kelly Pollard

Introduction

Long before the collapse of the Soviet Union, domestic public interest groups were involving themselves in transnational social movements affecting US foreign policy (Solomon 1999; Isaacs 1963). The end of the Cold War created an environment wherein intermestic politics centered on the connections between domestic and international politics came to play an important role in global affairs. The proliferation of intergovernmental organizations (IGOs) and non-governmental organizations (NGOs) allow for the reconfiguration of international relations based on increased roles of non-state actors, although governments are not about to disappear and have actually become quite adept in coopting and controlling NGOs. Furthermore, the nascent stages of global civil society offer alternatives to traditional Lockean preferences against citizen diplomacy (Morgenthau 1978, 152-55; 535-39; 545-50; 558; Locke, 1690, 145-7). Close links between local and world politics promote the involvement of subnational governments (e.g., the Prefecture of Okinawa) and transnational pacifist public interest groups in world affairs. These new actors pursue transborder preferences and affect foreign policies of powerful governments.

This chapter utilizes a variety of theoretical perspectives to explore how anti-base activists in Okinawa might facilitate the closure of US military operations on the islands. Emphasizing political and telecommunications globalization and drawing on futures studies, this study compares the experiences of the Filipinos and Okinawans in seeking the removal of bases. What lessons should Okinawans draw from the successful experiences of the Filipinos' Anti-Bases Movement? What geopolitical realities impede or facilitate the potential for base closure?

---

* The author appreciates Wenjing Wang's comments on earlier drafts of this chapter.

What obstacles do *Uchinanchu*– Okinawans– face which the Filipinos did not have to surmount? These questions are explored in the context of global and domestic political realities affecting Japan.

Several developments affect possible futures of Okinawa. Under governors of different political parties, Okinawa has been a venue for subnational diplomacy between the prefectural government and the Japanese national government and for direct lobbying in the United States. The history of Okinawa and the nationalism associated with it, in addition to the treatment of the *Unchinanchu* as second-class citizens, forced to assimilate into Japan, yet never fully achieving the benefits of reversion to Japan in 1972 complicate matters. In the case of the Philippines, NGOs first collaborated with a skillful minority of Constitutional Commissioners drafting a post-Marcos *Konstitusyon* (Constitution) in 1986 to restrict presidential foreign policy making powers and later with key Senate leaders to defeat President Corazon Cojuangco Aquino's proposed extension of the US-Philippines Military Bases Agreement. The Okinawa case also involves a national government supportive of the bases and quite willing to keep most of them relegated to Okinawa.

Traditional Okinawa's Relationship with China and Japan

The literature of ancient China and Japan tells of a decentralized Okinawa. The three kingdoms of Nanzan, Chuzan and Hokuzan emerged in the 1100s (Rabson, 1999, 134) and some three hundred years later, a united Shoshi Kingdom was established in the Ryukyu Islands. Much of the Kingdom's success resulted from trade and merchant activity as a port-of-call for ships en route to China, Japan, Korea and Southeast Asia. To survive, the Shoshi Kingdom exercised dual diplomacy, placating the Satsuma clan in Japan and the Ming dynasty in China. The Ryukyu simply could not compete with Japan or China militarily or economically. Four decades later, a Second Shoshi Kingdom was established in 1469. The Ryukyu kingdom traded with mainland Japan, China, Korea, and Southeast Asia for economic survival.

While paying tribute to Chinese emperors of the Ming Dynasty (1368-1644) and to their Manchu successors until late in the Qing Dynasty (1644-1911), Okinawa also began paying tribute to Japan in the early years of the Tokugawa Shogunate (1603-1868), after subordination by the Satsuma *han* (clan) in 1609. Simply by keeping Chinese Emperors uninformed about Okinawan court's dual loyalties, the Okinawan court probably avoided conflict. The Meiji Restoration coupled with the atrophy of the governing structures in the kingdom signaled major changes in the second half of the nineteenth century that would bring the kingdom into mainland control.

In a political revolution, the Meiji Restoration toppled the Tokugawa Shogunate (1600-1868) and restored the Emperor Meiji (1868-1912). In Japan, Meiji-era rulers selectively undermined older social structures, borrowed from the West, raised educational levels, promoted pro-imperial *Shinto* ideology and increased capitalist production. The Ryukyu were formally incorporated as a prefecture of Japan in 1879. Forcible incorporation marked the end of the monarchy. Within the next quarter-century, Japan initiated aggression against China, Russia and Korea.

Before World War I (1914-8) and throughout the *Taisho* era (1912-26), no noteworthy military bases were located in Okinawa. Instead, the etiology of foreign bases in Okinawa lies rooted in the early years of Japan's Showa-era (1926-89). Based on a design for the self-styled Greater East Asian Co-Prosperity Sphere, Japan created numerous bases on Okinawa, in particular a major naval submarine facility in southern Okinawa. Furthermore, the *Uchinanchu* became targets for assimilation and colonization by the Japanese. Local language, culture, and history became suppressed and supplanted by Japanese nationalism and culture.

The US viewed Okinawa as a crucial initial step for an all-out assault on the Japanese mainland to end World War II. The Battle of Okinawa– the only land battle fought on the Japanese homeland– devastated the *Uchinanchu*. Aerial bombardment of Okinawa began in late 1944 and an invasion force larger and more powerful than that for D-Day in Europe landed on 1 April, 1945. Organized Japanese resistance ended in late June but the Battle of Okinawa involved a terrible toll for *Uchinanchu*. Most Okinawan civilians participated unwillingly, and they became bystanders and then victims in the horrific slaughter. In addition to 107,000 Okinawan and Japanese conscripts, the Okinawan death toll exceeded 150,000 civilians, including many children and elderly people; some were forced to commit suicide by Japanese troops and were killed outright if they hesitated (Ota, 1999 and 1981; Gonzales, 1995; Appleman, and et. al, 1992 [1948]; Belote and Belote, 1970). Lingering questions remain in the minds of Okinawan nationalists and peace activists. Did the Japanese acquiesce in such huge civilian casualties because the Okinawans were not Japanese? Also, why must Okinawans continually manage to deal with powerful neighbors that disregard the long-term interests of the *Uchinanchu*?

US Occupation and Administration after World War II

Okinawa first fell under the control of the US Navy and, later, the United States Civil Administration of the Ryukyu Islands after the war. American bases became a permanent fixture on the island, with the primarily expeditionary Marine Corps, as well as a lesser Army, Navy and Air Force presence on the Islands. While Japan's main islands experienced a six-and-a-half-year occupation by the Supreme Allied Command in the Pacific, opportunities presented by the Cold War (especially its proximity to China, Korea and the USSR) and the San Francisco Peace Treaty allowed the United States to maintain bases on Okinawa. Even Okinawa's incomplete 1972 Reversion to Japan did not allow for the closure of the main bases (Gakken Okinawa Ha, 1982).

A series of bilateral international treaties and executive agreements between Japan and the United States evolved as successive rationales for U.S. military facilities in Okinawa. Okinawa became trapped in the purgatory of the Cold War. While US Presidents and Japanese prime ministers invoked national security, who protected the security of the *Uchinanchu*? The only reason why Okinawa housed American bases was to further the interests of two major powers.

On 8 September, 1951, the Security Treaty between the United States and Japan was signed in San Francisco. Instruments of ratification were exchanged on 28 April, 1952. On 19 January, 1960, a Treaty of Mutual Cooperation and Security between Japan and the United States of America was signed. Protests involving 6,000,000 Japanese that year led to an unprecedented cancellation of the Government's invitation to US President Dwight D. Eisenhower to visit Japan. Japan's National Diet ratified the agreement, although the uproar forced the resignation of Prime Minister Kishi Nobusuke. On 15 May, 1972, Reversion of Okinawa to Japan took place.

These agreements outlasted the collapse of the Soviet Union while leaving behind earlier arguments for US military facilities in Okinawa. Three decades after Reversion, the US continues to control substantial tracts of land, water and airspace in, around and over Okinawa. As Japan's economy doubled several times during the postwar years, the Liberal Democratic Party-led government increased its financial commitment to maintaining the military bases. If Japan's 'host-country' appropriations towards maintaining US military facilities are added to Self-Defence Force expenditures, Japan's total annual military budget has ranked second to that of the U.S. and no lower than fifth since the collapse of the Soviet Union (Sköns and et. al, 2000).

While some bases, including Makiminato, Naha port, and several minor ones closed, Okinawa continues to host a disproportionate share of bases in Japan and in East Asia. Meanwhile, several major bases, including Tachikawa closed over the past couple decades on the mainland. Early in the George W. Bush Administration, US Secretary of Defense Donald Rumsfeld publicized the need for additional base closings internationally. However, even if Secretary Rumsfeld gets his way, there is no reason to believe he wishes to pull out of Okinawa. Lastly, the closure of Subic Bay Naval Base in the Philippines in 1992 made the Okinawan bases that much more important as part of the US Pacific strategy, although development of deep-water ports in Guam and the Republic of Belau (Palau) have been discussed as fall-back alternatives.

Disproportionate Burden Sharing by Uchinanchu

For decades, seventy-five percent all of the US forces stationed in Japan and the same proportion of military base land used by the US military concentrated in Okinawa-*ken*, a prefecture with 0.6% of Japan's land area. Outcomes of this course of military development have generated negative consequences for the daily lives of *Uchinanchu*. Since 1945, an expanding series of Okinawan grievances against the US and Japanese governments periodically erupted in open protest. Especially before the end of the Cold War, media coverage of Okinawan grievances received limited attention in the United States and Japan but very critical coverage in Okinawa. While American and Japanese news coverage attempts to frame the issue according to US-Japan relations, Okinawan coverage attests to the tripartite nature of the base issues. Since the mid-1990s, coverage since the mid-1990s, "newspaper reporters in the United States, mainland Japan and Okinawa 'framed' their stories in ways that supported the ideological hegemony of cultural elites with their particular societies" (Hollstein 2000, 1). Clearly, the objectives and goals of the Japanese government differ significantly from that of many *Uchinanchu*.

Alternative media, in particular electronic mass communications, including the internet provide alternative perspectives about the issue of American troops. Summarizing a variety of sources (Johnson, 2000, 34-64; JAALA Solidarity Committee, 1998; Okinawa Prefecture Council Against Atomic [and] Hydrogen Bombs, 1968), the main grievances consist of the following:

- continued US military occupation of real estate that might otherwise be devoted to agriculture, tourism or industry– or left as open space;
- crimes of theft, battery and sexual assault by US servicemen against Okinawans;

- unresolved paternity claims made by Okinawan women;
- noise pollution-induced tinnitus and even deafness;
- physical damage and loss of life due to explosions of munitions during live-fire exercises;
- long-term risk from unexploded ordnance;
- crashes of fixed-wing aircraft and helicopters in populated areas; suspected (sometimes later documented) nuclear weapons; and
- environmental damage and threats to land, internal waters and surrounding seas, and to endangered species of plants, birds, animals and fish.

Unfortunately, these issues seem far from the everyday lives of most people on the main islands of Japan and rarely affect them. Living in a distant prefecture with little national clout, Okinawans seeking fundamental solutions to these problems have been routinely frustrated by the unwillingness of the Japanese government to address their concerns more directly.

Uchinanchu Divided

In addition to the lack of Japanese focus on Okinawan issues, the *Uchinanchu* themselves remain divided over the bases. These facts provide insight into a central question: How can substantial US military presence persist in Okinawa over a decade after the end of the Cold War while a majority of US military facilities in place around the world in 1945 have closed or reverted to host countries? The classification of the majority of US troops in Okinawa-*ken* as an expeditionary force (United States Department of Defense FY1998, 1998, Sec. 2.0), vitiates the claim that the US troop presence exists to defend the Japanese homeland. During the Vietnam War, Okinawan bases provided a springboard for US troops and bombing missions to Vietnam. If anything, the presence of US troops on Okinawa and in Japan made them both viable targets during the Cold War.

As referenda in 1996 and 1997 indicated, US military bases in Okinawa remain a divisive domestic issue in the Prefecture. In mid-2001, reports Japan's Cabinet Office, Okinawans responding to a government poll split almost evenly between supporters and opponents of U.S. military facilities (Japan Times Staff, 2001). According to US Navy veteran and journalist Mike Millard, "more than 8,000 Okinawans work[ed] on the US bases" in the late 1990s while many thousands more [were] employed in the entertainment and service industries around those installations" (Millard, 1999, 101). With an economic stake in the bases, they are probably represented among those favoring continuation of the bases. At the same time, however, the development of the local tourist industry and services on the island increased wages on the island. While the wages and the standard-of-living lag behind the mainland, some diversification of the Okinawan economy decreased the economic desirability of maintaining the bases since reversion.

Analysis of the Philippine Anti-Bases Movement

As in the Okinawa case, the US bases in the Philippines occupied large segments of land in specific locales. In particular, Subic Naval Base and Clark Air Force base provided the US with forward-deployed capability. However, during the colonial period, they were ineffective against Japan's invasion. And similar to the Okinawan case after World War II, the bases existed for expeditionary purposes rather than for the defense of the Philippines against an external threat. Filipino nationalists were well aware that US bases originated in the Philippine-American War and the overthrow of the constitutional Malolos Republic. In the 1970s, the bases were so vital to the US defense establishment that closure seemed unthinkable, especially with the 1975 closure of US bases in Thailand. Yet the very outcome considered unlikely by most military strategists and political scientists occurred in December 1992. Nonetheless, the base closing in the Philippines was not inevitable. And while natural calamity inflicted by the Mount Pinatubo eruption that spewed tons of ash on US facilities, the volcano did not destroy Subic Naval Base. Because of the similarities and differences of these two cases, the Filipino Anti-Bases Movement case provides some useful insight about the future of US bases on Okinawa.

From a comparative perspective, what lessons might Okinawan organizations discern from the success of the Filipinos' Anti-Bases Movement in preventing President Corazon Cojuangco Aquino (1986-92) from renewing the US-Philippines Military Bases Agreement fifteen months earlier? Precisely, what strategies and approaches provided the pivotal pressure on the Filipino government?

Okinawan, regional, and international movements supporting the closure of American bases need to exercise constant flexibility in creating the appropriate strategies and opportunities. Intensified networking among social movements will be enhanced if they develop 'institutions of foresight' (Slaughter, 1994, 181-201) by systematically discerning, focusing on, and evaluating early indicators of emerging trends, particularly those in and affecting East and Northeast Asia. The most significant change in the post-Cold War era, the fluidity of politics at the domestic and international levels requires analysis. For example, what emerging factors affect the prospects for a demilitarized Okinawa? (Cf.

Molitor, 1977) What do leaders and movements need to account for in order to maximize these prospects?

Lessons from the Anti-bases Movement in the Philippines

Inferences from the experience of Filipino anti-bases organizations from the 1950s until the early 1990s deserve careful study by concerned Okinawan organizations, their allies on Japan's four largest islands, and transnational supporters in other countries. Several lessons of particular importance suggest the success of a broad array of organizations working together to promote the removal of bases.

Perhaps the most important element of success involves the development of a long-term perspective driven and sustained by participants' commitment to offset disadvantages of size and scale. Filipinos strongly favoring a country unoccupied by foreign military bases became a majority of the population until only *after* the US bases left. Because the power of governments dwarfs that of NGOs, intransigence of governments requires prolonged attention to potential and emerging weaknesses of those governments.

Networking among the NGOs and subnational and transnational actors creates opportunities for anti-base movements to address effectively disadvantages of size and scale. In the cases of the Philippines and Okinawa, network formation involved subnational and transnational actors exchanging information, collaborating in actions of solidarity and protest, and gaining media coverage to offset powerful national governments. However, political and telecommunications globalization allows these groups to operate transnationally in a less state centric world with sustained attentiveness to local and global developments facilitating rapid responses to suddenly changing domestic and international situations.

Broad-based solidarity in the case of the Philippines proved crucial for ending the American presence. The anti-imperialist National Democratic Front imploded in factionalism following the Communist Party of the Philippines's unwillingness to participate in the four-day protest actions that toppled the Marcos dictatorship in February 1986 (Pollard, 1993, 38-49). However, a working coalition of Filipino women's organizations, anti-nuke coalitions, farmers' organizations and industrial workers' unions had the vision and persistence to see the campaign through to its conclusion. In the case of Okinawa where traditional Japanese anti-militarist parties have shown hesitancy in recent years, a Green and Red coalition may yet prove important.

Despite important leadership roles played by elected political leaders (especially in the Senate of the Philippines), extraparliamentary political activity drove the agenda and facilitated legislative action. Although one wing of the anti-bases movement (especially, the New People's Army) engaged in armed struggle against the government, non-violent political activity involved larger numbers of participants in the final, successful phase. To make this point is not to claim that armed struggle was ineffective– only that it was insufficient. Some national and local political leaders supported an end to the Military Bases Agreement in order to remove a central nationalist issue from the Communist Party of the Philippines. With increasingly widespread support for the withdrawal of bases, the high opportunity cost (potential loss of political capital by President Aquino) inhibited her future chances of extending the US-Philippines Military Bases Agreement during the 1986 Constitutional Commission (Pollard, 1998a, 101-5; Locsin, 1996; Special Interviewee #1, 1995; Aquino, 1995).

A negative lesson from the Philippines' experience needs assimilation into the Okinawa case. From the middle to late 1980s, member-governments of ASEAN (characterized in 1995 as 'free riders' by former President Aquino in an interview with the present researcher) ostensibly benefiting from the US military facilities refused Aquino's direct requests to absorb the political heat associated with her endorsing continuation of the Military Bases Agreement (Aquino, 1995). During the mid-and late 1980s, the United States, the Philippines and some pro-US bases ASEAN (Association of South East Asian Nations) member-governments repeatedly tried but failed to elicit the Association's public support for renewal of the Military Bases Agreement (Pollard 1998b, 162-67, 187, 189-90).

The governments of Indonesia and Malaysia resisted pressure from Filipino diplomats under the Marcos and Aquino administrations publicly to state their privately expressed preferences favoring an extended stay for US military facilities. Yet according to former Ambassador of the Philippines to Indonesia Narciso G. Reyes, Indonesia, Malaysia and other ASEAN member-governments emphasized privately their desire that the bases remain. "They are," he asserted, "happy about having the bases in the Philippines, period" (Reyes, quoted in Hernandez and et al, 1987/1986, 178). In other words, discounting the anti-colonial rhetoric of the 1967 ASEAN Bangkok Declaration, the implicitly anticommunist ASEAN's behavior shows that it preferred that the 'temporary' foreign bases remain for an unspecified, lengthy period of time (Pollard, 1970, 255).

So even if the Japanese government decides to seek support for the closure of US bases, the Philippines example suggests that support from East and Southeast Asian nations may never materialize for such a move. Given the unwillingness of Japan's leaders to deal openly with its imperial past, leaders of Korea, China, Taiwan and some of the ASEAN nations presently prefer American bases in Japan as a check on its potential future aggression.

In the case of Okinawa, the Movement to Demilitarize Okinawa faces formidable opponents in Washington and Tokyo. If not for reasons of 'pacifist' strategy (e.g., Sharp, 1973) then tactical considerations require grounding the Movement to Demilitarize Okinawa in 'nonkilling global political science' (Paige, 2001) based on principles of non-violence. Simple reliance on expectations of sympathy for Okinawans' plight or on the moral force of their case for demilitarizing the Okinawan archipelago will be insufficient. Violent activity, on the other hand, would only antagonize domestic and international supporters of a base-free Okinawa. Okinawan peace activists need to remain focused on non-violence by convincing the majority of Okinawans about the social, cultural, political, and economic value of total base removal.

Often viewed pejoratively by Japanese on the main islands, Okinawans face a complicated challenge. The disproportionate concentration of US military facilities in the southerly Okinawan archipelago usually segregates and compartmentalizes awareness from their day-to-day existence in the mindset of most Japanese. Until recently, 'out of sight' usually meant 'out of mind'. In this respect, the central government in Tokyo's support for the Security Treaty remains the biggest political obstacle facing anti-militarist Okinawans. In contradistinction to the Okinawa case, Filipino anti-base sentiment in the 1980s and 1990s became stronger in the National Capitol Region than in areas immediately surrounding the US military facilities.

The Movement to Demilitarize Okinawa faces coming challenges only partly reminiscent of the Philippines in the mid to late 1980s where barely one fifth of the total population felt that removing foreign bases was a high priority (Ateneo de Manila University and Social Weather Stations, 1986; *idem*, 1987). An even smaller Japanese minority opposes strongly *Ampô*– acronym for the United States-Japan Security Treaty– currently. Continuous high profile crimes committed by Okinawa based US Marines during late 2000 and early 2001 coupled with insensitive and inflammatory statements by commanding officers and the *US Greenville*'s deadly crash into the *Ehime Maru* created increased awareness of U.S. military facilities (Funabashi, 2001).

Reinforcement of 'not in my back yard' or so-called NIMBY-type resistance to a wider dispersal of the bases in Japan may be a likely short- or long-term effect of these developments. These sentiments may cause the US military and the Japanese central government to relegate the bases to Okinawa indefinitely. At the same time, renewed and strengthened activism resulting from increased attention to the base issues could energize the anti-bases movement as evidenced in several cases elsewhere.

For example, after forty years of target practice and a decades-long campaign from the *Kanaka Maoli* (Native Hawaiian) community and their supporters, the US Navy ceased shelling, strafing and bombing Kaho'olawe Island in 1991. Its current activities include supporting ordnance removal, revegetation and cultural restoration of Kaho'olawe (United States Kaho'olawe Island Reserve Commission, 1996; United States Kaho'olawe Island Conveyance Commission, 1993).

Other examples outside Japan exist. For example, one fifth or more of O'ahu Island (in the State of Hawai'i) is occupied by the US Armed forces. Yet in Makua Valley, O'ahu, the US Department of Defense finds itself on the defensive from local residents (Cole, 2001, 1). Similarly, longterm anti-bombing campaigns focused on Vieques Island in the Commonwealth of Puerto Rico and a more recent one in Saipan (American Broadcasting Company, 1991/1979; Associated Press, 2001) equally deserve attention. These efforts have already led to increased cooperation among anti-base movements to increase leverage on the US government.

Japanese Domestic Politics

Since the Japanese 'economic bubble' burst in 1989, political uncertainty dominated domestic politics. Throughout the past decade, economic stagnation, deficit spending, and attempted reforms, characterized the political environment. With the Liberal Democratic Party's (LDP) monopoly on power temporary shattered and public opinion polls citing increased contempt and distrust of elected officials, the bureaucracy, and political parties, political legitimacy dramatically weakened. To the extent that Japanese citizens are willing to listen to alternative perspectives and not blindly trust the government bodes well for social movements. In particular, local governments and social movements increasingly emphasize the need to resist the central government.

Local Government Assertiveness in Japan

For perhaps the first time since the mid-1950s and early 1960s, local governments in Japan have new legal openings to challenge the central government. Article 92, 'Local Autonomy', of Japan's 1947 Constitution, enshrines governmental decentralization in general terms: "Regulations concerning organization and operations of local public entities shall be fixed by law in accordance with the principle of local autonomy". Despite that language, strong unitary government remained the reality until the 1990s. Japan's revised Local Autonomy Law of 1991 and the Law to Promote Decentralization of 1995 have facilitated prefecture-level challenges to the central government on a variety of issues (Smith, 2000a, 1-74), including military facilities in Okinawa (Smith, 2000b, 75-114). Other local challenges to central government authority include student and community-based interference with remilitarizing the high school curriculum (Aspinall and Cave, 2001, 77-93).

In the late 1960s and early 1970s many progressive governors and mayors won elections signaling public discontent with the LDP led national government. In the late 1990s, a similar trend seemed likely, with local voters defying an entrenched LDP. These new governors and mayors sought decentralization and represent a wide gamut of ideological beliefs, including the nationalist orientation of Shintaro Ishihara of Tokyo. Social forces on the left and right in Japan may temporarily find it to their mutual convenience to converge in open antipathy towards foreign military facilities and personnel. Article 9, 'Renunciation of War', of Japan's Constitution abjures "the threat or use of force as means of settling international disputes" and the maintenance of "war potential". However, any debate over Article 9 of Japan's ostensibly pacifist Constitution presents both opportunities and dangers for the Movement to Demilitarize Okinawa. Supplanting of US forces with Japanese troops fails to adequately resolve the bases issue for the *Uchinanchu*. Nationalists may seek to maintain bases in Okinawa, albeit Japanese ones.

Meanwhile, the traditional leftist political allies of progressive groups like the Movement to Demilitarize Okinawa continue to evince disorientation and disintegration. First, the Socialists made a major retreat from opposing *Ampô* in 1989 and eventually allied themselves with the LDP. Ultimately, the Social Democratic Party of Japan lost considerable electoral clout due to its strategic partnership with the LDP and new electoral rules for House elections. Furthermore, according to interviews with Diet members, the same contributors of the LDP financially supported the Japanese Socialist Party for many years (Kuroda 1994; cf. Compton, 2000, 131).

The Communists also caved into mass sentiments. By February 2000, the 'lovable' Japanese Communist Party (JCP) took still more awkward half-steps toward mainstream respectability by toning down earlier partisan stands against *Ampô* (Japanese Communist Party, 2000, 12). However, the JCP's attenuation began much earlier (Hayes, 2001, 107-9; Compton, 2000, 137). Perhaps ironically, by moving in a more centrist direction, the JCP probably weakened its ties with Japanese militants firmly opposed to foreign bases.

Lastly, when put to the test in the middle to late 1990s, even the peace planks of the religiously oriented New *Komeitô* (Clean Government Party) program sometimes became indistinct with its willingness to embrace the Liberal Democratic Party in ruling coalitions. In one astonishing example, *Komeito* failed to endorse publicly a gubernatorial candidate in the November 1998 Okinawa Prefecture Election. Although it endorsed Ota during his earlier reelection campaign in 1994, it abstained from doing so when he ran for a third term against a candidate backed by Liberal Democratic Party money and personnel. Instead, New *Komeitô* merely permitted individual Party members to vote according to their consciences in that contest (Smith, 2000b, 76). In a defeat for the Movement to Demilitarize Okinawa, the LDP-backed candidate won. Even more importantly, ostensibly anti-militarist or peace-oriented parties whose leadership minces words when it comes to the bases in Okinawa are likely to be standing on the sidelines when the Movement picks up steam and concerned activists ask which party's rhetoric was matched by deeds.

The Changed Face of the Movement to Demilitarize Okinawa

While the political landscape becomes increasingly treacherous for the LDP and established political institutions, extra-parliamentary grassroots organizations continue to exert increased pressure on the political system. In contrast to earlier compensation-oriented environmental movements of Minamata and Yokkaichi, new social movements emphasize more contemporary orientations and values regarding progressive social issues.

A demographic shift has been underway in the composition of the Movement to Demilitarize Okinawa. On the one hand, Okinawan holders of titles to land parcels expropriated for the use of the US military remain active, even expanding their specific influence by subdividing their plots of land currently occupied by the bases. On the other hand, a content analysis of activists depicted in a recent Okinawa-produced advocacy video indicates that elderly residents and teenagers– notably high school women– joined with environmentalist organizations to protest the continued foreign military presence (Pollard, 2001; JAALA Solidarity

Committee, 1998). Thus, the oft-noted involvement of women and women's groups in anti-military campaigns during the past four decades suggest yet another crucial potential global ally.

Although Japanese NGOs and networks of NGOs does not match the level of the Philippines or that of many other countries, another source of support for demilitarization derives from environmental movements. The Green-Red alliance acknowledges the intricate connections between environmentalism and militarization. Furthermore, given the environmental decay on Okinawa, environmentalists and anti-militarists share a common foe in a recalcitrant and entrenched Japanese central government. With skillful use of mass communications media and reliance upon appropriate clauses of human rights of women and indigenous people and references to environmental treaties, the prospects for internationalizing the anti-militarist agenda increases. International environmental groups, including Greenpeace for example, object to Japan's treatment of maritime species facing extinction. Japanese fishermen receive worldwide condemnation for their government sanctioned fishing practices. One such species, the dugong, appears headed for extinction by boating and silting in Japanese waters. However, current Japanese law does not yet designate the dugong as an endangered species (United Nations Foundation, 2000, Sec.15). In early 2000, an estimated sixty dugong survived in a small area estimated to comprise thirty square miles north and south of Henoko, Okinawa (Efron, 2000; Nowak, 1997). The campaign to protect dugong, coral and other creatures (JAALA Solidarity Committee, 1998) readily lends itself to assistance from transnational nongovernmental organizations and interest groups.

The following case demonstrates the type of linkages among national grassroots movements currently taking place. In South Korea, the Civil Network for a Peaceful Korea (CNPK) made initial inroads toward pressuring Korean politicians for base removals with its 2000 declaration to then-President Clinton and U.S. presidential candidates that "We East Asians Are Against NMD [Nuclear Missile Defense]/TMD [Theatre Missile Defense]" (Civil Network for a Peaceful Korea, 2000). The CNPK cooperates with the Nago-Okinawa Peace Cyber Cycle's (NGPCC) website (1997-2001) by sharing links on each other's websites. Futhermore, that organization's home page is linked to organizations in Hawai'i, Washington State, Puerto Rico and 'Green Korea United'. The 'Red Card Movement' held an anti-bases protest at the July 2000 G-8 Summit Meeting in Okinawa and it occupied space on the NGPCC's website. In turn, the organization translated material from Bahasa Indonesia and English.

The complete reversion of bases on Okinawa would improve land-use conditions and overcrowding, if the prefectural government effectively establishes appropriate policies. Environmental groups and anti-militarist groups share many common goals based on the principle of citizen empowerment and shared issues of the environment, demilitarization, and democratization. The explosion of information technology and the weakening of the state due to globalization will increase the linkages among these groups. At the same time, international NGOs seek to join forces with domestic organizations and movements to pressure governments to reform policies. The global anti-militarist movement appears headed in that direction.

Geopolitical Obstacles to Base Closure

Despite the progress of networking among various interest groups on a global scale, governmental foreign policies of Asian nations remain an obstacle. New leaders regarded as progressive by some of their supporters in some ways behave remarkably similar to conservative opponents whom they have defeated. For example, with President Kim Dae Jung of South Korea, US military bases remain in that country. By the time Socialist Prime Minister Tomiichi Murayama began leading a three-party coalition government including the LDP (1994-6), his own Party had already abandoned its opposition to the US-Japan Security Treaty five years earlier. While Chinese and North Korean rhetoric sometimes suggests that they are insisting that the US immediately withdraw from bases from Japan and South Korea, their preferences seem more conflicted. The spread of representative democracy in East and Southeast Asia has not yet created an environment conducive for demilitarization of Okinawa. Instead, the status quo orientation of American bases became firmly implanted in America's Asian allies.

South Korean Reluctance to Demilitarize

South Korea's government under President Kim Dae Jung refrained from calling for the removal of US military personnel from the region and his likely successors cannot be expected to do so either. Even North Korea appears complacent about US bases in South Korea. In a remarkable turnaround in mid-2000 from past political pronouncements, Kim Jong-Il twice informed Kim Dae-Jung that he had no objection to a continued US military presence in South Korea (Reuters, 2000, A-7; Naming, 2000, A-10). As euphoria over steps towards opening up North Korea wore off,

Kim Jong-Il repeated his more familiar criticisms of US military bases. In any case, if the content of placards of demonstrators against US military bases in South Korea provide a valid index of increased citizen activism, media-savvy citizens and civil society need to consistently emphasize a broader regional view of US military facilities in Northeast Asian region. In the future, if this begins to occur more often, the opportunity cost of reassuring Japan's prime ministers about maintaining US bases in Japan could eventually become intolerable for vote-seeking incumbent and prospective political leaders in South Korea.

China's Conflicted Perceptions of a Demilitarized Okinawa

In the People's Republic of China (PRC), middle-level and top-level officers of the People's Liberation Army privately provide perplexing perspectives about the prospect of a US military pullout from Okinawa. Given Okinawa's proximity to China and Taiwan, US military facilities in Okinawa place irritating limits on the PRC's verbal threats and possible blockading, bombarding or invading Taiwan. Yet for historical reasons dating back to the Sinn-Japanese War of 1931-45, the PRC mistrusts Japan's leaders. In light of that deep mistrust, perhaps it is not altogether surprising that one source in the late 1990s reported backhanded PLA (People's Liberation Army) support for a continued US military presence in Okinawa if the alternative is greater Japanese military assertiveness (Anonymous, 1997).

Therefore, as civil society evolves in the PRC, Okinawa activists might consider looking for ways to engage their potential Chinese in a dialogue about a demilitarized future. Even if Chinese public opinion is divided on the bases (Special Interviewee #2), discussing and debating this topic is safer than a number of other more sensitive topics. For historically conversant Chinese, calling for the withdrawal of the US from Okinawa has historical continuity with opposition to US militarily intervention in China in 1900 and 1945, as well as during its direct clash with the PLA during the Sino-American War in Korea. If political liberalization ensues in earnest, the Chinese press and student groups could provide clues as to coming changes in Chinese public opinion about US bases in Okinawa. And even if moments of ambivalence were detected in the late 1990s, China's public position may change if it decides that US concern with the PRC (and not some loosely defined 'rogue state' or nonstate terrorist group) is what really underpins its determination to stay in Okinawa.

Taiwan

Based on the Taiwan Relations Act of 1979, the US is the largest arms supplier to Taiwan. If the US-China rivalry escalates, Taiwanese governmental support for demilitarizing Okinawa will probably be difficult to obtain. If the US-China rivalry escalates, the Chinese military rapidly modernizes and Taiwanese identity formation increases, then Taiwanese support for maintaining US commitment in Asia may increase rather than decrease over time. Hong Kong and Macao's assimilation into China suggests that a Taiwan unified with the PRC in the near future could not maintain its distinct political system without significant interference by PRC. In other words, Taiwanese public opinion leaders calling for US presence in the Pacific and for military aid to Taiwan and a fear of assimilation by PRC are obstacles to supporting Okinawa's demilitarization remain strong.

Perhaps initially by emphasizing some common cultural ties in traditional culture, Okinawa women, peace groups and environmental organizations will figure out how to reach some common political ground with their counterparts in Taiwan. Ironically, a comparison between the Taiwan and China relationship with that of Okinawa and Japan reveal similar historical patterns and current realities. Both were colonized by Japan and in the future both Okinawa and Taiwan face possible political and cultural assimilation into larger political entities. Thus, both Okinawa and Taiwan face similar pressures and challenges.

Conclusion

Political and telecommunications globalization changed the rules for defenders and opponents of militarized Okinawa. For better or for worse, will political globalization make any difference in the future success or failure of the Movement to Demilitarize Okinawa? Both encouraging and discouraging signs become evident upon close examination of domestic and international politics. Domestically, the problems facing the LDP coupled with increased public visibility of crimes committed by American servicemen provide ammunition for demilitarizing Okinawa. Increasingly, the demilitarization issue has become a mainstream issue of political discourse on Okinawa. Furthermore, the emergence of the Green and Red coalition offers hope that grassroots organizations could take advantage of both increased political difficulties facing the LDP and movement toward decentralizing the country's unitary system. Globalization allows these interest groups to broadcast their message throughout the world and coordinate activities with sister organizations in other countries as well as NGOs.

The geopolitics of Asia suggest less than encouraging prospects for a demilitarized Okinawa. With US interests in maintaining the status quo of military intervention, coupled with the national security reality of Japan's neighbors, significant pressures exist for the maintenance of US troops in the entire Asia region. Surprisingly, even North Korea and the PRC could acquiesce in continued American troop presence. If the Movement for a Demilitarized Okinawa can seek alliances with sister organizations in these countries the environment could change. These sister organizations could bring pressure on their governments to apply diplomatic leverage against Japan and the United States to end the miniaturization of Okinawa. This in turn will depend on thoroughgoing domestic changes in the countries involved so as to raise the level of trust.

Globalization makes the task of envisioning and implementing a vision for a demilitarized Okinawa very difficult but not impossible. Assimilation of appropriate lessons from other antimilitarist movements and systematic scanning aimed at discerning early indicators of changes could lead to the demilitarization of Okinawa in the future.

References

American Broadcasting Company, (1991/1979), *Trouble in Paradise*, Videotape Telecast in 1979, Capital Cities/ABC Video Enterprises, New York.
Anonymous, (1997), Former Commissioned US Military Officer [Not-for-attribution comments], Honolulu.
Appleton, R.E., and et al. (1992/1948), *Okinawa: The Last Battle*, Center of Military History Publication 5-11, U. S. Government Printing Office for the Historical Division, Department of the Army/Center of Military History, Washington, D.C.
Aquino, C.C. (1995), Former President of the Republic of the Philippines (1986-92), Audiotaped interview with Vincent Kelly Pollard, Jose Cojuangco Building, Makati City, 10 August.
Aspinall, R. and Cave, P. (2001), 'Lowering the Flag: Democracy, Authority, and Rights at Tokorozawa High School', *Social Science Japan Journal*, vol. 4, pp. 77-93.
Associated Press, (1997), 'US Urged to pay UN Arrears in Full; and Germany and Japan Want Permanent Seats on the Security Council', *Honolulu Star-Bulletin*, A-7. 24 September.
Associated Press, (2001), 'Environmental Groups Ask Court to Halt Vieques [Puerto Rico] Bombing', Fox News 8 June, http://www.foxnews.com/story/0,2933,26834,00.html Downloaded 9 June, 2001.
Ateneo de Manila University and Social Weather Stations (1986), 'The Public Opinion Report of June 1986', *Public Opinion Report*, Quezon City.
Ateneo de Manila University and Social Weather Stations, (1987), 'The Public Opinion Report of October 1986 and March 1987', *Public Opinion Report*, Quezon City.

Belote, J.H. and Belote, W.M. (1970), *Typhoon of Steel: The Battle for Okinawa*, Harper & Row, New York.

Civil Network for a Peaceful Korea (CNPK), (2000), 'We East Asians are Against NMD/TMD', Website. http://www.peacekorea.org/eng/index_eng.html Downloaded 21 May, 2001.

Cole, W. (2001), 'US Military Losing Land Wars', *Honolulu Advertiser*, A-1 and A-7. 3 June.

Compton, R.W., Jr. (2000), *East Asian Democratization: Impact of Globalization, Culture, and Economy*, Praeger, Westport.

Efron, S. (2000), 'Doing Wrong by Japan's Dugong? Timid Marine Mammal Could Be Eliminated from the Waters Off Okinawa if a Deal with the US Military Goes Through', *Los Angeles Times*, 19 May, http://www.cosmos.ne.jp/~miyagawa/nagocnet/data/latimese.html and http://www.latimes.com/news/science/environ/20000519/t000047362.html Downloaded 21 May, 2001.

Freedom House, (2000), *Annual Survey of Freedom Country Scores 1972-73 to 1999-00: All Countries' Scores, 1972-2000*.

Funabashi, Y. (2001), '100,000 American Troops Isn't a 'Magic Number', *Asahi Shimbun Online*, 13 March 2001 http://www.asahi.com/paper/columnist/en/efunabashi/ef010313. html Downloaded 14 March 2001.

Gekkan Okinawa Sha [comp.], (1982). *Laws and Regulations During the U.S. Administration of Okinawa, 1945-1972*, Ikemiya Shokai, Japan.

Gonzalez, J.A. (1995), 'Kadena Commemorates Battle of Okinawa', *Air Force News*, Air Force News Service, Online ed. http://www.af.mil/news/Jun1995/n19950630_699.html Downloaded 1 June, 2001.

Hayes, L.D. (2001), *Introduction to Japanese Politics*, 3rd edition, M.E. Sharpe, Armonk.

Hernandez, C.G., and et. al (eds.), (1987/1986), *Issues in Socio-Political Transformation in Asia and the Pacific: The Recent Philippine Political Experience– Papers and Proceedings*, 30-31 May, 1986, Center for Integrative and Development Studies, University of the Philippines, Quezon City.

Hollstein, M.C. (2000), *Framing Security: A Tri-Cultural Discourse Analysis of Newspaper Reports About the American Military in Okinawa*, Ph.D. Dissertation, University of Hawai'i at Manoa.

Isaacs, H. R. 1963. *The New World of Negro Americans*. A Study from the Center for International Studies, Massachusetts Institute of Technology. New York: John Day Co.

JAALA [Japan-Asia-Africa-Latin America] Solidarity Committee (1998), 'Withdraw U.S. Bases! Appeal from Okinawa', Videotape, Cinema Okinawa, Naha City, Japan.

Ministry of Foreign Affairs, (2000), *Diplomatic Bluebook 2000: Toward the 21st Century– Foreign Policy for a Better Future*, http://www.mofa.go.jp/policy/other/ bluebook/2000/II-1-a.html#1, Downloaded 21 May, 2001.

Japan Times Staff, (2001), 'More Okinawans Accept Presence of US Military', *The Japan Times Online*, 20 May, http://ww.japantimes.co.jp/cgi-bin/getarticle.pl5?nn200105 20a 6.htm, Downloaded 21 May 2001.

Japanese Communist Party, (2000), 'Problems of U.S. Military Bases in Okinawa', February, http://www.cosmos.ne.jp/~miyagawa/nago/jcp.html, Downloaded 16 March, 2001.

Johnson, C.A. (2000), *Blowback: The Costs and Consequences of American Empire*, Henry Holt and Company, New York.

Kaplan, A. (1964), *The Conduct of Inquiry: Methodology for Behavioral Science*, Chandler Publishing Company, San Francisco.

Kelly, T. (1994), Public Information and Cultural Affairs Officer. Consulate-General of Japan. Honolulu, Hawai'i, Telephone interview by Vincent Kelly Pollard.

Kuroda, Y. (1994), Lecture, 'Japanese Politics' graduate seminar, University of Hawai'i at Manoa. Notes by Vincent Kelly Pollard, Fall 1994 Semester.

Locke, J. (1690), 'Of the Legislative, Executive, and Federative Power of the Commonwealth', In idem, *Second Treatise on Civil Government*, A. and J. Churchill, Ch. XII.

Locsin, T.L. (1996), Journalist and editor; former speech writer for candidate and President Corazon Cojuangco Aquino; and former Minister of Information (1986-87), Republic of the Philippines, Interview (audiotaped) with Vincent Kelly Pollard, Macrima Building, National Capitol Region, 14 March.

Mallard, M. (1999), 'Okinawa: Then and Now', In Chalmers Johnson (ed.), *Okinawa: Cold War Island*, Japan Policy Research Institute, Cardiff, pp. 92-107.

Molitor, G.T.T. (1977), 'How to Anticipate Public-policy Changes', *S.A.M. Advanced Management Journal*, vol. 42, pp. 4-13.

Morgenthau, H.J. (1978), *Politics Among Nations*, Fifth, rev. ed., Alfred A. Knopf, New York.

Nago-Okinawa Peace Cyber Cycle, (1997-2001), Website, Nago, Okinawa, http://www.cosmos.ne.jp/~miyagawa/nago/, Downloaded 21 May, 2001.

Namkung, K. A. (2000), 'North Korea, US Are on the Verge of Relations', *Honolulu Advertiser*, A-10, 10 October.

Nowak, R.M. (ed.), (1997), *Walker's Mammals of the World Online*, Johns Hopkins University Press, http://www.press.jhu.edu/books/walker/sirenia/ sirenia.dugongidae.dugong.html, Downloaded 21 May, 2001.

Okinawa Prefecture Council Against Atomic [and] Hydrogen Bombs, (1968), *Okinawan White Paper*, The Council, Naha.

Ota, M. (1999), 'Re-examining the History of the Battle of Okinawa', in Chalmers Johnson (ed.), *Okinawa: Cold War Island*, Japan Policy Research Institute, Cardiff, pp.13-37.

Ota, M. (1981), *This Was the Battle of Okinawa*, Naha Publishing Company, Naha.

Paige, G.D. (2001), *Nonkilling Global Political Science*, Xlibris, Philadelphia.

Pawsat, C. (1994), 'NGOs Learn Fine Points of Advocacy Campaigning', *Japan Times*, 13 November.

Pollard, V.K. (2001), Review of JAALA [Japan-Asia-Africa-Latin America] Solidarity Committee, 'Withdraw U.S. Bases! Appeal from Okinawa', Cinema Okinawa, Naha, 1998, in *Journal of Asian Studies*, vol. 60.

Pollard, V.K. (1998a), 'Electioneering, Constitution Writing & Foreign Policy Making During Early Redemocratization', *Philippine Political Science Journal*, vol. 39-42, pp.73-125.

Pollard, V.K. (1998b), *Executive Power in Foreign Policy Making: Stretched Organizational Pluralism and Social Process in the Philippines and Japan*, Ph.D. Dissertation, University of Hawai'i at Manoa.

Pollard, V.K. (1997), 'Delphi/Scanning Methodologies: An Electronic Futures Symposium', *Manoa Journal* [Hawai'i Research Center for Futures Studies], vol. 9, pp. 1-12.

Pollard, V.K. (1996), 'Entering Global Civil Society: Japan's ODA Policy Making Milieu from June 1992', *Japanese Studies*, vol. 16, pp. 35-61.

Pollard, V.K. (1993), 'Democratizing the Philippine Revolution: Squaring the Circle for the Communist Party of the Philippines', *Conference Proceedings*, School of Hawaiian, Asian and Pacific Studies, University of Hawai'i at Manoa, pp. 38-49.

Pollard, V.K. (1970), 'ASA and ASEAN: Southeast Asian Regionalism', *Asian Survey*, vol. 10, pp. 244-55.
Rabson, S. (1999), 'Assimilation Policy in Okinawa: Promotion, Resistance, and "Reconstruction"', in Chalmers Johnson (ed.), *Okinawa: Cold War Island*, Japan Policy Research Institute, Cardiff, pp.133-48.
Reuters, (2000), 'North [Korea] Agrees US Troops Stabilizing Influence, Kim Says', *Honolulu Star-Bulletin*, A-7. 18 August.
Sharp, G. (1973), *The Politics of Nonviolent Action*, Extending Horizons Books, P. Sargent, Boston.
Sköns, E. and et. al (2000), 'Military Expenditure: Table on the Fifteen Major Spenders in 1999', in *SIPRI Yearbook 2000; Armaments, Disarmament and International Security*, Oxford University Press for the Stockholm International Peace Research Institute, Oxford, Ch. 5. http://projects.sipri.se/milex/mex_major_spenders.html Downloaded 16 March, 2001.
Slaughter, R. (1994), 'How Institutions of Foresight Protect Future Generations', in Kim, Tae-Chang and Dator, J.A. (eds.), *Creating a New History for Future Generations*, Institute for the Integrated Study of Future Generations, Kyoto, pp. 181-201.
Solomon, M.. 1999. "Black Critics of Colonialism and the Cold War." In Michael L. Krenn (ed.), *The African American Voice in U..S. Foreign Policy Since World War II*. New York and London: Garland Publishing, Inc. 53-87.
Smith, S. (ed.) (2000a), *Local Voices, National Issues: The Impact of Local Initiatives in Japanese Policy-Making*, Michigan Monograph Series in Japanese Studies 31, Center for Japanese Studies, University of Michigan, Ann Arbor.
Smith, S. (2000b), 'Challenging National Authority: Okinawa Prefecture and the U.S. Military Bases', in *idem*, *Local Voices, National Issues: The Impact of Local Initiatives in Japanese Policy-Making*, Michigan Monograph Series in Japanese Studies 31, University of Michigan, Center for Japanese Studies, Ann Arbor, pp.75-114.
Special Interviewee #1 (1995), A high-ranking diplomat, interviewed by V.K. Pollard, not for direct attribution, Makati City, 9 August.
Special Interviewee #2 (2000), Chinese professor, interviewed by V.K. Pollard, not for attribution, 1 June.
United Nations Foundation (2000), 'Briefly Noted: Environmental news from Around the World [Dugong]', *UNWire*, Item 15, Para. 1. 26 May. http://www.unfoundation.org/unwire/archives/UNWIRE000526.asp#14, Downloaded 16 May, 2001.
United States, Department of Defense (FY1998), *The United States Security Strategy for the East Asia-Pacific Region*, 25 November, http://www.defenselink.mil/pubs/easr98/ Downloaded 21 May, 2001.
United States, General Accounting Office (1998), *Overseas Presence Issues Involved in Reducing the Impact of the U.S. Military Presence in Okinawa: Report to the Honorable Duncan Hunter, House of Representatives*, Microfiche GAO/NSIAD-98-66, General Accounting Office, Washington, D.C./Gaithersburg.
United States, Kahoʻolawe Island Conveyance Commission (1993), *Kahoolawe Island: Restoring a Cultural Treasure*, The Commission, Wailuku.
United States, Kahoʻolawe Island Reserve Commission (1996), *KIRC Summary Report on Observations, Lessons Learned and Recommendations: Model Unexploded Ordnance Cleanup Project*, Kahoʻolawe Island, Kahoʻolawe Island Reserve Commission, Honolulu.

Index

AIDS 1
Amsden, A. 68
APEC 4
ASEAN 4, 8
Asian Economic Crisis 10, 16, 19-21, 25-7, 126-9 (also see Indonesia, Japan, and Korea S.,)
    authoritarianism and 27
    contagion 25
    IMF and 27
    Indonesia impacted 126-9
    recovery from 24
Asian environmental assessment 154-5
Asian geopolitics 80
Asian values (see Confucianism, human rights and political development)
Australian policy toward Indonesia 122-4, 125-6, 128-31
authoritarianism 5, 86 (also see political development)
    Asian crisis and 26-7
    globalization and 6

Bretton Woods 6, 13
    currency systems 25-6
        devaluation 26, 126

Canada (see middle powers)
China (also see Deng, Great Leap Forward, Mao, and SEZ)
    economic development 50-6, 57-9
        corruption 54-5, 57-9
        decentralization 51
        SEZ 50, 52-4
        SOE 55-6, 61
    economic chaos
        1950s 45-9
        1980s 50-7
    elites (also see Deng Xiaoping and Mao Zedong)
        impact of SEZ 57-9
        internationalists 41-3, 49-50, 60-1
        moderates 43-4, 60-1
        nativists 40-1
        environmental policy cooperation with Japan 156
        WTO 61
Cold War 3, 11-4, 19, 71, 75, 78-9, 100-2, 115-6, 119-23, 175, 180, 183-6

    Indonesia, impact on 115, 119-24
Confucianism 86-8 (also see developmental state, Japan, and political development)
Culture (see human rights, Japan, and political development)
Cumings, B. 17
currency devaluation 25

Democratization 7
Deng Xiaoping 42, 49-50, 58
Dependency theory 38
Developmental state 2, 3 5-6, 27-9, 37-9 (Also see mercantilism)
    autonomy of state in 91
    China 39
    Confucianism 72-3
    Flying Geese Model 16,18
    future of 27-30
    insular nature of 5 (also see Japan)
    political development 27-30
    psychological crises in 3
    utility as a development model 29

East Asian miracle 3,7, 14, 17
    autonomy of state in 91
    Confucianism 72, 83
    revisionist view 18
East Timor (also see Indonesia)
    East Timor 115-34
    FRETILIN 118-9
    Indonesia and 117-9, 130-2
Economic development (see developmental state, export led growth, China, and Japan)
Elite economic beliefs
    China 39-44
    South Korea and Taiwan 38
Elite pluralism 7 (also see developmental state, FDI, and political development)
    configuration of 6
    Japan 71
    China 40-4 (also see Mao Zedong)
Environmental aid (see Japan; environmental aid)
Environmental impact assessment 155

Export led growth 10, 17
  bottlenecks in China 50-2 (also see SEZ)
  Flying Geese Model 16, 18
  Foreign policy change and 10
  Internationalization of economy 92-3

Fewsmith, J. 42, 43, 57, 58
FDI 94
foreign aid (see Korea S. and Japan)
Foreign policy change 100
Freedom House 91
Friedman, Thomas 2, 11, 12, 71-2, 84
Fukuyama, F. 11

Gill, S. 26
Garon, S. 74
GATT 6 (also see WTO)
Globalization 84-5
  defined 11-2
  critics of globalization thesis 11-3
  economic impact 10 (also see export led growth)
  foreign policy impact on 8
  history of 11-3
  IMF and, 24, 26, 127, 133
  immobilism 7
  information power 23
  internet and, 15
  international division of labor 17
  international division of power 17
  liberal view of 18
    McWorld 13-4
  Marxism and 19
  North-South divide in 14
  Post World War II 84-5
  Speed of 14
  stages 13
  state control over society and 31, 90-1, 97-8
  uneven nature of 14-6
Great Leap Forward 36, 46-9

Habibie, BJ and Indonesia 130-31, 133
Haggard, S. 17, 25, 37, 68
Hirst, P. 2
human rights (also see Lee Yuan Yew, political development, and NGOs)
  Asian values and 173-4
  Culture and 171

Economics and 170-1
Functionalism and 162-4
Huntington, S. 86, 87

IGO (See NGOs)
IMF 27, 78 (also see currency devaluation)
  Indonesia and 127-28, 133
  Japan and 143
Import Substitution Industrialization (ISI) 39
Indonesia 115-34
  US policy toward 115-6, 124-5, 128-31, 133
  Australian policy toward 122-24, 125-26, 128-31
  Habibie 130-31
  IMF and 133
  Japan's failed environmental policy towards 154
Internationalists in China 41-2, 49-50

Japan
  administrative reform and consolidation 141-3
  as a closed society 71
  banking crisis 76
  budget deficit 76-7
  community values 71
    in and out groups 74
  culture and power 70, 72, 83
    citizenship and 79
  depopulation and immigration 79-80
  economic dislocation 69, 75-7
    culture and 76-7
    lack of political will 77, 80
    macroeconomic problems 77
  economic inefficiency 75
  environmental activism 138
  environmental aid 141-5, 147, 150, 153, 156-9
    public opinion in lieu of economic problems 140
    Ministry of Foreign Affairs and (MFA) 141-3
    MITI and 142-3, 145, 152, 156-7
      Green Aid Plan 152
    environmental cooperation with China 156

future of 80
LDP (see Liberal Democratic Party)
Meiji 68, 70, 73
Okinawa 181-97
    Peace network 193
Reverse Course 73
Johnson, C. 10, 68

Korea, South 100-13
    IMF 78
    middle power and 100-5
    multilateral aid 112
    ODA 101, 103-4, 107-11
        loan types 110
    Peacekeeping 105-7

Lee Kuan Yew 69, 72, 86 (also see human rights and political development
Liberal-Democratic Party (LDP) 73-4, 139, 191-2, 196-7
    Maintenance of US bases and 191-2, 196-7

Mao Zedong 45-7
    Economic development policies 45-6, 48
Meiji (see Japan)
Middle power
    Canada as 100-5
    Korea as 100-5
    Korean ODA 101, 103-4, 107-11
    Strategies 100-5

Nativists in China 40-1
NGOs 2, 140, 150-1, 180-1, 187, 192-4, 196
    Japan's support for 150-2
    Human rights 161-78
    Leadership characteristics 164-5
    Issues of sovereignty 167
    Okinawa 187
    Post Cold War and IGOs and 180

NICs 16-18 (also see developmental state)
Neomercantilism 37 (Also see developmental state)

Okinawa 180-200 (also see Japan)
Okinawa and geopolitics 194-6

Political development 29, 31, 68, 69
    (also see human rights, Lee Kuan Yew, authoritarianism, and Japan)
    Asian culture and 3, 70-1, 86-9
    Asian values 69, 173-4
        Lee Kuan Yew and 69, 86
    China 36-40 (also see China)
        economic opening, impact on 57-9
    Confucianism 37, 83, 72, 85-7 (also see Asian values, authoritarianism, and Japan)
    developmental state and 27-30
    declining legitimacy 68-9
    Freedom House 91
    Japan 68-80
    Lee Kuan Yew and 72 (also see Lee Kuan Yew)
Peace Network (See Japan)
Pempel, T.J. 10
Philippines 187-8
Post Cold War (also see NGOs)
    Japan and 79-80
    political development 6 (also see political development)
    regional economic development 4
    US policy 115-6, 119-122

Radelet, S. 18
Reardon, L. 36, 42, 44, 60
regulatory state 28
RIGHRO 161, 164-7
    resistance to 173-76

Sachs, J. 88
SEZ 53-7
    illegal activity in 54-6
Soros, G. 26
state power
    decline of 2

United Nations (UN)
    South Korean involvement with peacekeeping in 105-7
    Security Council and Indonesia 118
US policies (also see Indonesia and Okinawa)
    Hawaii 190
    Vieques 190

Wallerstein, I. 16-7

Woo-Cumings 10
WTO 30
   Chinese elite division over 61

Yoshida, S. 73